"Racoosin is a natural and gifted storyte
H. Wallis Anderson's life and wartime sei ̴ ̴ ̴ ̴ ̴ ̴ ̴ ̴
it is a deeply moving story of an American citizen and hero, an honest and unusually realistic look at what it was like to serve on the ground in World War II, and a fascinating description of the role of a combat engineer. Finally, Racoosin's book tells of an older America and its best virtues. You are introduced to Colonel Anderson at the beginning, and by the end, you truly miss him and all he stood for."

—JOE WEISBERG, Emmy Award–winning creator, writer, and producer of *The Americans*, and author of *An Ordinary Spy*

"Written by a former Navy SEAL and grandson of a true citizen-soldier, *Combat Engineer* is a superbly researched, fast-paced account of Colonel H. Wallis Anderson's experiences in establishing and leading US Army combat engineering units in two wars and a lesser-known Mexican excursion by General John Pershing. A highly decorated colonel by the end of World War II, Anderson's great leadership and doggedness in dealing with the Army bureaucracy while having to constantly train new troops and fight is well covered by the author. Using Anderson's letters to his wife and other primary sources, this book provides unique, firsthand insight into the wartime importance of combat engineers in army operations and is a must-read."

—CAPTAIN BOB GORMLY, USN Ret., author of *Combat Swimmer, Memoirs of a Navy SEAL*

"It's not often that a book comes across my desk that covers such an important but relatively unknown figure in the well-tread field of World War II history. Racoosin does just that with Col. H. Wallis Anderson, who led 'the damned engineers' in the ETO."

—JEREMY COLLINS, director of conferences and symposia at the Institute for the Study of War and Democracy, The National World War II Museum

"This book provides a wealth of detail about combat engineers, the development of the National Guard, and the life and accomplishments of an unjustly obscure citizen-soldier, Col. H. Wallis Anderson. I believe in the future, *Combat Engineer* will become a standard reference book for those seeking information on the Battle of the Bulge and men behind the Rhine crossing."

—**A. H. LLOYD**, author of *Long Live Death: The Keys to Victory in the Spanish Civil War*

"A combined biography, leadership study, and account of the German offensive and the 1111th Engineer Combat Group's active response throughout the Ardennes/Bulge. A very readable chapter and verse of how Colonel Anderson and his engineer detachments got the job done against the odds. In civilian life, he was a career maintenance manager with a regional railway, the son of a railway man, entranced by matters to do with rails, roadways, and bridges. As emphasized in this account, he was modest, unassuming, unflappable, and soft-spoken. The most interesting aspect to me is that he was a reservist, and not career Regular Army."

—**CELIA HAYES**, author of *My Dear Cousin: A Novel in Letters*

"The tip of the spear thrust deep into American lines at the Battle of the Bulge, on the verge of ripping open the American defensive line. One more bridge, that's all—then Victory! Just one bridge, held by combat engineers . . . .

"In a moving and comprehensive memoir of his grandfather, Colonel Harry W. Anderson, John Racoosin details the blunting of that spear, the crucial action that doomed Peiper and his 'Kampsgruppe Peiper' to defeat. Defeat at the hands of the 1111th Engineer Combat Group, an outfit commanded by Anderson. An American victory that led SS Obersturmbannführer Peiper to mutter, 'Those Damned Engineers.' High praise, indeed."

—**MICHAEL VAN NESS**, author of *GENERAL IN COMMAND: The Life of Major General John B. Anderson from Iowa Farm to Command of the Largest Combat Corps in World War II*

"*Combat Engineer* is Racoosin's homage to the often under-sung heroes of military operations. Meticulously researched and clearly written, the book brings back to life Colonel H. Wallis Anderson and his gift for leadership."

—**BRUCE J. BRITTAIN**, author of The *Chow-hound (B-17)* and *Brother Daniel's Good News Revival*

"What began as a labor of love and proceeded to become a five-year journey for John Racoosin has culminated in the literary tale of Wallis Anderson, an unheralded but historical hero. John's descriptive account of COL Anderson's rise from humble beginnings to exemplary leader in the most tumultuous of situations is a captivating page-turner that I highly recommend for all military history enthusiasts. John has artfully crafted this narrative that does justice to the valiant protagonist in this story, his grandfather."

—**BEN WARNER,** author of *20-YEAR LETTER: An Afghanistan Chronicle*

"Written by John Racoosin, this thoroughly researched work delivers little-known facts concerning those famous battles. Anderson's actions can be judged to have played a significant part in stopping the German offensive and, indeed, shortening WW2."

—**CSM DENNIS WOODS**, USA Ret., author of *Black Flag Journals, One Soldier's Experience in Americas' Longest War*

Combat Engineer:

The Life and Leadership of Colonel H. Wallis Anderson,
Commander of the Engineers at the Bulge and Remagen

by John Racoosin

© Copyright 2021 John Racoosin

ISBN 978-1-64663-282-4

Published by

◤ köehlerbooks™

3705 Shore Drive
Virginia Beach, VA 23455
800-435-4811
www.koehlerbooks.com

Colonel H. Wallis Anderson, Corps of Engineers, US Army

COMBAT ENGINEER

The Life and Leadership of Colonel H. Wallis Anderson, Commander of the Engineers at the Bulge and Remagen

JOHN RACOOSIN

VIRGINIA BEACH
CAPE CHARLES

FOR JULIET, WIFE AND MUSE

TABLE OF CONTENTS

Prologue 1

Introduction 4

Chapter One: Beginnings 7

Chapter Two: Mexican Border 19

Chapter Three: The Great War 27

Chapter Four: Between the Wars: Career, Family,
and Tragedy 56

Chapter Five: A New War 73

Chapter Six: The Calm 102

Chapter Seven: Into the Storm 114

Chapter Eight: Winter 140

Chapter Nine: The Ardennes 149

Chapter Ten: Prelude 200

Chapter Eleven: Distant Thunder 207

Chapter Twelve: Crisis 215

Chapter Thirteen: Collision 243

Chapter Fourteen: Into Germany 283

Chapter Fifteen: Remagen 293

Epilogue 339

Bibliography 326

Index 332

PROLOGUE

The panzers had one more bridge to cross. The commanders in their turrets strained to see ahead in the dusk; crossing that bridge meant—finally—good roads. One more bridge, and the ruthless, black-uniformed SS men would reach the open country leading to their objective . . . with no more enemy to their front.

Starting a mere sixty hours earlier, the SS forces had driven through an enemy—the American First Army—in disarray, and had encountered sleeping troops, haphazard and unprepared defenders, panicked withdrawals by American units, fighter-bombers taking huge risks to fly in miserable weather, and unarmed convoys blundering into their forces. Just moments before on this Monday afternoon, a rear-echelon American staff officer and his driver, thinking they were safe so far behind the lines and oblivious to the presence of the panzers, had swerved their jeep along the Belgian back roads directly into the SS guns, with fatal results for the Americans.

Yet the *obersturmbannführer* commanding the SS column had serious problems of his own. His initial advance had been delayed from the onset due to lack of aggression by the assault troops whose job it had been to punch a hole through the lightly defended American lines. When he finally got his column advancing behind

1

the American front, he found his assigned road network more suited to bicycles than heavy armored vehicles. The December weather in the Ardennes Forest added to the misery and difficulties. And even with all the chaos and confusion caused by the lightning thrust of the SS panzers, not all Americans had broken and fled; some had stood their ground and faced his column—the most powerful, best-equipped assault force of the entire German offensive. Combat engineers and hastily assembled infantry had resisted along the way, with the engineers causing most of the delays and problems. Their determined defiance had caused critical delays and disruption to the carefully planned SS timetable.

Kampfgruppe Peiper was behind schedule, and time was critical. Named for its commander, SS-Obersturmbannführer Joachim Peiper, the SS column had had to improvise along the way, detouring from its assigned route due to unanticipated American resistance. Speed was everything; delay meant the stronger and better-supplied Americans could bring up reinforcements that Peiper's stormtroopers would be unable to match. Delay meant defeat.

No matter. After two days of frustrations dealing with detours, bad roads, miserable weather, unexpectedly stiff resistance, insane air attacks, stubbornly defended roadblocks, and outposts that blew up bridges in their face, *finally* the Waffen-SS panzer column was on the brink of success. With determination, aggression, and resourcefulness, Peiper had led his column to within a mere thirty kilometers of his objective, the Meuse River. And twenty-five more kilometers beyond—less than an hour's drive—lay the port of Amsterdam. Approaching La Lienne creek, his panzers were poised to roll on toward a victory that would provide the Nazis with some respite, and possibly disrupt the inexorable advance of the Western Allies into Germany. Peiper knew there were no organized forces to impede his progress once he cleared the bridge. His panzers could surely deal with anything the desperate American army could put in his path.

Peiper's senior, 6. *Panzerarmee* commander SS-*Oberstgruppenführer* Josef "Sepp" Dietrich, had personally issued a grim challenge to Peiper before the Ardennes offensive began: reach the Meuse, even if all he had left from his column was *one panzer*. With one bridge to go, in fact Peiper still had more than sixty.

One more crossing remained, over a tiny creek; although narrow, its banks were steep. In the gathering gloom of the winter day, the panzers rumbled forward, taking the curve to the right, as the bridge came into view.

INTRODUCTION

The man most responsible for defending the sector behind the First US Army front lines at the point Peiper's armored column broke through and raced for the Meuse was a fifty-four-year-old grandfather of three, a thirty-two-year Army veteran who had served during the US Army's punitive action against Mexico, even before America's entry into the Great War.

Colonel Harry Wallis Anderson, Corps of Engineers, commanded the 1111th Engineer Combat Group, arrayed in a sixty-mile arc in the Belgian Ardennes Forest, some twenty miles behind the front lines facing the Losheim Gap. Under Anderson's command in December 1944 were four battalions of engineers, two of which, the 51st and 291st Engineer Combat Battalions, held positions directly in the path of the most powerful element of the entire German offensive.

Beginning early in the morning of December 17, the second day of the offensive, the German panzers charged directly into Anderson's area of responsibility, which occupied the key town, road, and bridge network in the path of the SS assault force. The German objectives were to cross the Meuse River and to race to Antwerp, driving an armored wedge between the Allied army groups and cutting off the northern half from their supply depots. Such a split would cause a severe crisis, isolating the British, American, and Canadian forces north and east of the Meuse; the entire Allied northwest European campaign would have suffered a massive setback.

The meager force of engineers were the only organized combat units in position behind the front lines. Failure to stop the panzer column would have allowed the Germans to reach the Meuse, and beyond.

Anderson was truly a product of his times and a uniquely American version of the citizen soldier. The presence of the right man in the right place at the right time during the crisis of December 1944 was no pure accident, nor was it inevitable. That he was in position for a critical battle was due to chance and choice, and the culmination of circumstances, both civilian and military, that began decades before. The result was a leader who was highly proficient and inspiring to his troops, even under severe stress.

A study of the life of H. Wallis Anderson soon reveals two long-running, comparable themes: the railroad and the military. Although battles are the most obvious and popular means to relate to armies and the military, all serious students of military history know it is the monotonous, mundane, and mandatory training, organization, logistics, preparation, and readiness that truly make an army, and account most for its success or failure. Actual battles, while spectacular and significant, are but rare events, interspersed periodically throughout long timelines of peacetime preparation and wartime positioning.

In the same manner, the glory and glamour of railroads are most popularly focused on the terminals deep in the center of metropolitan capitals. The names and locations of these storied venues reflect the success of the primary purpose of the railroad: to connect major population centers. And while a Grand Central Terminal or Sirkeci serves its purpose with style and distinction, a more disinterested appraisal concludes that it is the miles and miles and *more* miles of tedious, parallel tracks of hot-rolled steel that make a railroad, more so than the gleaming terminus basking within the glow of the capital.

Anderson's dedicated, steadfast, and patient pursuit of the routine, without drama or distinction, led to measured yet critical military success. His steady hand provided confidence to the officers and men looking to him for guidance and leadership. In two historic instances, Anderson and the troops under his direct command accomplished decisive objectives: the destruction of key bridges literally in the face of the charging enemy, preventing a disaster; and building a strategically critical bridge while under heavy fire, allowing the rapid buildup of forces that inflicted the final defeats on the German Western Front armies.

After, Anderson left it to others to proclaim their own significance. In his unpublished account of the Ardennes campaign, the largest battle fought by the US Army in World War II, and its most dramatic crisis, Anderson's extreme modesty is evident. He merely notes—in less than a page—briefly and vaguely the activities of "Group Tactical Hdqrs." without ever noting his own critical orders, or even that *he* was the group commander. He consistently chose to highlight others, rather than himself.

Anderson, how he responded to crises, and how his young engineers met critical challenges are the subjects of this book. Although the outcomes are well known, what is not as widely appreciated is how much the decisions and actions of this seasoned and steadfast leader influenced the results. Anderson's actions can be properly judged to have played a specific, direct, and significant part in stopping the German offensive and, indeed, shortening the war.

CHAPTER ONE

BEGINNINGS

Harry Wallis Anderson was born October 2, 1890, in a Frankford suburban home in northeastern Philadelphia, Pennsylvania. The firstborn of John Henry and Ida Woodington Anderson, young Wallis was later joined by sisters Adeline and Rebekah (known as Betta). John Henry, or J. H., worked for the Pennsylvania Railroad (PRR) as an accounting clerk, which provided for a stable and solid middle-class status for the Anderson family. Wallis, who was called, inevitably, Wally or Andy, enjoyed a comfortable upbringing, without frills but with modern conveniences of pre-turn-of-the-century America.

Anderson wrote of his life in two accounts, *Military* and *Civilian*, recorded shortly before his death in 1973 at the age of eighty-two. In his formal, somewhat spare and wry writing style, he revealed a life of tight-knit neighborhood friends and families, and a childhood in an old-fashioned America.[1] He was born in his parents' house, one of three new brick row–type houses owned by Ida's father, James Woodington. Woodington had replaced his single-family frame with the three row houses, one of which he lived in, the remaining two given to Ida and her older brother Fred.

When Anderson was still a toddler, J. H. moved the family to another Philadelphia suburb to the south, Folcroft (two miles northwest of present-day Philadelphia International Airport), in the area that came to be more generally known as Sharon Hill. Anderson's commentary reflects a life that centered around the railroad and the post office, as the small community was considered outside Philadelphia's downtown, though only ten miles distant.

His life in suburban Folcroft was a time that included doctor's house calls (which included the performance of minor surgery!), telegraph operators, stone masons, and one-room schoolhouses. Most roads were dirt, with only a few major ones "macadamized." Water was provided via wells; Anderson's Folcroft house had a pump in the kitchen with a tank in a closet on the second floor. Hot water resulted from a "hot water back" in the coal-fired kitchen range.[2] Early on, there was no sanitary plumbing, nor any electricity; lighting was provided by oil lamps. Eventually, city water, gas, and then electricity became available, and J. H.'s status as a railroad executive meant he was one of the first in the community to have his house thus furnished.

Turn-of-the-century American life included tragedies that struck with not uncommon occurrence. Three members of a neighboring family were killed by carbon monoxide from an improperly functioning gas hot-water heater. They were discovered by the father, who worked out of town every other day. Fires too were not rare, and Anderson's narrative records numerous such incidents as he grew up.

Anderson also described severe weather events—a reminder of the much more evenhanded battle between man and elements than present day. With life centered on the railroad, extreme cold and snowstorms affected life in ways understood in modern times only in far more remote regions, rather than a scant ten miles from one of the country's major metropolitan centers. In a notable example, the blizzard of 1898, all rail transportation was suspended for several days. When a work train finally arrived in Folcroft, it delivered shovels and brooms to assist the local populace in digging itself out.[3]

The Andersons enjoyed another aspect of railroad life that set them apart, and they seemed to have taken full advantage: free regional railway travel. The Andersons used the railroad and its network to enjoy a degree of mobility and freedom that provided wonderful opportunities for a small boy. Anderson related how J. H. took him and his friends on camping and fishing-crabbing trips to the Chesapeake Bay, fifty to sixty miles distant from Folcroft. In true Anderson style, the bridges crossed while in transit to the campsites receive more attention in his notes than do the fishing or crabbing ("At that time the Susquehanna Bridge was low level and the Bush and Gunpowder [bridges] were timber trestles with an 'A' frame draw-span").[4]

Using the train as free and convenient transportation, J. H. took his family to presidential inaugurations in Washington, DC, regularly. Anderson remembered being present for William McKinley's first inauguration in March 1897, as well as similar events in 1901 (McKinley's second) and 1905 (Theodore Roosevelt's). Of the latter, Anderson commented on the influx of "cowboys and pseudo-cowpokes, some complete with cow ponies"[5] to celebrate the event, and dryly noted that "had even a small fraction of those appearing for the inauguration also been at San Juan Hill the success of the attack would have been assured."[6]

The second of the dual themes that carried through Anderson's life—railroad and military—was also established early on. Wallis's paternal grandparents and other relations lived in Leiperville, a township on the northeastern boundary of Chester, a little more than a mile or so from the Folcroft residence. The Pennsylvania Military College (PMC) was located nearby, a former private boys' school with a strong military tradition that had transitioned into a full-fledged martial institution with federal ties. PMC was the second-oldest military academy in America, after West Point, upon which PMC was modeled.[7]

Anderson attended several of the annual PMC commencement ceremonies with his aunt Annie Rebekah during the late 1890s. More than seventy years later, Anderson recalled the excitement of watching the PMC graduation exercises, which included not just "the usual oratory, ceremonies and awards in the morning, but also a mock battle in the afternoon." The cadets, having exchanged dress uniforms for field-service duds, "conducted an assault across the parade grounds against the college's main buildings—always gallantly defended by a small group of loyalists with a couple of smoking hot Gatling guns."[8] These ceremonies left a lasting and enjoyable impression on young Wallis.

In February 1898, the US battleship *Maine* was sunk in Havana harbor, sparking the Spanish-American War. Consequently, the National Guard prepared, and volunteers were called to enlist. With his father, seven-year-old Anderson visited a National Guard camp in nearby Middletown, where Company K of the 6th Pennsylvania National Guard Regiment was being mustered. Years later, during similar mobilizations for troubles with Mexico and for World War I, Anderson commanded this same infantry company—an example of the enduring and community nature of American citizen soldiers.

Also as a result of the Spanish-American War, Anderson enjoyed the excitement of witnessing Admiral George Dewey's Asiatic Squadron of the US fleet in the Hudson River, following their triumph over the Spanish Navy in Manila Bay, May 1898. J. H. had arranged for the family to ride the Pennsylvania Railroad ferry between New York City and Jersey City, New Jersey, in order to observe the victorious fleet, then at anchor in the Hudson. With no radio, satellite, television, internet, or even current photographs to supplement the occasional newspaper accounts of a foreign war conducted halfway around the world, the opportunity to see the actual recently victorious battle fleet must have been an indescribable thrill to a curious population.

Around 1900, when Anderson was ten and living in Folcroft, he joined the newly formed "Boy's Brigade," a military-themed youth organization started up by the community—probably inspired by Baden-Powell's similar efforts in Britain at the time—for the purpose of instilling and encouraging martial qualities of patriotism and "field" skills in young boys. Anderson recalled attending weekly meetings in the church basement and conducting marching drills using wooden rifles. The unit was very loosely organized, and its members had no uniforms or real equipment.

J. H. was transferred by the PRR to Hollidaysburg, outside Altoona in central Pennsylvania, when Anderson was about twelve. Hollidaysburg was more of a small country town than Folcroft, and Anderson's reminiscences reflect the differences. He recounts traveling operas, circus visits, and local bands performing in the town square ("the Diamond") during Saturday evenings. Partaking in the local and regional travel provided to members of the railroad family, and the freedom it represented, Anderson appears to have ranged all over the state, even as an adolescent. He and a friend still in Folcroft, E. P. "Ted" Bliss, visited each other's homes regularly, a one-way trip of more than 200 miles. Wallis and Ted also traveled alone, as thirteen-year-olds, to Pittsburgh, to visit the Carnegie Museum and other places—a one-way excursion of 100 miles.

Another visit by Anderson back to his former home in Folcroft as a young teenager had a more far-reaching result: he met Elizabeth Elsie Cobb, who had moved back into the same Folcroft-Sharon Hill neighborhood. Born in Sharon Hill in 1890, Elizabeth had moved with her family to Charleston, South Carolina, as her father was a member of a five-and-dime store chain. When Cobb senior was subsequently transferred back to Sharon Hill in 1903, the conditions were set for Wallis to meet "Betsey," his future wife.

J. H. and his family returned to Folcroft in 1904, with another PRR reassignment. Moving back into their same house, which had not been occupied during the Hollidaysburg posting, Anderson began to focus on achieving the best possible education available. Either he or his parents seem to have manipulated (and falsified) various residential records in order to qualify for higher-quality, inner-city schools that were convenient to the rail lines that Wallis used for commuting. Eventually, after an incident or two (including the mysterious disappearance of student residence records), Anderson was admitted to the Central Manual Training School, CMTS, for his secondary education.

In 1906, at the age of fifteen, Wallis landed his first job—with the railroad, of course. He joined the PRR Construction Department survey corps as his first regular summer employment. The work involved preparing for railway line adjustments in and around Mount Union, 190 miles west of Philadelphia. He and other members of his corps stayed in a hotel and worked long days as the railroad cut new channels to relocate the Juniata River and shift the rail line to the north. Anderson was put on a work detail in Mexico, Pennsylvania, 150 miles northwest from Philadelphia, an assignment that doesn't seem to have impressed Wallis very much, as he only noted that he was still able to return home on weekends.

It is worth mentioning the type of work he was assigned at this young age: assisting the surveying for eventual track-line development and installation or rerouting. He would have helped to evaluate all aspects of rail-line management—cuts and curves, grades and excavations, even related river relocation. As a teenager, Wallis Anderson began to professionally develop an eye for terrain, and to understand all aspects of the impact of topographic features on transportation issues. In Mexico, for example, his work was to assist in estimating, section by section, a projected large cut being made to change the path of the rail line.

The Construction Department survey corps again transferred young Anderson toward the end of his first working summer, this time closer to home, to a project in Camden, New Jersey, across the Delaware River from Philadelphia. This allowed Wallis to live at home while he worked on various survey projects as a rod and plumb-bob man.

Anderson returned to CMTS for his senior year, graduating in June 1907 at age sixteen. Wallis planned to attend college immediately after high school and applied for a scholarship inaugurated by the PRR, the Frank Thompson Scholarship program. The railroad had begun to award two four-year scholarships each year—one each for an offspring of PRR employees east and west of Pittsburgh. The awards were competitive and based on examinations conducted in conjunction with annual college entrance exams; he was not selected for this award.

Lack of financial assistance notwithstanding, Anderson was accepted into the University of Pennsylvania (Penn) in the autumn of 1907. He naturally gravitated toward the civil engineering program. He went back to work in the PRR engineering corps during the summer of 1908, again working in Camden, and once more Anderson applied for the PRR's Frank Thompson Scholarship, this time winning one of the two awards. His Penn college work continued, as did his PRR employment during the summer breaks, for the most part.

The summer of '09 interrupted Anderson's normal school-break PRR employment routine. Wallis traveled to Quebec to visit a school friend for a month. The field trip and visit to Canada precluded another summer pastime he normally enjoyed—being a member of the local Sharon Hill baseball team. Showing early yet typical signs of his maturity and sense of responsibility, Anderson worked as an umpire for the county baseball league when he was available.

Anderson graduated from Penn in 1911 with a bachelor of science degree in civil engineering, and then transitioned directly into the PRR engineering corps. His summer work assigned him to Elkton, Maryland, where he and other corps members lived in company housing at "Felton House." Once again, his work involved surveying to prepare for line adjustments and the elimination of grades, and other topographic measurements.

Due to the happy coincidence of his heavy engineering curriculum and program requirements, Anderson discovered that an additional year of coursework would qualify him for a degree in economics from Penn as well. With the fourth year of his Frank Thompson scholarship funds still available, he took leave from his PRR employment and continued his studies, this time at Penn's business school, the Wharton School of Finance and Commerce.[9]

Armed with his engineering and economics degrees, and coupled with his practical background and experience in railroad engineering (at this point, the railroad executive's son had worked for the PRR six of the previous seven summers), twenty-one-year-old Wallis Anderson had an exceptional beginning to his career. It is equally evident, seeing into the future, that his role as an Army engineering officer also had an outstanding foundation.

NATIONAL GUARD

Anderson's interest in the military continued throughout college. He had many friends who joined the local unit of the National Guard of Pennsylvania, Company K of the 6th Infantry Regiment. At various musters and bivouacs and training events, Anderson tagged along, once noting that he was considered the company "mascot." Anderson even accompanied the company on occasional field deployments, including once to Gettysburg—140 miles west from his Folcroft home. His friends naturally tried to convince him to join up officially, which Wallis finally did after completing his studies at Penn.

In the autumn of 1912, a vacancy opened for a lieutenant in Company K. Wallis Anderson, with the objective of eventually obtaining a commission, and at the urging of his friends, enlisted as a private on October 15, 1912, just after his twenty-second birthday.

The National Guard was a community affair as well as a somewhat democratic institution; assignments and promotions were handled rather informally "in-house" and based upon recommendations and even elections. Accordingly, Anderson moved up the ranks rather swiftly, based upon his seniors' evaluation of his evident competence and ability to handle increasingly broad responsibilities. In March 1913, he was promoted to the rank of corporal; subsequently, after a flurry of personnel moves, elections were held for new Company K leadership positions. Anderson was elected as second lieutenant, NGP, on July 26, effective for August 1, 1913.[10] Interestingly, and as a commentary on a traditional (and archaic) custom, Anderson was required to execute a bond of $1,000 upon acceptance of his commissioning. That is, he was required to pay for his commission as an officer. As a second lieutenant in the NGP, his commander in chief was the state governor, John K. Tener.

In spring 1914, Anderson attended a week of Officers' Instruction Camp, held at Mount Gretna, PA, about eighty-five miles west and north from Philadelphia. Mount Gretna was used as a central mustering location for the entire NGP. Throughout his life, Anderson had a remarkable tendency to make friends with a vast array of people, many of whom he would encounter again, in a variety of situations. His week at Mount Gretna was one such example, as his tent-mate was Butler Windle, a colleague from West Chester, near Anderson's Folcroft home, and a future Pennsylvania judge. Likewise, one of his instructors was Captain Walter Krueger, with whom Anderson would serve along the Mexican border in 1916, and in Europe more than twenty-five years hence.

Anderson was promoted again, to first lieutenant, on August 8, 1914. This advancement was also the result of an election; another bond of $1,000 was required for this promotion as well. (Note that a junior officer's pay was around $5 per day of service at the time.) Yet another promotion to captain followed, on May 25, 1915, along the same lines—election, appointment, bond payment ($2,000 this time).

Thus, by summer of 1915, twenty-four-year-old Anderson had already gained experience commanding troops, albeit in a part-time role with the NGP. He had been advanced from enlistment as a private to captain in little more than two and a half years, almost two years of which had been as company commander. During this early career, as he was working full time for the PRR, Anderson's National Guard duties consisted of routine drills and training periodically with other Pennsylvanian units.

TRANSITMAN

Meanwhile, as his part-time military career took shape, Anderson embarked on his permanent, full-time career as a railroad employee. Switching from his collegiate summer construction jobs, Anderson was assigned to the Maintenance of Way (MW) operating department. He was assigned to the Trenton Division, working out of the headquarters in Camden, New Jersey.

He recorded his first important assignment in the aftermath of an accident. A main track bridge near Glen Loch, PA, twenty-five miles west of Philadelphia, had failed the night of November 27, 1912, resulting in the derailment of a passenger train. Four passengers were killed and fifty injured. The cause was determined to be a major flaw in the bridge's construction, which had apparently been overlooked during periodic inspections by qualified and experienced bridge inspectors, and during annual inspections by a committee of senior engineering officials as well. The Glen Loch bridge was of steel construction, and the defect regarded the assembly of the steel. Despite Trenton Division's preponderance of arched masonry bridges (i.e., significantly different from Glen Loch's), railroad management subsequently ordered an immediate inspection of all bridges.

Anderson joined this system-wide effort, his team using a locomotive and combined car and carrying a commandeered rowboat used to inspect the underside of bridge arches. Although this months-long effort did not identify any major defects, several minor yet potentially problematic flaws were discovered by Anderson's crew and subsequently remedied.

During the period leading up to America's entry into World War I, Anderson took part in other railway emergencies, including a flood that stopped track operations (1913), a severe snowstorm that halted much of the New York Division (1914), and derailments due to various causes. Anderson's roles were varied and required problem-solving across a vast spectrum of railroad-related activities. He reported erecting telegraph poles that had been downed due to wind and icing. He rode in a "plow" locomotive for snow-clearing, and used brooms and shovels as well; at one point his crew shoveled snow into the water tank to operate the locomotive. Interestingly, his commentary includes references to working alongside African-American railroad workers during these crises, which entailed long, arduous days of continuous work while train and engine crews were rotated, and subsisting almost entirely on sandwiches for days on end.

As mentioned previously, Anderson had a knack for making friendships and connections, ones that not only endured but also paid professional and social dividends throughout his life and career. For the most part, during his assignment to the Trenton Division Maintenance of Way Engineer's Office of the PRR, Anderson stayed at the Camden YMCA. At various times there, he met and became friends with individuals who went on to become prominent personalities, including the president of the Campbell Soup Company, the superintendent of the Camden school system, a Navy admiral, and a New Jersey city executive.

By spring of 1916, Anderson was a senior rodman, soon to be promoted to transitman. His alter ego, Captain H. Wallis Anderson, Company K commander of the 6th Infantry, National Guard of Pennsylvania, however, was about to become involved in a national crisis along the border with Mexico—the actual country this time, not the township in central Pennsylvania.

Once again eyeing the future, a summary assessment of Anderson at this point is useful. Following his collegiate studies, Anderson had embarked on two professional interests—the railroad and the Army, in the form of the National Guard. This allowed Anderson to develop skills along two parallel lines, and he made the most of both. He was about to experience his first period of operational leadership.

ENDNOTES

1   Modest to a fault, Anderson almost always refers to himself with first person plural pronouns ("we"), or in the third person altogether ("the writer").

2   H. Wallis Anderson, *Memoirs—H. Wallis Anderson, Sr,* (unpublished, 1972. Henceforth cited as "HWACiv"), 3.

3   Another aspect of Anderson's pastoral early life was timeless, bridging generations: pet dogs. One such was a collie and shepherd mix, Bob, who was noted as being exceptionally intelligent, capable, and likable. Not only was Bob "harness broken," he knew his reins and could pull either sled or express wagon—surely a benefit like no other to a small boy and his neighborhood friends. Bob was known for at least one other skill, the value of which is hard to calculate: he could be sent, by himself, to the post office to retrieve mail. Apparently, this act sometimes included periodically defending himself against a "perennial neighborhood adversary." During these contests Bob would lay the letters down, perform his civil defense duties, and then resume his task after again collecting the mail.

4   HWACiv, 6.

5   Ibid, 9.

6   Ibid.

7   The school formerly known as the Pennsylvania Military College is now conducting business as Widener University; PMC's last class of cadets graduated in 1972.

8   H. Wallis Anderson, *Some Military Experiences* (unpublished, 1972. Henceforth cited as "HWAMil"), 2–3.

9   The University of Pennsylvania's Wharton School, as it is now known, opened in 1881 as America's first collegiate business school, and is routinely considered to be among the country's top business school programs.

10   War Department, Adjutant General's Office, Officer's 201 File (Service Record) for Harry Wallis Anderson (O-187089).

CHAPTER TWO

MEXICAN BORDER

"Gentlemen, we don't want you to cross the border;
we want you to push the border ahead of you."

F rom the end of the Mexican-American War in 1848, well into the second decade of the twentieth century, the political situation in Mexico had been chaotic and violent. Some of this turmoil surged up to the southern border of the United States.

During this period, the entire international boundary was only vaguely and intermittently marked, sparsely populated, and barely controlled in a few places. The violence along the border was conducted in both directions, and involved Mexican bandits, American outlaws, hostile Indians, Mexican and American irregular militia–type bands, and sometimes US and Mexican troops. One group would carry out some raid or act of brigandage, then bolt across the border, as that usually stopped the pursuit by whatever law enforcement was available.

The various and numerous rebellions, revolts, and revolutions in Mexico invariably involved the American border.

In the decades before the Columbus Raid, the American army had conducted numerous incursions into Mexico in pursuit of Mexican bandits. These were typically small-scale affairs, and rarely accomplished anything useful other than a temporary lull in violence, at the cost of stirring up the local Mexican population and government to anti-American resentment. In fact, Mexican revolutionaries conducted raids to provoke US retaliation, specifically calculated to garner patriotic support from the local populace.

The exception to the rule took place in 1914 in Vera Cruz, a Yucatan port that was due to receive a shipment of arms that President Woodrow Wilson deemed contrary to US interests. The resulting seaborne invasion and occupation by the US was large-scale, lasted six months, and cost hundreds of lives combined, on all sides (American, Mexican government, and anti-government revolutionaries). In 1915, scores of raids across the border into the United States were undertaken by Mexican revolutionaries.

In response, the US Army deployed troops along the border, usually in small outposts, some of which went so far as to build emplacements with trench lines, barbed wire, machine-gun positions, and artillery battery parks.

Francisco "Pancho" Villa, a Mexican revolutionary whose power had ebbed and flowed for years, was losing support and influence in northern Mexico by 1916. Attempting to regain some of his dwindling popularity, he directed violent provocations across the border. The most severe incident came on March 9, 1916, when a raiding party of about 600 Mexican irregulars crossed three miles into the US at the border hamlet of Columbus, New Mexico. Columbus was the site of "Cavalry Camp Columbus," an outpost of the US 13th Cavalry Regiment. In the ensuing clash, the raiders were repulsed and fled south across the border, where they were pursued by the US cavalry a dozen miles into Mexico.

Eventually the chase was abandoned, and the American cavalrymen returned to the US. The raid was an abject failure for Villa. Eight US servicemen were killed, along with ten civilians. Against these numbers, Villa's band lost around 150 men, and he was forced to clear out from the border region.

The larger result of the Villa raid, however, was that it spurred US president Wilson to declare a national emergency, and to authorize a punitive expedition into Mexico, led by the commander of the troops at El Paso, Brigadier General John J. Pershing. Pershing had had an active and varied military career to this point. He had campaigned and fought across America's far-flung territories, including against the Sioux, Geronimo's Apaches, the Moros in the Philippines, and the Spanish in Cuba; he had obtained a law degree from the University of Nebraska; and had served as military attaché in Japan during the Russo-Japanese War. President Theodore Roosevelt (perhaps remembering him from the Battle of San Juan Hill, where both had served) had promoted Pershing to general from the rank of captain (bypassing three grades—major, lieutenant colonel, and colonel—as well as 835 more-senior officers). Political patronage undoubtedly helped, as Pershing had married the daughter of a Senate member of the Military Appropriations Committee.

In order to supply and support the troops conducting the incursion into Mexico, to ensure their lines of communication, and to provide for border security, more troops were required than were available on active duty. With the war raging in Europe since 1914, Wilson realized how vulnerable the US was, should a more extensive national defense crisis arise. The war in Europe (not yet a "world war") was approaching its second full year, with no end in sight. President Wilson was staunchly opposed to entering the European war; he had concluded it was not in America's interest to join the fight, as no direct threat to American interests had yet developed. Nevertheless, the troubles in Europe and the Mexican border highlighted America's woefully inadequate and unacceptable military defense preparedness.

While he and Congress sought to increase the size of the military, Wilson also ordered into federal service the National Guard, and mobilized those units to be sent to the border with Mexico.

This was the first such widespread activation and deployment in American history, and while it provided an immediate augmentation to the active-duty forces, the call-up came with limitations. The most important of these was that National Guard units were not allowed to cross borders and be used outside the territorial boundaries of the United States.

At the time, the National Guard of Pennsylvania was organized as a division of four infantry brigades of three regiments each, one battalion of signal troops, one battalion of engineers, two field hospitals, three ambulance companies, and one regiment of cavalry. Captain Anderson, as commander of Company K, 6th Infantry Regiment, was part of the 2nd Brigade.

Pennsylvania units were of course included in the federal call-up, and on June 22, 1916, the National Guard of Pennsylvania (NGP) was called into federal service. Anderson thereupon formally began his active federal service from this date; he became Captain H. Wallis Anderson, Infantry, US Army.

At the time, spring 1916, Wallis Anderson's civilian job title was senior rodman. Upon call-up with the National Guard, he was able to extend his railroad service, albeit in absentia, by taking two weeks' leave, even after having reported for military service. This two-week period was just long enough for the PRR to promote him on July 1, 1916, to transitman in the Office of the Chief Engineer– MW, Trenton Division. (A transitman performs survey duties using specialized measurement equipment.) Throughout the period of federalized service, PRR policy allowed employees to remain on the rolls as "furloughed for military duty."[11]

Once ready, units were transported by rail to the Texas border region, mostly around El Paso, Texas. By June 24, NGP units had begun the process of being reshaped and renumbered in order to fit into the federal table of organization. Captain Anderson's K Company thus came into service with the 3rd Battalion, 16th Infantry Regiment of the United States Army. The 16th Infantry had been stationed along the US-Mexico border for years, in the region of El Paso.

Anderson observed one difference wrought by the shift from state to federal service—namely, the treatment of African Americans. His Company K had included two serving as cooks, as was common practice. Upon being federalized, however, these two service members (a father-son duo named William and Foster Polk, respectively), who Anderson deemed "very able, competent, and esteemable,"[12] were not allowed to muster into US service due to federal regulations of the time. Their appointed successors were considered to be a significant downgrade. The total experience of the replacements—one of whom was a boilermaker by trade, the other a bookbinder—upon selection as cooks was a couple days each as potato peelers, which made them the most qualified.

Anderson's battalion departed Mount Gretna and traveled to El Paso by way of Reynoldsville, PA, the Wabash River, and Fort Smith, Arkansas. Stops along the way were allowed for exercise and administrative activities. On arrival in El Paso in July 1916, the Pennsylvania units were assigned to a desert area along the El Paso and Southwest Railroad, a mile or so north of the main post of Fort Bliss (itself on the north end of the city). A large Army camp was established, with state units positioned in designated areas. A brigade from Kentucky was located four miles northeast of the city, near the municipal waterworks. Near the Pennsylvania troops were Ohio Guard units as well. Other state units rotated in during the ensuing months, as selected state units were returned home. The post was named Camp Stewart, after the long-serving adjutant general of Pennsylvania, Thomas J. Stewart.

Initially, the major objectives of the federalized units were to "establish a livable base camp, to acclimate the largely urban civilians to military field service, maximize their physical fitness and equipment, increase their military knowledge, training, and combat readiness and prepare for contingencies and eventualities of a military nature."[13] The sudden and extreme change from a northeastern civilian life to a southwestern desert military existence meant challenges for all company officers. One example of the training was a four-day, forty-mile route march with tactical objectives. Deficiencies were identified and steps quickly taken to resolve them as the entire Army adapted to the new routine and environment.

With such a large force along the border, the situation became calm, and the mission evolved into what Anderson characterized as a "watch and wait" routine. The chances of actual combat action dwindled for the border troops, and eventually units were returned home as 1916 drew to a close. A main concern for the latter months of the expedition was managing the weather conditions. Temperature changed dramatically in the desert, as Anderson reported that "a low of 30 at 3 a.m. and a high of 80 at 3 p.m. on the same day were not uncommon." He reported "appreciable" snowfalls, particularly at night.

Anderson also recorded an interesting anecdote. Local El Paso citizens hosted a dinner for University of Pennsylvania alumni, which Anderson attended. One of the speakers, a local businessman who had commercial interests in northern Mexico and who had "undoubtedly profited materially by the influx of troops and major increase in business due to their presence," had remarked, "Gentlemen, we don't want you to cross the border; we want you to push the border ahead of you."[14]

Eventually, Pennsylvania regiments were gradually released from their federal obligation at the rate of one per month. Other National Guard units were still arriving, and elements of Pershing's incursion column were returning to El Paso as well. Camp routine continued for those units that remained. Improvements in tents and meals made both more tolerable. Nevertheless, Anderson reported that "the flies, sandstorms, and high winds frequently added little to the pleasure of outdoor living." A planned Christmas feast, which included "many,

many turkeys complete with fixins" were provided; however, a severe sandstorm limited the troops' enjoyment. Anderson, meanwhile, managed to arrange to take leave, and thus missed the Christmas turkey sandstorm.[15]

While back home in Philadelphia for ten days' leave over Christmas, Anderson became engaged to Betsey Cobb, his neighbor for more than twelve years. Although Wallis had to return to El Paso after his leave, the 6th Regiment was selected for return home shortly after Christmas 1916. The contingent entrained on February 12, 1917, and arrived in Philadelphia on February 22. Their arrival was delayed and timed so that they would arrive at Broad and Washington Streets in the morning of George Washington's birthday, in order to conduct a marching parade up Broad Street, around City Hall, then west on Market Street, and out Lancaster Avenue to the Armory on Forty-First and Mantua Avenue. The regiment was formally mustered out of federal service on February 28.

Resuming his employment with the PRR, Wallis enjoyed only a brief period as a civilian; the international situation once again threatened to intervene as America's slide toward war with Germany gathered momentum. During his absence he had nevertheless been advanced from junior to senior transitman, and in fact was in line to become a branch line assistant supervisor with the next vacancy.

Despite the uncertainty of a pending conflict, Anderson and his fiancée, Betsey Cobb, were married shortly after his return. To complicate what must have been a difficult decision, it was understood that due to the high level of preparedness resulting from their service along the Mexican border, especially compared to novice units being formed from the civilian population to meet the new wartime demands, those units federalized in 1916 would be the first ones called up for the European war. As a result, twenty-six-year-old newlywed Captain H. Wallis Anderson, Infantry, US Army, soon found himself headed back into active service and toward combat in the largest conflict in history thus far.

ENDNOTES

11   HWACiv, 15.

12   HWAMil, 6.

13   Ibid, 7.

14   Ibid, 8.

15   Ibid, 9.

CHAPTER THREE

THE GREAT WAR

After more than two years of ambivalence, America entered the war in the spring of 1917. With both houses of Congress overwhelmingly giving President Wilson the declaration of war he had requested, America joined the fray with characteristic exuberance, seeking "to make the world safe for democracy," and to be a part of the "War to End All Wars."

A mere five months before declaring war, however, America had reelected Wilson on a campaign built around the slogan "He Kept Us Out of War." The war was viewed by many as being a clash between competing European empires—the German, Ottoman, and Austro-Hungarians (with the Kingdom of Bulgaria) on the one side, against the Triple Entente on the other: primarily Britain, Russia, and France.

Nevertheless, by spring 1917, Americans finally viewed Germany[16] as the clear aggressor whose behavior had become so abhorrent that sending American boys thousands of miles away from home to fight was deemed appropriate.

Once committed to war, however, surely one of the most overarching questions facing the War Department of the Wilson administration had to have been "Now what?" From a military standpoint, the nation's situation was not ambivalent—it was dire. Transforming what was essentially a modest and widely dispersed border authority into a force able to fight alongside the massive allied armies—millions were by then engaged—of France, Russia, and Britain was a gargantuan task.

The state of the US Army at that moment was by any measure abysmal when measured against what was expected of it. Hopes ran very high; America was supposed to win the war, and soon, before the bankrupt and exhausted Allies collapsed. To those involved in carrying out this effort to completely reinvent the US Army, there had to have been immense trepidation.

When Brigadier General John J. Pershing returned with the American army from dealing with the Mexican border situation (without any real resolution), the Army was at a half-century peak of preparedness and organization. However, this "peak" revealed just how inadequate the Army was at the onset of America's entry into the Great War.

The combined American army comprised approximately 260,000 total troops. This number reflects the Regular Army plus the mobilization of the National Guard, which of course caught up Wallis Anderson. Ranked against the other Entente and Allied Powers, the American army numbers at the time of the war declaration were anemic: France's army numbered 3.6 million at the outbreak, heading toward a war-long mobilization of 8.7 million; Britain numbered 750,000, working toward 3.8 million; Russia 5.25 million, working toward 15 million; and the Kingdom of Italy had mustered 1.5 million, working toward 5.6 million.

Another comparison highlights the daunting size and scope of the war the American army was joining. Shortly after the American declaration of war, a joint French-British offensive kicked off, intended to drive back the German invaders in the Chemin des Dames region of France. Named for the aggressive French commander in chief, Robert

Nivelle, the plan called for occupying and distracting the Germans with attacks by the British to the north in the vicinity of Arras; when German reserves were committed and depleted, the French would launch a powerful thrust intended to achieve a decisive breakthrough.

The Nivelle Offensive (known as the Second Battle of the Aisne) involved three British and two French armies, forces totaling around 850,000 troops. Opposing them were two German armies, with around 480,000 total troops. No breakthrough occurred; the net result of the combined offensive was the territorial gain of a few square miles of blood-soaked soil. French casualties were around 187,000, with the British suffering an additional 160,000. German casualties totaled 163,000 for both sectors. Thus, in a mere six-week period, Allied and German *casualties* combined were double the size of the entire American army.

Nevertheless, the prospect of America joining the fight was a cause for optimism for France and Britain, and of equal concern to the Central Powers. After all, America was a democratic republic with a population of 103 million. Once Congress authorized a full mobilization with conscription, the Allies could expect millions of American soldiers to fight side by side with French and British armies. Plans were made for the US to provide 100 divisions by spring 1919, making it larger than the entire French Army. Germany knew this as well and calculated that they could win before the full weight of American arms could be brought to bear in the trenches.

The German estimation was based on the other aspect of American military status in April 1917, beyond mere numbers: preparedness. The last major war the American army fought was the Civil War, now fifty years distant. All subsequent conflicts had involved actions at military-unit levels far below that being waged in France along the Western Front. In *seventy-five years* of fighting the various Indian Wars in the American West, the US Army had involved about 100,000 troops total, incurring about a thousand casualties—total—in that entire time.

Even the Spanish-American War (1898–1902) only involved combat by units at the infantry brigade or regiment level, a regiment at the time being about a thousand men. The largest and most decisive action of that ground war was the battle of San Juan Heights (including San Juan Hill and Kettle Hill), in which about 8,000 US troops were involved.

By 1917, no American commander had any actual combat experience with troops larger than this number. Congress took steps to address this deficiency with the National Defense Act of 1916, which created the structure for larger Army formations, on par with the Allies.

Another challenge to be overcome was matériel. At the start of 1917, the US Army was equipped largely in the nineteenth-century fashion, with cavalry units still integral in the order of battle. While by 1917 in France, heavy artillery and machine guns had established battlefield dominance, the US Army was woefully deficient in both.

Again using the Nivelle Offensive of April to May 1917 for comparison, the French and British amassed more than *7,000* heavy guns and howitzers for the supporting bombardment, including calibers up to 400 mm (16 inches). The heaviest artillery pieces fielded by the US Army at that time were the 120 mm (4.7-inch) M1906, and the 152.4 mm (6-inch) M1908 howitzer. The entire US Army had only sixty of the M1906 guns and forty-two of the M1908 howitzers.

Similarly, in April 1917, the US Army had fewer than 450 machine guns scattered throughout its entire force.[17] The European armies had by this time equipped their combat units with *tens of thousands* of machine guns; the British Army had even established a Machine Gun Corps, on par with their air force (Royal Flying Corps).

In all, with the entry into the war, the US Army faced three simultaneous upheavals: massive expansion, a complete reorganization, and unprecedented modernization. All three of these changes were underway in spring 1917 when Wallis Anderson was called up, after an all-too-brief spell of civilian life.

CAMP HANCOCK

Having been mustered out of federal service on February 28, 1917, Anderson returned to his job with the Pennsylvania Railroad. Momentous events occurred swiftly during that spring. He and Betsey Cobb wed on March 21, three weeks to the day from the end of his federal service obligation. He was notified of his advancement to branch line assistant supervisor in the Maintenance of Way Department, to be assigned to Olean, NY, starting May 1. Reporting for work in Buffalo, Upstate New York, Anderson left his new wife, Betsey, back in Philadelphia, no doubt with one eye on world events and anticipating only a brief stint as a civilian.

On July 15, the expected call came as the National Guard of Pennsylvania was once again called into federal service. On that date, Anderson, still commanding Company K, once again returned to service with the US Army. His initial processing took place in Philadelphia, after which the NGP division shifted to Augusta, Georgia, for training and reorganization.

At the new Camp Hancock (run by Lieutenant Colonel I. Price Ewing; naturally, Anderson knew him, as Ewing had come from the Pennsylvania 6th Infantry) in Augusta, the Pennsylvanians, now designated as the US Army's 28th Division, began training and reorganizing, with the attendant confusion one would expect when undertaking such a massive retooling effort. To better handle modern warfare (and, grimly, the expected mass casualties), the 28th Division's regiments were effectively doubled by combining two of the Guard regiments. New units (for machine guns and trench mortars) were created, while traditional components, such as the horse cavalry regiment, were eliminated. The Company K that Anderson commanded in Mexico earlier in 1917 had consisted of about sixty-five men, with a captain (himself) and two lieutenants as junior officers. In Georgia, infantry companies were more than doubled in size, to around 150 men per company, with six officers assigned.

For a brief period in November, Anderson was assigned as a "surplus" officer in the 111th Infantry, leaving his Company K after having served there since his enlistment in 1912, and as commanding officer since 1915. He was briefly assigned to the 109th Infantry, in November to December 1917.

AN ENGINEER OFFICER

Army engineers have two essential functions: to build and to destroy. In an offensive role, engineers enable the army to close with and to destroy the enemy. Engineers build and maintain the roads and bridges and remove obstacles such as minefields and defensive obstacles and fortifications, providing ground forces access to the enemy. On the defensive, engineers duly perform the opposite: they destroy the enemy's access to friendly forces. Engineers lay minefields, demolish roads and bridges, and they build fortifications and other obstacles to hinder the enemy's offensive efforts.

While "sappers" and "pioneers" (as engineers were sometimes known) had been a formal component of US Army since the Revolutionary War, the National Guard of Pennsylvania had only recently created such a specialized unit, in 1908. It was originally organized in Scranton, in order to take advantage of the skills of the local pool of manpower—coal miners, with their requisite expertise working with explosives.

When the division expanded, the engineer component was elevated from a battalion to a regiment. The larger engineer component required additional qualified officers. Anderson's civilian background, training, and education would have made this move from infantry a logical choice. Accordingly, H. Wallis Anderson became a member of the Army Corps of Engineers in January 1918, and was assigned to the 103rd Engineers under the command of Colonel Frederic Snyder.

As a specialized formation, the 28th Division's new 103rd Engineer Regiment was organized somewhat differently than line infantry units. It comprised only two battalions of three companies each. As the senior captain in the engineer regiment (despite having been relatively junior while with the NGP), Anderson was eventually assigned as adjutant[18] for the 1st Battalion, under Majors James Bradford and then Burt Sapp. The massive expansion then underway meant a much larger officer corps was needed as well. Anderson became a training instructor in the Third Officer Training Camp, and presided over a board to evaluate enlisted candidates for selection as officers.

At Camp Hancock, the 103rd Engineers engaged in a wide variety of support activities, such as construction to house and support the ongoing reorganization and training. This included barracks and firing ranges, and while this greatly benefited the division overall, it did not meet the requirements for training combat engineers. Considerable effort, then, was made to ensure that the regiment received adequate combat mission training.

Combat engineers received infantry training to augment their specialized "pioneer" or engineer skills. Infantry activities included close-order drill, guard duty, physical training, hygiene, and rifle and bayonet practice. As engineers, the regiment conducted trench construction, bridge-building, use of explosives, and mapmaking. These activities were carried out in as realistic and intensive an environment as possible, to simulate actual war conditions.

Captain Anderson's combined military and engineering value would have been evident. At twenty-seven, with five years' experience, including a seven-month operational deployment as a company commander, Anderson would have been a valuable asset in his battalion. In a February 1918 Army survey, he was able to claim either "expert" or "experienced" status with between five to eleven years' experience in civil engineering, surveying, topography, railroad construction, bridge construction, highway construction, reinforced concrete and structured steel construction, railroad maintenance of way and operation, mechanical and topographical drafting, and railroad transportation. He registered as "expert" in infantry drill, "musketry," topography, and training camp activities. Among the thousands of recruits then being pulled into service to fill out the massive expansion, Anderson's expertise would have stood out.

As the division's preparation for war continued into 1918, Anderson's wife spent much of that time with him in Georgia. Betsey returned north to suburban Philadelphia in early 1918 to stay with her parents, and to give birth to their first child. Bettie Anderson was born on February 24, 1918, in Sharon Hill; Captain Anderson was able to take leave and return to Philadelphia for the event. Betsey and Bettie remained with the Cobbs throughout the war.

TO FRANCE

In spring 1918, after more than nine months of reorganization, expansion, equipping, and training, the 28th Division was finally sent to France to join the American Expeditionary Force (AEF), under General John J. Pershing.

Leaving Camp Hancock on May 9, the 103rd Engineers moved by train to Camp Mills, Long Island, New York, to await transatlantic transport. The regiment departed Camp Mills, embarking on the Canadian Pacific Steamship (CPSS) *Metagama*, a passenger liner used as a troop transport during the war.

Due to the serious threat posed by German U-boat submarines, a convoy of the *Metagama* and twelve other vessels departed New York City on May 19 escorted by a battleship. The Atlantic crossing took thirteen days; it was uneventful apart from a submarine alarm and subsequent emergency actions on the last night at sea, May 30. The *Metagama* and several other ships fired at the reported sighting, and an accompanying British aircraft dropped a depth bomb as the convoy rounded the coast of Ireland. No further activity developed, and it was decided that the sighting had been false.

The *Metagama* pulled into Liverpool the next day, and the division disembarked; it entrained for Dover the same day. A daylong train ride across England ensued, which only afforded a nighttime glimpse of London en route to Dover. The division history notes that London's searchlights were visible as a defense against German bombers.

After only one night in Dover (quartered in underground facilities), Anderson's regiment embarked a channel steamer for the transit to Calais, arriving June 1, 1918. The 103rd Engineers remained in the vicinity of Calais for several days as it received training from the French Army, including defense against gas attacks. From Calais they embarked in the famous "Hommes 40, Chevaux 8" rail cars (designated to hold forty men or eight horses); they detrained at the Desvres railhead fifteen miles south of Calais (Anderson characteristically writes of railheads more so than major cities). The 103rd remained there eighteen days, attached to and provided training by British Army elements, including the 18th Northumberland Fusiliers and the Tyneside Pioneers, an engineering unit.

At Desvres, Anderson encountered a friend from his 6th Infantry days, Captain Clifford Arnold, Medical Corps, US Army. Captain Arnold's wife, Audrey, was spending the war living in Sharon Hill as well; she and Betsey Anderson became fast friends as their husbands served overseas. Anderson characterized this friendship as a case of sharing "mutual misery."[19]

The Americans expected to go into combat very shortly, in conjunction with the Allies. There was immense pressure to involve large numbers of American troops as quickly as possible. In the British and French view, this meant feeding the fresh but inexperienced American soldiers into British and French formations as replacements, a process referred to as "amalgamation." Pershing and Wilson, however, adamantly insisted that American units would serve on equal footing with their Allies, even if it meant some delay as the AEF was built up into an effective large-scale and independent army.

The debate between these opposing views was not an academic one: in March 1918, Germany had begun a series of massive offensives against the French and British armies, hoping to end the war before the addition of the American army tipped the balance on the Western Front in favor of the Allies.

Collectively, the Germans referred to these blows as the Spring Offensive, made possible by the release of huge numbers of German troops from the Eastern Front following the collapse of Russia, then in the throes of revolution. Unlike the previous Allied offensives, the German attacks had achieved some significant success; the French were being forced back, and by June, the German Army was again threatening to take Paris.

To meet the crisis, a compromise among the Allies was reached, allowing US divisions and brigades to be initially fed into battle alongside and interspersed with French and British formations, until such time as effective senior-level American units could be placed into the line.

When the 103rd Engineers arrived in Desvres in early June, the situation had become critical. The German Army had reached Château-Thierry, on the Marne River, only fifty miles from Paris suburbs. Although halted by combined French and American forces, the Germans were poised to continue attacks to break the Allies. Fighting around Château-Thierry (including Belleau Wood)—the German offensive's furthest penetration toward Paris—was intense, and continued for several weeks.

SECOND BATTLE OF THE MARNE

On June 22, the 103rd Engineers moved to the Château-Thierry battle area, along with other elements of the 28th Division. The division was attached to the 39th Division (French) for a final stint of training, before being placed into the line for combat service. Carried by train at night, south past Amiens (then under German artillery fire), and past Paris to La Ferte Gauche, a small town fifty miles east of the capital and twenty-three miles south of the front lines at Château-Thierry, the regiment detrained for active employment.

Six days later, the 103rd marched to take up positions ten miles to the north in support of operations then being conducted in the vicinity of Château-Thierry. Colonel Snyder ordered the 103rd Engineers around a bridgehead over the Marne, at Charly, seven miles southwest of Château-Thierry. Arriving on June 29, Major Burt Sapp's 1st Battalion, with his adjutant, Captain Anderson, established its headquarters in the town of Charly, along the Marne's north bank. The regiment joined French troops already in position.

During the move to the Marne, the 28th Division (under the command of Major General Charles H. Muir since December 15, 1917) suffered its first casualties, as five engineers from Company E, 2nd Battalion, were wounded by shellfire. Anderson recorded that the entire area was under sporadic German artillery fire during this period. He speculated that the Germans were probably trying to hit one of the bridges across the Marne, which would have disrupted support for the front lines.

Overall, though, Anderson does not seem to have been overly impressed with such harassing barrages, as he wrote that the engineers' "major discomfort was the annoyance of inopportune ducking into a basement for shelter—particularly at night."[20]

The 103rd's position was in reserve, seven miles south of the US 2nd Division, which included the brigade of Marines that had fought and stopped the German advance in Belleau Wood in early June. Here the 28th Division dug in and awaited a German attack, anticipated for July 4. For the engineers, this meant constructing trenches behind the French and American front lines. The German attack never took place, although the area was subjected to artillery barrages. On the night of July 8, gas shells hit near 1st Battalion's Company C billets—gas barrages being a fairly common and accepted occurrence at this point in the war, by both sides.[21] The engineers were shifted to defensive positions along the easternmost position for the entire 28th Division; the lines beyond were manned by French troops.

Although the Germans had chosen not to attack during the American national day, they did recognize the French equivalent,

Bastille Day, July 14. Calculating perhaps the French would be celebrating and thus relax their guard, the Germans planned one last offensive the next day, hoping to crack the French lines and win the war. Estimating the Allies would expect a drive toward Paris from the Château-Thierry salient, Ludendorff, the German chief of their general staff, instead planned a two-pronged assault on either side of Reims, a major industrial center seventy-five miles northeast of Paris.

The First and Third German Armies would drive south and southwest, from east of Reims; this was code-named "Reims" (a ruse either too clever by half, or brilliant, or unimaginative; the reader is left to decide). West of Reims, the Seventh Army aimed to drive southeast, across the Marne, to meet the advancing First Army units behind Reims, somewhere near Epernay. The Seventh Army's effort was code-named "*Marneschutz*" ("Marne Defense"), with the actual assault designated in planning documents as "Road Construction" (surely this would have pleased civil engineer Anderson, had he known at the time.). The three German armies, with more than 500,000 troops in fifty divisions, were intended to converge to cut off the city and destroy a major segment of the French and American defensive line. Such a success would have unraveled the French armies east of Paris and caused a major catastrophe.

The German offensive began with a massive heavy artillery barrage, starting around midnight, July 14 to 15, with gas and high explosives all along the line. French liaison officers with American units "said it was the heaviest bombardment they had any knowledge of."[22] It reached more than twenty miles beyond the front lines. Before dawn, German troops crossed the Marne on ponton bridges, ferries, and small boats. "*Marneschutz*" was underway.

The four regiments of the US 3rd Division (4th, 7th, 30th, and 38th Infantry Regiments) occupied trench lines along the Marne's south bank from Chierry upriver to Varennes. From there, the 28th Division's 109th and 110th Infantry Regiments were positioned along the river from Varennes east to Courthiezy. East of the Americans were units of the French 125th Division.

As troops from three German divisions assaulted across the Marne in front of the 28th Division, a tragic situation developed, exposing the flaws in the still-developing cooperation between Allied armies. Differing and mismatched tactics were being used—with severe consequences.

The Germans forces hit the US 3rd Division on the south bank, and after heavy fighting, were stopped less than two miles south of the river on a narrow front, sustaining heavy casualties. The American defenders, arranged in a traditional forward trench defense, held firm, even as they suffered many losses.[23]

However, farther east along the river, Americans of the 28th Division, in forward trench positions and ordered to "hold out at any cost," were surprised to learn that the adjacent French troops had adopted a "defense in depth" strategy. Accordingly, when the Germans attacked, they encountered lightly occupied forward French defensive positions; even these few troops quickly faded to the rear when the artillery barrage and assaults began. Strong French positions had been established several miles to the rear, along the line the Americans had placed their reserve forces.

Thus the 28th Division's right flank was completely exposed as Germans poured across the river opposite the now-empty French positions. The division's 109th and 110th Infantry Regiments were in danger of being outflanked, and were forced to give ground in the face of the overwhelming German pressure, as the French support on the right melted away to the rear. By day's end, the German 101st Grenadier and 100th Infantry Regiments held a line along a wooded ridge around St. Agnan. Opposite, across a narrow, shallow valley, the American 1st Battalion of the 109th defended the south side of the valley, in a wooded ridge spur named Bois de Rougis.

During the night, a counterattack for the next morning was ordered for the 1st Battalion of the 109th Infantry, to cross the valley and retake St. Agnan. The attack would be joined by the French on their right, with both efforts supported by French artillery. Major

Sapp, one and a half miles to the rear at Grande Fontaine with the 1st Battalion engineers in reserve, was ordered to take his battalion to occupy the 109th trenches; should disaster befall the attacking troops, the trenches behind them would be manned and defended.

Anderson reported that the trench positions were "incomplete and in some places hardly more than just a scratch on the ground a few inches deep—due to the rocky nature of the terrain." There were no underground bunkers or shelters, as the position had only recently been occupied as a reserve fortification, the battalion "P.C. (post command) being merely a shallow pit."[24]

Disaster befell. Per their offensive doctrine, the Germans had immediately replaced their assault infantry with machine-gun teams as soon as a defensible position (St. Agnan) had been reached. The French artillery barrage never took place, and the accompanying French attack on the 109th's right never materialized. When the Americans surged across the valley at noon, they were met with withering German machine-gun fire from St. Agnan and vicinity. The 1st Battalion, 109th Infantry, lost heavily in the failed attempt, and in the efforts that followed with the intent to retake St. Agnan, even with better preparation and artillery support. All were thrown back, with severe casualties, and failed to dislodge the Germans. These American counterattacks, and others up and down the lines by Franco-American forces, although initially futile and costly, had the overall effect of slowing, then finally stopping, the German advance.

Sapp's (and Anderson's) 1st Battalion remained on Bois de Rougis for three days, fighting from the exposed position in support of the infantry attacks. They endured severe German gas and explosives artillery barrages, infantry and machine-gun fire, and even German airplanes bombing and strafing their positions. Anderson noted later that a map was recovered from the body of a dead German officer; the map was marked with detailed information regarding their positions and had the notation "confirmed by airplane photograph."[25]

During the evening of July 18, the 1st Battalion Engineers, having been under fire continuously for three days, were withdrawn to their previous wooded bivouac at Grand Fontaine, a mile to the rear. The battalion had lost nine men.

The sacrifices and stiff resistance paid off. French and American reinforcements arrived all along the line, and on the Marne front the tide was reversed: as the massive German assault ebbed, the Allies pushed back. Exhausted and overwhelmed, the Kaiser's armies were forced to give ground, as the Allies vigorously battered the increasingly dispirited Germans. Ludendorff's *Friedensturm* ("Peace Offensive"), which he had hoped would finish the French Army and win the war, had failed.

In their first action with the enemy, the 28th Division's 109th Infantry (with the engineers providing close and steady support) had made a remarkable stand against the German veterans. General Pershing was said to have remarked, "Why, they are Iron Men" when informed of the Pennsylvanians' determined efforts. The sobriquet stuck, and henceforth the 28th Division referred to themselves as "The Iron Division."[26]

The French and Americans surged forward in the final days of July. After a rest, the 28th Division, now acting as a reserve force, followed the pursuit of the retreating Germans. Advancing north, the 103rd Engineers crossed, in turn, the Marne, Oureg, and Vesle Rivers. As ever, with his keen eye for terrain details and precise memory, Anderson made note that the Oureg was "more of a rill than a river."[27] During this period, the engineers reverted to their support role, repairing roads and bridges.

Throughout August, engineers constructed defensive fortifications south of the Vesle River line, demonstrating their respect for the still-formidable German Army, even as the Americans shifted to a more offensive posture. German positions held north of the Vesle in the vicinity of Fismes were strong and determined, stalling the Allied advance.

The 103rd Engineers were assigned a three-mile stretch of the line between Fismes and Courlandon, just behind the railroad track.

Here they built their defenses and maintained roads and supply lines while under artillery fire being directed from enemy observation along the high ground to the north. It was hard and dangerous work, and the division took numerous casualties, including a friend of Anderson's, former 6th Pennsylvania Infantry officer and fellow company commander Captain Edward Lynch, who was killed in the fighting along the Vesle River on August 12.

Due to combat losses and an American army program that sent officers home to provide experienced soldiers for newly formed National Army divisions, in August Anderson was reassigned to command Company E in 2nd Battalion. Combat is perhaps the most severe test of leadership, and it is commonplace at all levels— especially following a first action—for those who cannot measure up to be relieved. That Anderson was sent to command a company after the hard action around St. Agnan indicates strongly that he possessed a most precious quality: combat leadership ability.

Too often good leaders also become casualties. Even as Anderson reported to the 2nd Battalion CP at Arcis-le-Ponsart to command Company E, he discovered that the battalion commander, Major James Sydney Bradford, had been evacuated. The unfortunate major had first been gassed on August 12, then had contracted a severe case of dysentery, which was then "epidemic in the entire area."[28] Being the senior captain in the battalion, Anderson was reassigned on August 29 as the 2nd Battalion's commander.

The 103rd Engineers suffered other casualties during this August period. Major Burt Sapp, Anderson's 1st Battalion leader during the July actions, was wounded on August 7. Even more severe, however, was the loss of the regiment's executive officer, Major Frank Duffy, outside the Company F headquarters in Courville, three miles south of Fismes. Just as Duffy "stepped into a side car in front of headquarters on the evening of August 17th to make a tour of the lines, a huge shell exploded immediately behind him, killing him and the cycle driver immediately."[29]

The 103rd Engineers continued the hazardous duty of road and bridge repair and maintenance, under fire from shelling and machine guns, throughout August and into September. They constructed defensive fortifications as well, as the Germans were expected to be preparing yet another offensive in the area along the Vesle River. From July 28 through September 17, in the ranks of the 103rd, "thirteen were killed, eighty-five wounded, one-hundred thirty-seven gassed, six shell-shocked, and one was missing."[30]

Captain Anderson, commanding the 2nd Battalion, established his command post in the Bois de la Bruys, southwest of Fismes. His engineers worked primarily in support of the 56th Brigade (which included many former Pennsylvania 6th Infantry members, now organized as part of the US 111th Infantry). They built a dugout command post for an infantry regiment; erected barbed-wire entanglements in three fields; finished frontline trench construction "with the exception of fifty yards abandoned by the company detailed for that work on account of shelling";[31] constructed bridges over the Vesle; and repaired and cleared roads around three towns. Throughout, all "this work was done under very heavy enemy shell fire, including considerable gas."[32]

On September 7, the 28th Division withdrew from the Vesle arena and moved east, to the southern end of the Argonne Forest. A massive new Allied offensive was being planned, with the 28th Division placed front and center for Pershing and the American army's largest effort thus far.

THE MEUSE-ARGONNE OFFENSIVE

Following the resounding defeat of the last German attempt to break the Allied lines along the Marne, Marshal Foch, the French supreme commander of the Allied armies, sought to maintain his forces' momentum and follow up with a war-winning "continuous offensive"[33] of his own.

Despite his title, Foch did not have actual authority over the respective national armies ostensibly under his command. The Americans, with more than 1.25 million troops on the continent by midsummer, had formed the American First Army on August 10. After a period of sometimes contentious negotiation, Pershing and Foch reached agreement in early September; First Army would take part in a major offensive, fighting between two French armies along a line from Reims to Verdun, in a bid to drive north, pushing the Germans to the French-Belgian border at Sedan.

The sector assigned to the Americans was a twenty-mile-wide channel, with the Argonne Forest on the left-hand, or western side, and the Meuse River on the right. Just east of the rugged Argonne flowed the Aire River, which wound its way along this channel between the Argonne and the Meuse, along a twelve-mile-wide valley of uneven pasture and farmland—low, swampy ground interspersed with rugged patches of hills and ravines.

Wide and deep with no fords to threaten the American right flank, the Meuse flowed slowly north past Verdun, seven miles behind the front lines. The offensive's objective, Sedan, lay thirty-five miles behind German lines. Dominating the entire region were the Heights of the Meuse, northeast of Verdun, which had been held by the Germans for virtually the entire war and provided a base for heavy artillery and its direction.

Midway up the channel that was the axis for the American advance was Montfaucon, an 1100-foot-high butte, topped with a church and village long reduced to rubble. Montfaucon was the highest point of the Meuse-Argonne sector, and would be a focus for the American attacks. North from Montfaucon the terrain became even more rugged, and the front narrowed, as the Meuse on the right bent westward. Two broken heights, Cunel and Romagne, rose and split the channel into avenues leading north. Thus, at the top of the Argonne, there were three wooded positions of high grounds in a line, as a barrier to any advancing army. All three would have to be cleared before the ground flattened into a broad plateau for an advance north.

German defenses in the region had been developed continuously since 1914. Three east-west belts provided for a defense in depth. The three belts (or *stellungen*, German for "positions") were named for characters in Richard Wagner operas, the first two of which were anchored on the west by the Argonne.[34] From south to north, an advancing army would first run into Etzel-Giselher Stellung, three miles beyond the original front lines. Etzel-Giselher contained Montfaucon as its centerpiece.

Four miles north of Etzel-Giselher lay Kriemhilde Stellung, which included Cunel and Romagne heights and Grandpré, which capped the Argonne's northern tip. Freya Stellung, the weakest of the three defensive belts, was a further five miles to the north. Each belt included concrete, wooden, and earthen fortifications of bunkers, pillboxes, and redoubts. Interlocking trench systems and barbed wire were situated to provide mutual support between positions and to take maximum advantage of the terrain. Throughout their positions in the Meuse-Argonne, the German Army had placed field artillery batteries to provide additional firepower for the defenders.

Machine-gun positions provided the backbone for all German resistance. Hundreds of them were used throughout the entire sector. The Germans were especially adept at machine-gun placement: nests and approaches were provided with overlapping fire zones and supporting coverage. Often machine-gun nests faced north, in order to catch attackers in flank and rear as they passed by. Snipers, grenade throwers, and riflemen augmented the positions. Wagner was known for his complex, dense harmonies and orchestrations. With the comprehensive, intricate, multilayered, and interlocking defenses, the German positions had been well named.

The American First Army prepared for its first major offensive as an independent entity. Sixteen American divisions, each one twice the size of European counterparts, were to be used. Nine of these were assigned to the initial assault, including the 28th Division. Although the 28th had suffered serious casualties (8,772 in total) in the July to August fighting from the Marne to the Vesle, its value as a veteran force was a crucial asset; only three of Pershing's nine assault divisions had any experience. The 28th was provided such rest and replacements as could be found in August and September, and then assigned to advance along the eastern part of the Argonne Forest. They were arranged half in the woods (111th and 112th Infantry Regiments) and half out, with the 109th and 110th to advance alongside the Argonne in open ground to the Aire.

In the forest, to the 28th Division's left, was the 77th Division, another division with combat experience. The 77th was the leftmost (western) of the American divisions. Advancing up the channel east of the Aire and to the 28th Division's right was the new and inexperienced 35th Division. The 35th Division was another former National Guard division, largely from Kansas and Missouri.

The offensive began with a massive three-hour artillery barrage, with the infantry beginning their advance at 0530, September 26. Pershing's overly optimistic plan was to quickly move up to and through the German's first defensive line (Etzel-Giselher Stellung). To compound the challenges facing the Americans, the weather was cold and wet, which slowed, clogged, and fouled everything.

As the assault began, the difference in experience levels of the 28th and 35th Divisions was revealed. The 35th advance was ragged, and they suffered many casualties from German flanking fire. The main reason the 35th did not completely disintegrate was that to their left, the 28th Division methodically pressed forward and broke the German defenses around Varennes. Unlike the disjointed advance of the 35th, the Pennsylvanians conducted a coordinated, combined infantry and tank attack, maintaining unit cohesion and using their forces in a highly organized manner to unseat the German defenses, almost to Montblainville-Charpentry.

The left-hand half of the 28th, however, was mired in the forest; headway against German positions there was much more difficult to overcome. The resultant drag slowed down the division and prevented any major territorial gains.[35]

Anderson's 2nd Battalion, 103rd Engineers, advanced in the gap between the forest and the Aire, supporting the division's 55th Brigade. Anderson placed Lieutenant E. D. Hill in charge of a platoon to assist the 344th Tank Battalion. For the successful employment of tanks, whose purpose was to deliver firepower on the battlefield while protecting the crew, it was first necessary to deploy wire-cutting teams of very much non-armored men in advance to clear the way. In this case, "while preceding them and leading his men, Lieutenant Hill was severely wounded. Sergeant Dewey of the same company, in command of a wire-cutting instructors attached to the One Hundred Tenth Infantry, was killed by a German machine gun sniper during the advance."[36] Such were the hazards of engineers in combat.

To the left of Anderson's 2nd Battalion, in the dense Argonne, a leadership crisis had developed. Major Burt Sapp, recovered from his earlier wounds, had had difficulties to the extent that Colonel Snyder relieved Sapp of command of the 1st Battalion. By the end of the very first day of this grueling action, Snyder had only one battalion leader for his two battalions engaged in combat—Captain Wallis Anderson. To deal with this dilemma, Snyder eliminated the battalion organization, consolidating all engineer companies under himself, with Anderson as second in command. In this way Snyder, with Anderson assisting, could more effectively exercise direct command and control.[37]

The 28th Division's advance continued through September 27 as it pushed north of Varennes-en-Argonne past Montblainville, despite heavy casualties. In the forest, the division barely managed any headway, under extremely difficult conditions. The engineers were engaged in a variety of combat-support activities, demonstrating the versatility and usefulness of engineers. They repaired roads (usually filling in craters from shelling) and even built and maintained a light railway, used to resupply frontline units. They fortified gun positions, allowing artillery to support the offensive actions of the infantry.

Periodically they served as reserve infantry, as with the previous Marne actions. Others supported tank attacks, assisting by removing wire and other obstacles.

After the first three days, the entire offensive was struggling as all the divisions took heavy casualties against the strong German positions. By September 30, much of the American drive to the north had stalled. Although the plight of the American First Army was severe, overall Foch's Anglo-French offensives were having the desired effect: the German Army suffered all along the line from the continuous Allied pounding. German casualties were as bad as or worse than the Allies, forcing Ludendorff to abandon positions and retreat everywhere except Meuse-Argonne. On October 1, Pershing allowed the American First Army to rest and reorganize. Additional American and French units were added to the Argonne sector, and the offense resumed.[38]

The 103rd Engineers supported the drive north alongside the Argonne, to just beyond Châtel-Chéhéry. Anderson celebrated his twenty-eighth birthday on October 2, recording no comment, although he almost certainly spent it under shellfire, as the entire area was still being contested vigorously. By October 5, the engineers were in reserve for the infantry in Varennes, while still engaged in road repair and clearing operations, as well as other activities directly supporting the assault.

The engineers constructed field artillery positions, brought ammunition up to the front, built trenches, camouflaged fortifications, and emplaced machine guns during this period. Company E built a bridge over the Aire, east of Châtel-Chéhéry, on the night of October 6, when the location was still considered "No Man's Land." The soldiers worked in chest-deep water and hid from German patrols until they completed the job; during their return to Varennes they had to dodge enemy shellfire. Anderson described the engineers' work during this period as "mostly normal and routine."[39] The division continued to take casualties and slog their way north.[40]

After dark on October 8, the entire division was relieved and brought off the line as another fresh division (82nd) took its place to continue the offensive. The 28th was reassigned to the Thiaucourt sector, a relatively quiet sector compared to Meuse-Argonne. Although still active combat, the intensity was much reduced, as reflected in the soldiers' epigram from the period, "A meter in the Argonne is worth a mile at St. Mihiel."[41]

The 103rd Engineers established its headquarters at Euvezin while conducting the usual support: road repair, fortification construction, ammunition-dump guarding, infantry drill, and equipment maintenance. The regiment again reorganized, resuming a more conventional structure under the reestablishment of Captain Anderson as 2nd Battalion's commanding officer, with Companies D, E, and F assigned under him.

Although nothing like the intensity of enemy action in Meuse-Argonne, the Germans still harassed the Americans with artillery and machine-gun fire. Patrols and raids were conducted across the lines, with engineers accompanying the infantry as demolitions experts for such dangerous work. This activity continued right up through the declaration of the Armistice at 1100 hours on November 11. That afternoon, Anderson took the opportunity and "reconnoitered [their] front—keeping close to [their] own positions—but on horseback and without gas mask, as never before."[42]

ARMISTICE, AND HOME

With the cease-fire, the 28th Division and 103rd Engineers remained in the Thiaucourt area, headquartered in Heudicourt. Engineers spent weeks cleaning up some of the war damages. The removal of German mines presented a particularly dangerous pastime. Germans had constructed rows of antitank mines in front of their positions, some consisting of six-inch (150 mm) artillery shells in wooden boxes, wired with pressure-sensitive detonators.

Higher headquarters decided to use the American engineers to clear the area instead of requiring the Germans to do so. The chore was made even more hazardous because friendly artillery fire had disrupted minefields, leaving some disarrayed and sensitive. On November 20, nine days after the cease-fire, while attempting to render safe the German mines, "Sgt. Henkels and a detail from E started the job but unfortunately encountered a badly damaged mine and Henkels with [all] of his men were killed instantly."[43] This type of danger was not an isolated incident.

All told, the 103rd Engineer Regiment had suffered 639 casualties from July 28 through November 30. Although these numbers were not on par with frontline infantry units, they were substantial.

The end of hostilities led to inevitable administrative adjustments for the regiment. A major from Army headquarters arrived to assume command from Anderson for 2nd Battalion, relegating the captain back to command of Company E. Anderson, now armed with a camera, took the opportunity to snap dozens of pictures throughout the area. True to form, many of these show fortifications, obstacles, defensive positions, and transportation-related subjects (how exciting it must have been for him when, returning home, he was able to show his bride, family, and friends such snapshots labeled "Barbed wire – N. of Toul").

The US Army remained in France to provide stability for the initial period of the Armistice. Troops carried on with maintenance and custodial duties, training courses were established, and educational opportunities were generated, along with furloughs and leave. Anderson was apparently unable to avoid such "busy work" when he was ordered to attend the Second Corps combat engineer training school, at Châtillon-sur-Seine. He and five colleagues, all of whom had "previously been too busy with combat activities to attend such things[,] went to the school to learn how the war should have been fought—and found one of the instructors to be one of [their] former Lieutenants," who had been sent there months before "in order to get him out of the way."[44]

They arrived at the school on Christmas Day and enjoyed a dinner of canned salmon. The original concept for the training course was to familiarize newly arrived officers with the necessary information for them to join combat units in place. After the war concluded, however, the usefulness of the school no longer existed. To make matters worse, as noted above, the students were often substantially more experienced than the faculty.

Anderson noted his admittedly flippant attitude toward the school: "The War is over; we won after a rather tough job; now let's call it quits, have a good time, and get home!"[45] However, the faculty took their assignment quite seriously and struggled to understand why the students were not in the best frame of mind for learning. By January 1919, the logic of the situation asserted itself; the faculty, after "a valiant resistance," finally gave up and disbanded the school. Anderson's was the final class.[46]

On March 10, 1919, at Barizey-aux-Plain, General Pershing conducted a formal review of the 28th Division, and battle honors were presented. Finally, on April 28, the 103rd Engineers embarked on the troop transport SS *Mongolia* for the voyage home. Anderson was assigned duty as a policing officer for the return transit. Upon arrival in Hoboken, New Jersey, on May 8, he was required to remain behind, conducting final inspections to ensure all troops had cleared out, causing him to miss the departing troop train.

In order to rejoin the division, Anderson conducted independent rail travel from Hoboken. He traveled to Philadelphia to change trains, a fifty-mile detour that bypassed the division at Camp Dix; this stop allowed "a night at home."[47] The next day he reversed north back to Camp Dix to rejoin his division. Sometimes being a railroad man had distinct advantages.

To welcome the 28th Division's return, a homecoming parade was held in Philadelphia on May 15. The division marched through the streets in an eight-mile-long procession, viewed by a crowd of two million, more than the entire population of Philadelphia. The parade route concluded with a leg up Broad Street to Shibe Park (later named Connie Mack Stadium) for a final celebration. For such formal events, the officers were mounted; Major Anderson (he had been promoted on March 6) commented, "For me, the high light of the parade was my very fine mount—courtesy of the Philadelphia Police Department."[48]

The 28th Division, having served just shy of one year overseas, began mustering its troops out of federal service immediately after the celebration. The Army's Chief of Engineers Office issued a slightly different muster-out policy for engineer officers, who were required to report to Washington, where they were given leave and ordered to report back after Memorial Day (Friday, May 30). Anderson was formally discharged, returning to civilian status, on May 31. He promptly returned to his position with the Pennsylvania Railroad Company.

ENDNOTES

16   America's declaration of war pointedly did not include Austria-Hungary, nor the other members of the so-called Quadruple Alliance, Bulgaria and the Ottoman Empire.

17   The US Army employed the hand-cranked Gatling Gun—first used in combat in the 1860s, through 1911.

18   In the Army, adjutants are basically administrative assistants for the commanding officer. In combat units, as will be seen, the position provides a "holding tank" for officers who can then be sent to replace leaders as casualties mount.

19   HWACiv, 15.

20   HWAMil, 14.

21   German gas artillery shells had three categories: diphenylchlorarsine, a "sneeze" gas marked by and referred to as blue cross; mustard gas, marked by a yellow cross; and phenylcarbylamine, a "tear" gas, marked by a green cross.

22   The General Service Schools, *The German Offensive of July 15, 1918*, Fort Leavenworth, Kansas: The General Service School Press, 1923, 893.

23   To this day, the US 3rd Division's motto is "Nous Resterons Là," French for "We Shall Remain There." The division had entered the line for the first time the day before the German offensive, July 14. The division earned its nickname, "Rock of the Marne," the next day, July 15, by its tenacious defense that stopped the Kaiser's army.

24   HWAMil, 15.

25   Ibid.

26   Colonel Edward Martin and E. S. Wallace, editor, *The Twenty-Eighth Division (Pennsylvania's Guard) in the Great War, Vol. 1* (Pittsburgh: The Twenty-Eighth Division Publishing Company, 1924), 80.

27   HWAMil, 16.

28   Ibid. Bradford would recover and was promoted, returning to lead 1st Battalion in December, and then as regimental executive officer in March 1919.

29   H. G. Proctor, *The Iron Division (National Guard of Pennsylvania) in the World War* (Philadelphia: The John C. Wilson Company, 1919). Duffy's F Company motorcycle driver, also killed, was Private First Class Frank G. Fiore.

30   Martin and Wallace, *The Twenty-Eighth Division (Pennsylvania's Guard) in the Great War, Vol. 3*, 461.

31   Ibid, 466.

32   Ibid.

33   Edward G. Lengel, *To Conquer Hell* (New York: Henry Holt and Company, 2009), 49.

34   Wagner's *Der Ring Des Nibelungen* opera series includes Etzel (AKA Attila), king of the Huns; Giselher, warrior-king of Burgundy, brother

of Kriemhild; Kriemhild, princess of Burgundy; and Freya, goddess of love, youth, and beauty.

35   28th Division commander Major General Charles H. Muir, while observing his troops on the day of the opening of the offensive, decided to take part as a rifleman. Before his staff could stop him, he rushed onto the battlefield, dodged shot and shell, and assisted his infantry in eliminating a German machine-gun position. Task completed, he returned to his stunned staff.

36   Martin and Wallace, *The Twenty-Eighth Division (Pennsylvania's Guard) in the Great War, Vol. 3,* 472. Lieutenant Hill survived his wounds. Sergeant Theodore R. Dewey was killed in action, September 26, 1918.

37   The engineer regiment's top two leaders presented a stark contrast in appearance. The barrel-chested Snyder was tall, powerfully built, and in photographs displays determined looks, very much suggesting a combat leader. By comparison, the shorter Anderson was lean and wiry. In photographs, he always seems to present a look of mild bemusement, although his actions reveal a strong and resolute boldness.

38   Fighting alongside the Pennsylvanians in the 35th Division during this period was artillery officer and future president of the United States Captain Harry Truman.

39   HWAMil, 17.

40   Martin and Wallace, *The Twenty-Eighth Division (Pennsylvania's Guard) in the Great War, Vol. 1,* 109. By October 7, none of the 109th Infantry's three battalions had an effective strength of even 300; nominal strength of each battalion was around 750, and 3rd Battalion was commanded by a sergeant by the time it was withdrawn after ten days' fighting.

41   Proctor, *The Iron Division,* 1981.

42   HWAMil, 18.

43   HWAMil, 18. Martin and Wallace, *The Twenty-Eighth Division (Pennsylvania's Guard) in the Great War, Vol. 5,* 461. Killed on November 20, 1918: Sergeant Paul W. Henkels; Corporal Donald T. Shenton; Privates Frank Smith, Raymond W. Drown, and Thomas R.

Cullington. Shenton was brother to the artist who created the sketch of the shallow trenches overlooking St. Agnan. Ed served in Company B, while Donald served in Company E.

44   HWAMil, 18.

45   Ibid, 19.

46   Ibid. Anderson's 201 personnel file lists "2nd Corps School, Chatillon, 1 term, 1919" as a service school attended. While returning to their units by rail, their train spent the night in a marshaling yard, near a French tank car carrying *vin ordinaire*; Anderson commented it was probably headed to provision some French unit. He noted the tank car was partially depleted during their delay.

47   Ibid, 20.

48   Ibid.

CHAPTER FOUR

BETWEEN THE WARS: CAREER, FAMILY, AND TRAGEDY

With the war's end, Anderson renewed his career with the Pennsylvania Railroad (PRR), starting in mid-1919. Throughout the next few years, Anderson pursued a routine career with the company, with periodic reassignments throughout its operating area, in and out of state. He had departed the railroad in 1917 as a newly promoted main line assistant supervisor. When he resumed his work, admittedly "really quite green and inexperienced as to track work"[49] due to his absence for military duty, he was bumped back to a branch assistant, and assigned to the Maintenance of Way (MW), Trenton Cutoff Line of the Philadelphia Division. With wife, Betsey, and eighteen-month-old-daughter, Bettie, he made his home in Norristown, PA.

In November 1919, Anderson transferred to a main line position in Paoli, fifteen miles northwest from downtown Philadelphia.

As MW track assistant supervisor, his work involved a variety of tasks, including clearing wreckage from accidents and, for a few days during a worker strike, actual engine maintenance, which included oiling pins, filling hard grease caps, etc., for locomotives. Anderson found the Paoli work, the location, and his management very agreeable. His supervisory skills were apparently developing satisfactorily, as his boss, A. E. Prebble, assigned Anderson de facto responsibility for the western half of the entire Paoli zone.

Another example of Anderson being given assignments of increasing responsibility occurred in 1921, during a period that preceded a bituminous-coal strike. PRR management had decided to prepare for this by staging coal cars to be ready, should coal deliveries be stalled. Anderson was given responsibility for this major effort, which included building rail lines to hold the coal cars.

Wallis and Betsey added another family member, Harry Wallis Anderson Jr., in February 1920, almost exactly nine months to the day from Wallis's detour home to Philadelphia (bypassing Camp Dix) upon his arrival with the 28th Division's troop ship. In May 1922, thirty-one-year-old Anderson was transferred back to Norristown, this time as the line supervisor. He wrote it was a "major business management lesson: regardless of how much authority or responsibility one may have thought they had as an assistant—any 'assistant'—the picture changes when you are placed in the boss's seat and realize you are in complete charge—and alone."[50]

Anderson's tour as supervisor of the Trenton Cutoff track was mostly routine. Early in his stint the passenger service was discontinued, so most of his traffic consisted of coal and freight trains. He recorded incidents and accidents, some fatal. He noted route adjustments and PRR line changes, including the elimination of his position during a reorganization in 1925.

Meanwhile, throughout all the railroad service, Anderson's duty with the National Guard of Pennsylvania (NGP) continued. The wartime reorganization in the fall of 1917 had cut across state regional lines. In Georgia, regiments had been created by combining units from opposite ends of the state. Returning to postwar status, however, required a complete readjustment, as the location of units had to be considered in order to manage the citizen soldiers, who had to balance part-time military service with civilian jobs.

In addition, the wartime modernization had resulted in equipment changes for the US Army that Pennsylvania now had to accommodate. This included such significant developments as the transition from animal to mechanical transport; Anderson's engineer units now had to operate and maintain trucks, bulldozers, graders, and bridge equipment. Thus, the NGP undertook significant reorganization and adjustment as units were merged and relocated, and new, more modern armories were built to store and manage new and different equipment.

Anderson accepted a commission to continue his service with the Guard, which eventually reverted to the federalized designation, 103rd Engineer Regiment. Serving as regimental plans-and-training officer, Anderson participated in NGP camps and activities during this initial postwar period.

Recognition for his wartime service came through, as it did for hundreds of thousands who saw active service in France. Anderson was authorized to wear a Victory Cross, with five battle clasps for his participation in combat, for the following:[51]

- Champagne-Marne (July 15–18, 1918; during this period, the 103rd Engineers occupied the trenches south of St. Agnan in the bloody fighting to stop the final German offensive of the war.)

- Aisne-Marne (July 18–August 6, 1918; in this phase, the American army pushed the Germans back across the Vesle River, at Fismet.)

- Oise-Aisnes (August 18–November 11, 1918; this included a broader time and location criteria, encompassing combat throughout the entire sector.)

- Meuse-Argonne (September 26–November 11, 1918; the 28th Division's brutal struggle against the heavily fortified German defensive lines is well documented.)

- Defensive Sector (The criteria for this was general service in a defensive role, not actually tied to a specific battle. The final phase of the 28th Division's service east of St. Mihiel, among others, would have qualified.)

However, as his railroad responsibilities accumulated, Anderson "welcomed a military connection that would be less demanding and more consistent with [his] civilian occupation."[52]

Coincidentally, the US Army had been negotiating with various major American rail lines to establish "railway operating battalions" that would allow the US government to assume operation of railroads in an emergency. Experienced railroad personnel were required, and the PRR contributed three such battalions. For Anderson, this development fit his circumstances quite well.

Anderson's commission as a major in the Guard, effective November 22, 1919, was for a five-year term, set to expire on October 31, 1924. Under the new circumstances, he let this obligation expire while he accepted a commission in the federal Officers Reserve Corps (ORC) on November 27, 1923, once again as a major in the Corps of Engineers. He was assigned to the 492nd Railroad Operating Battalion, a "very satisfactory and appropriate assignment"[53] that likely would have continued had not tragedy struck in 1929.

As the 1920s roared along, PRR company reorganizations resulted in some professional turmoil for Anderson. His supervisor position in Earnest was eliminated in 1925, forcing Anderson to take a temporary slot in the Philadelphia Terminal Division. This West

Philadelphia interim assignment resulted in a move from Norristown closer in, to Wayne, where Anderson moved his family in the spring of 1926. The Andersons now included another daughter, Helen, born January 19, 1923, in Norristown.

This assignment, too, was cut short by yet another sudden railroad reorganization. Instead of a planned family holiday on Lake Erie in August 1926, Anderson was ordered to Chambersburg, 100 miles to the west. (His family still went on holiday without him, although how much of a "vacation" it would have been for Betsey with their three children, ages eight, six, and three, Anderson didn't record.)

The PRR reorganization, reassignment, and relocation merry-go-round had one last revolution, even before 1926 ended. On December 1, Anderson was sent to New Brunswick, New Jersey, seventy-five miles northeast of Philadelphia, on the New York Division as a maintenance of way supervisor. Anderson was responsible for a total of twelve tracks connecting South Elizabeth, Rahway, South Amboy, Perth Amboy, New Brunswick, and Princeton.

To add to his supervisor load, the railroad was beginning a major improvement project throughout his region. The PRR was in the process of raising all the main tracks two feet onto a sub-ballast of cinder, in order to improve drainage and to provide for a more stable roadbed.

With Anderson as the track supervisor, his subdivision received a railroad rating prize ("Improvement"), despite the heavy track raising and related ballast-cleaning projects. After the 1927 to 1928 maintenance year (which ran fall to fall), he was promoted to division engineer and transferred almost 450 miles west, to Akron, Ohio, on December 1, 1928.

After several years in the hectic Philadelphia Terminal and New York Divisions, Akron was a considerable contrast, with a "relaxed tempo." This drop in intensity coincided with a less stressful job as well, as Anderson took on division-engineer duties instead of track supervisor. Even so, a major part of his work involved dealing with accidents—derailments, collisions, and breakdowns, many of which he dutifully recorded.

Sadly, in Akron, Anderson suffered the most devastating loss of his entire life, the death of his wife, Betsey. Expecting their fourth child, Betsey experienced difficulty breathing in mid-March 1929, before the due date. The attending doctors decided to hasten the delivery, and daughter Audrey was born at 3 p.m., March 20, an apparently routine birth. However, a half hour later, with Wallis at her side, Betsey told him, "Now I believe I'll take a little nap,"[54] whereupon she turned slightly, and passed away.

That evening, Anderson walked the couple blocks from the hospital to their home, to tell his three children—Bettie, age eleven; Harry Jr. (the family called him Bud), age nine; and Helen, age six—the news that their mother had died while giving birth to their new sister.

For Wallis, the loss was shattering. He had known Betsey, the girl from his neighborhood, for twenty-six years, since he was twelve years old. Together they had endured his separation and service on the Mexican border and in France, where combat meant a constant fear of his never coming home. She had been with him throughout his budding railroad career, with its long hours and unpredictable assignments and transfers. She had given birth to their three older children and carried the burden of raising them while he attended to his civilian and military careers.

The railroad personnel and extended family pitched in as best they could to assist Wallis in dealing with this sudden catastrophe. He called upon friends or family to help him shoulder the burden. Initially, Wallis's mother, Ida, stayed with them to help. Infant Audrey spent her first two years with close family friends Clifford and Audrey Arnold,[55] the same Army Medical Corps doctor with whom Anderson had served along the Mexican border and in France. The Andersons were also greatly assisted by a series of domestic helpers through the years.

He moved the family back to Philadelphia while he finished out his one-year tour in Akron, after which he was reassigned on

December 1, 1929, as the division engineer for the West Jersey and Seashore Line (WS&J, in the Atlantic Division) in Camden, New Jersey. Importantly, this put Anderson and his young children much closer to supporting friends and family. The line was "an intensive summer operation and practically dormant during the rest of the year,"[56] as summer holidays to the beaches were conducted mostly by train; automobile road travel was not yet ascendant.

Anderson's railroad work was assisted occasionally by his remarkably extensive network of colleagues. In one instance, he and his boss, Superintendent Ben Hudson, had to address a train-scheduling problem involving two major corporate clients, electronics giant RCA-Victor and Campbell Soups. Hudson and Anderson attended a conference to sign agreements resolving the issue, hosted by the president of Campbell Soups. Anderson recounted,

> After an appropriate wait in the ante room we were finally solemnly ushered into the august presence in the inner sanctum where upon the president finally raised his glance from the papers on his desk, looked us over and blurted, "Hello Andy, how are you? Long time no see" . . . and we spent the next five or ten minutes discussing events of some 15 years previously when we—as bachelors—had neighboring rooms in the local YMCA. Meanwhile the others present—and our draft agreement—just cooled off.[57]

Amid all the Pennsylvania Railroad and personal turmoil, Anderson's continued military service was also affected. His initial five-year ORC commission expired in 1928. Although he had been offered a new appointment, Anderson had to adjust his priorities with Betsey's passing. Raising his family and his railroad career took more of his time; he could no longer devote the time necessary for his Army work. For the first time in sixteen years, thirty-eight-year-old combat veteran Wallis Anderson no longer served in any military component.

In early 1931, the PRR again promoted and transferred Anderson, this time back to central Pennsylvania, as the division engineer on the Middle Division, based in Altoona. This assignment was more in the "main stream of operations,"[58] which suited Anderson just fine after more leisurely work routines in Akron and Camden.

The Altoona operation was undergoing significant changes when Anderson arrived. The track was being upgraded to the heaviest-weight rail in the PRR system, and the Middle Division business offices were being rebuilt as well. As always, Anderson recorded some of the mishaps and accidents (including fatal ones), as well as the organizational aspects of the railroad, which, like all bureaucracies, functioned—or failed to—depending on the management personnel.

As often occurs with far-flung and complex management structures, there was a continual friction between the functional departments (Anderson reported to the MW engineer, based in Harrisburg 130 miles to the east), and the regional operations (Middle Division, where he sat in Altoona). The division superintendent expected Anderson to respond immediately to his directives, while the department head in Harrisburg expected the same. Oft times, Anderson was caught between the two, who had a heated and antagonistic rivalry. Office politics appear to be a universal and unavoidable human condition.

Throughout this period Anderson's job entailed inspections, maintenance, and repair efforts. Very much a hands-on manager, he spent many hours personally climbing in and on various railroad equipment and structures to get a personal appreciation of some issue. However, being a capable and steady performer is no protection when the winds of mismanagement blow. During the late spring of 1931, a "sleet and ice storm which hit the division about noon really crippled [them]. Poles and wires went down like ten pins and for several days [they] were practically without wire service."[59] Emergency repair efforts were undertaken, with the eventual restoration of service, as the railroad struggled to deal with the unexpectedly bad weather.

Shortly thereafter, Anderson was called for an audience to the PRR general manager's office in Philadelphia, for which no advance explanation or warning was provided. As a middle manager, he was not expecting the admonishment that followed. After all, the service disruption had been caused by severe weather, not faulty maintenance. Worse followed bad, as Anderson was then summarily demoted and transferred, which caught him equally off guard.

After thirteen straight years of annual PRR promotions and steady upward progress, he suddenly found himself rocked by an unexpected and seemingly unjust career derailment. Coming on the heels of his personal tragedy (just over two years had passed since his wife had died), Anderson faced a time of crisis, personally and professionally. With his Army service on hiatus, he must have felt particularly alone and adrift. Writing forty years later, when pain had been subsumed by wisdom, he described his feelings regarding this "adjustment" period: "First, the collapse of possible hope for advancement on the Railroad so soon after our loss of Betsey combined with that tragedy . . . constitute a shattering blow to our pride, ego, life plans, family development and dreams for the future. We eventually picked up the pieces but life can never be the same."[60]

Anderson noted later that it had been suggested that he could have registered his protest and even resigned. Such a recommendation failed to consider that at age forty, he had the sole responsibility for a family of four young children during the middle of the Great Depression.

So off to Harrisburg in central Pennsylvania Anderson moved his family, where he was given a management job in charge of the combined engineering MW and Philadelphia Division engineer drafting office. He replaced Ed F. Snider, for whom Anderson heaped praise and admiration. Naturally, Snider had been an acquaintance of many years, and Anderson considered him a true friend, a gentleman, and a professional of the highest order. Anderson's tenure in Harrisburg ran for around seven years, from 1931 to 1938.

His work in the drafting room was of course far less demanding than railroad operations or maintenance. He was able to witness railroad business and management in a different light and learned lessons that surely helped him in the future. He saw "an unbelievable number of incidents of deceit, mismanagement, and perfidy," although he "eventually learned to relax, take matters in stride, and even be amused by some of the episodes." Thankfully, over the years, he "achieved a position where [he] probably, as an aide, [was] given greater confidence and had more real power than [he] had in [his] own name."[61]

Anderson's young family continued to develop. The move to Harrisburg was accomplished with comparatively little disruption; he was able to bring longtime domestic helper Nonie Green as well. During the fall football season, Anderson would "listen to the U of Penn games Sat. afternoon and diagram the plays of the game."[62] Life carried on, as the Andersons settled into a pleasant routine.

Ironically, Anderson's move to Harrisburg set into motion events that resulted in unexpected opportunities, for both military service and the PRR, that would have seemed unlikely—if not impossible—two years earlier. Redemption lay ahead; that he persevered and eventually triumphed after serious setbacks is a tribute to the depth of his character.

Anderson had been militarily inactive since early in 1929. His PRR transfer to Harrisburg was fortuitous; as the state capital of Pennsylvania, it was also the headquarters for the National Guard of Pennsylvania. Inevitably, Anderson ran across old colleagues from the NPG and the 28th Division headquarters. It was "only natural that they should soon prevail upon [him] to resume [his] former activities in that direction."[63] With a more routine and less taxing work schedule, Anderson eventually accepted, and on October 7, 1933, he was again commissioned as a major with the 2nd Battalion, 103rd Engineers—his former wartime outfit.

This led to a follow-on appointment as commanding officer of the 125th Engineer Squadron, a PNG inactive reserve unit. An examination on military-knowledge qualifications followed, in which Anderson scored highly on tactics and technique of separate arms and services, function and duties of division commander and staff duties during combat, tactical principles and decisions, troop leading, methods of supply and movement, and even horsemanship.

Promoted to lieutenant colonel on February 19, 1934, Anderson held concurrent positions with the National Guard of Pennsylvania and the National Guard of the US. His work with NGP at this point required minimal commitment of time, as it was an inactive reserve assignment.

His October 1934 NGP physical examination revealed that Anderson, at forty-four years of age, was still remarkably trim and fit. He had 20/20 eyesight in both eyes, normal hearing and digestion, and "clear skin." His height was listed as sixty-five inches, his weight at 110 pounds, with a blood pressure recording of 108/76. The physician listed him as "slim and underweight, but apparently healthy and vigorous. Low blood pressure, not considered significant."[64]

In May 1936, Anderson was assigned to the G-1 (personnel section) on the 28th Division staff. He served in this position for almost five years, which, along with the Harrisburg PRR drafting section assignment, provided a period of unusual—and probably welcome—stability. Both assignments with mundane-sounding titles provided him the opportunity for professional growth, of which he took full advantage.

The 28th Division G-1 job was not overly active, with only one annual field-training trip (typically to Indiantown Gap, twelve miles away). But Anderson found the largely administrative work to be "very congenial, interesting, and instructive."[65] In addition to the aforementioned bivouac in Indiantown Gap, he participated in periodic division staff meetings, command post exercises, and occasional tours and meetings involving other military unit staffs.

All these developments played a part in preparing Anderson for senior command once the nation moved again to a war footing. He was a proven combat leader who had moved up in the military staff hierarchy, despite his broken service. His reputation was intact and respected, as shown by his ever-increasing responsibilities.

Meanwhile, after years of patient, diligent service in the drafting office, in 1938 Anderson finally caught a break. A series of retirements, demotions, and firings set the stage for a first in Anderson's PRR career: he was offered a posting rather than merely being assigned. Moreover, it was for a MW supervisor position (Supervisor #46, in PRR terminology), in a familiar place: Altoona. Although he had no illusions as to any continued potential for upward advancement, he still viewed it as partial vindication, and accepted the offer immediately.

Members of the Anderson family, meanwhile, were at thresholds of independence. Betty, twenty, had married Donald Danner and moved from home, and had a daughter, Donna, that same year. Bud, eighteen, was attending Perkiomen, a boarding prep school seventy miles east in Pennsburg. Helen, fifteen, was boarded at George School, a private Quaker boarding high school in Newtown, a northern suburb of Philadelphia. Audrey was the only one living at home with Wallis. For the move back to Altoona, Audrey was entered into Highland Hall boarding school in nearby Hollidaysburg, while Wallis took up residence at the Penn Alto Hotel in downtown, where he could walk to work.

Anderson's quasi-bachelor period did not last long, however. On November 25, 1938, in Union City, New Jersey, Anderson wed Marietta Jones, a friend of Anderson's family for many years. Marietta, originally from Brooklyn, had been Betsey Cobb's maid of honor when she married Wallis in 1917. During the years after Betsey died, Marietta had acted as a "synthetic aunt"[66] for the children.

Taking up work again as track supervisor on a busy line, Anderson set about on his usual round-the-clock routine, dealing with operations, accidents, derailments, repairs, and equipage issues. Anderson's track territory of responsibility included Altoona to Tyrone, fifteen miles northeast, toward State College. Displaying remarkable discipline, dedication, and an appetite for hard work, Anderson began personally inspecting his entire track line at least once a week. He would take the early-morning #42 train to Tyrone, arriving before 8 a.m., then walk the fifteen miles back to the office. This routine was far beyond an occasional symbolic gesture. Anderson could speak with authority about every aspect of every foot of the track for which he was responsible.

War began in Europe September 1939. Although not as unprepared as before the previous World War, the country was still woefully short of full military readiness. According to Anderson, "Even during our field training with the Corps at Ogdensburg in 1940 the situation in Europe made it appear inevitable that the Division would be called into service in the near future."[67] The PNG, anticipating this eventuality, began to ensure that all units were "adequately staffed with personnel with maximum chance of passing prospective examinations and qualifying for acceptance into Federal Service."[68]

Eminently qualified, in January 1941 Anderson applied for and was assigned as the executive officer of the 103rd Engineer Regiment, his old wartime unit. Shortly thereafter, on February 17, the PNG was federally mobilized, and Anderson "received orders to also report for extended active duty."[69] Once again, the railroad issued him a furlough for military service. Anderson's wife, Marietta, decided to move with Audrey back to Harrisburg, and to await the situation from there.

The transition to federal service once again resulted in some personnel failing to meet the standards; in this instance, the commanding officer of the 103rd Engineers failed to pass the required physical examination. (He then retired.) Anderson succeeded him, becoming the commanding officer of the regiment on February 18. Promotion to full colonel followed on May 15.

The division and Anderson participated in several major army-maneuver exercises in the ensuing months, as preparations for war continued. The Pennsylvanians trained in Virginia at Fort A.

P. Hill near Fredericksburg in summer 1941. Anderson described the conditions there as "a larger, and undeveloped area where it was possible to train major units under more realistic field conditions that were a closer approach to those which might be encountered in actual combat. The terrain was rather tangled and rugged and the amenities few. Major exercises were in order."[70]

Continued training and large-scale maneuvers continued throughout 1941. The 28th Infantry Division, as it was now designated, traveled to take part in the Carolina Maneuvers in the fall of 1941. The division was assigned the mission of "defending the coastal area from North Jersey to the Capes against invasion."[71]

It was during the division's New Jersey defense mission that word came of the Japanese surprise attack on Pearl Harbor, and America was once again plunged into war. Anderson and the division were back in Pennsylvania for the Christmas holiday, attending to various support functions that came with the sudden radical shift of a nation at war: the engineers were "constructing sand bag revetments to protect the planes at airfields in the area. This was arranged without delay and with particular attention to Philadelphia Airport and Dover Air base in Delaware."[72]

Other changes were underway, reflecting preparation for a very different kind war than was fought in France in 1918. The division reorganized once again, and "the Engineer component was reduced from a Regiment to a Battalion—in contrast to the change in 1917." Initially the table of organization and equipment called for "the grade of colonel for the Division Engineer regardless of the fact that his command was merely a battalion."[73] However, this was bound to be adjusted. In the Army, lieutenant colonels command battalions; full colonels command regiments.

As this situation was sorting itself out, in early January 1942 the 28th Infantry Division was sent to Camp Livingston in Louisiana for more training and field maneuvers. While there, Anderson's being "overgrade in job" finally caught up with him. With the American military's massive expansion then underway, concurrent with the comprehensive reorganization, new units were being created, and there was a dire need for experienced officers to command those units at all levels. As a result, his "position was quite vulnerable."[74] In August 1942, Colonel H. Wallis Anderson, Corps of Engineers, received orders to report to Camp Bowie, Texas, to take command of the newly created 51st Engineer Regiment (Combat).

For the first time in his already long and faithful service, which stretched back to 1912, Anderson was required to leave his beloved Pennsylvanians. For thirty years, on and off, he had been associated with state and federal versions of that commonwealth's National Guard. He had literally grown up with Pennsylvania's military establishment. As a youth, Anderson had been active in neighborhood "maneuvers" with wooden guns; had deployed to the Texas border to defend against Mexican brigands; had joined more than a million countrymen to travel to France, and in brutal, bloody trench-warfare combat had helped to turn the tide against Imperial Germany; and he had served in the unglamorous and underappreciated task of preparedness for most of the twenty-three years between the wars. Throughout, he had endured severe hardship of difficult duty, many extended separations from family, the stark terror of combat, violent deaths of friends and colleagues, military and civilian career setbacks, and heartbreak from personal loss.

Now, for the first time without a cohort of Pennsylvanians around him, he began anew. Wallis Anderson was a seasoned combat veteran and world wise, had significant senior staff and organizational abilities, and was in excellent physical condition, active and vibrant as he approached his fifty-second birthday. He represented the living embodiment of the nation's concept of the citizen soldier. Anderson was now on a direct path—a rail—to command troops in decisive actions that led to victory.

ENDNOTES

49   HWACiv, 16.

50   Ibid, 17.

51   H. Wallis Anderson, Major, Engineers, Form 740-a "Application for Victory Medal," approved April 23, 1921.

52   HWAMil, 22.

53   Ibid, 23.

54   HWACiv, 20.

55   Arnold's brother was Henry Harley "Hap" Arnold, who later became the first general in the US Air Force.

56   Ibid, 21.

57   Ibid. Arthur C. Dorrance (1893–1946) had become president of Campbell Soup Company in 1930. He was responsible for launching numerous successful initiatives, including radio advertising and the company's famous chicken noodle soup.

58   Ibid, 22.

59   bid, 25.

60   Ibid, 27.

61   Ibid. Toward the end of his life, Anderson wrote that in retrospect, the less stressful job and his attitude adjustment was probably for the best, so far as his health was concerned. He noted that he had outlived most of his contemporaries, practically all of whom had careers end with demotions or being relieved from their responsibilities.

62   Helen Anderson Racoosin, Memoirs.

63   HWAMil, 23.

64   HWA Officer's 201 File (Service Record), medical report dated October 8, 1934. Throughout his military career, Anderson was routinely rated as "underweight" in his official medical physical examinations.

65   HWAMil, 24.

66   Ibid, 28.

67   HWAMil, 24.

68   Ibid.

69   HWACiv, 28.

70   HWAMil, 25.

71   Ibid, 27.

72   Ibid, 28.

73   Ibid, 29.

74   Ibid.

CHAPTER FIVE

A NEW WAR

"I am he. I am Colonel Anderson."

After years of incursions and incidents, Imperial Japan followed up its invasion and occupation of Manchuria (1931) by brazenly attacking China proper in 1937. Similarly, following several years of increasingly aggressive territorial grabs, Nazi Germany attacked and invaded Poland in September 1939, launching the Second World War. By the time the United States entered the war, the Army's readiness posture was alarmingly low, despite the twenty-seven months between the start of the European war and Pearl Harbor.

The Army and its Corps of Engineers had made modest efforts to prepare, although they were merely a prologue for the massive changes after December 1941. Military levels rocketed quickly upward: "The Army as a whole increased five and a half times in that period [fiscal year 1941]; the Engineers, almost seven-fold."[75]

As with the First World War, additional massive expansion followed once war was declared.

For the Corps of Engineers, the missions for which its units were responsible continued to expand. Observing the German success in defeating France and the Low Countries with its blitzkrieg methods, the US Army noted that "the modern trend toward motorization and mechanization [demanded] a much larger proportion of Engineer and other technical troops with the combat troops than formerly."[76] The American engineers "were particularly interested in improving means for hasty road repair, emergency bridging, and construction of airfields."[77]

This new emphasis on mobility meant new equipment. Even as recently as 1930, the engineers relied on manual labor and horse- and mule-driven machinery. A new army would require mechanization. Anderson's troops had to augment their traditional tools—picks and shovels, which they referred to as "anchors and banjos"[78]— with motorized versions. Bulldozers, power shovels, dump trucks, graders, and many other devices now were issued.

Manpower would have to be adjusted as well, to operate the new technologies. Army engineers traditionally enjoyed having high-quality personnel assigned. Not content to rely on the service-academy pipeline for its officer contingent, the Corps "looked to the construction industry, whose ranks were filled with graduates of technical colleges, to furnish many such officers in an emergency"; the civilian/military connection was established "through the civil works activities of the Corps and through mutual membership in the Society of American Military Engineers (SAME) and other national engineering societies."[79]

The need for a high-quality workforce was not restricted to the engineer officer corps, as an enlisted component with a great variety of specialized backgrounds was also required; while there was much demand "for carpenters, construction foremen, truck drivers, toolroom keepers, riggers, mechanics, and demolitions men, the Engineers needed 91 different kinds of specialists at a rate of 727 per thousand."[80]

The corps' long-standing self-image as a specialized segment of the Army was displayed by their own distinctive and sentimental clothing accoutrements, including "the cherished Engineer button, different in design from the standard Army button and to be seen only on the uniforms of members of the Corps of Engineers."[81] Reflecting a similar pride, "confidence marked the Engineers' tendency to translate its motto, *Essayons*, as 'Let us succeed' rather than 'Let us try.'"[82]

51ST ENGINEER REGIMENT (COMBAT)

In the fall of 1940, American military preparation was gathering steam in anticipation of the nation's entry into war. In September 1940, training camps were established throughout the United States, one of which was Camp Bowie, located just south of Brownwood, 130 miles southwest from Fort Worth, in Central Texas. By the summer of 1942, the camp had grown to over 100,000 acres; new units were being created and trained there for service in the now-global conflict.

On May 5, 1942, the War Department constituted the 51st Engineer Regiment (Combat) on paper and activated the regiment at Camp Bowie on June 13. Initially, the 51st included "a Headquarters and Service (H&S) Company, two battalions (the 1st and 2d), and 3 letter companies in each battalion, A, B, C in the 1st Battalion, and D, E, and F in the 2d Battalion."[83] Reflecting how new the regiment was and how quickly the US Army was expanding, the initial regimental commanding officer was Martin F. Massoglia, who held the rank of first lieutenant. Several weeks of rapid expansion followed as new recruits were transferred from other units or from basic training depots. On June 21, command passed to Colonel Edwin P. Ketchum; after more reshuffling, Ketchum was shortly thereafter reassigned as corps engineer, replacing a Colonel Bill Heavy.

Soldiers and officers continued to flow in throughout the summer. The vast majority were volunteers and draftees from the civilian world, not from the preexisting Army. At least forty-one of the regiment's fifty officers at the time had only just graduated from the Engineer Officer Candidate School (OCS) between June 24 and July 22. The new officers had "basic combat engineer training as enlisted men and three months of officer indoctrination and development at Officer Candidate School (OCS) Fort Belvoir, Virginia. Many were recent college or high school graduates" and "only a few had any formal professional engineer training."[84]

The new regiment's initial activities included administrative organization and unit assignment, as well as "close order drill, marches, physical conditioning, unarmed defense, and organized athletics."[85] Being engineers, they constructed their own facilities, including "company supply rooms, mess halls, storerooms, and recreational buildings."[86] In-house schools were established, as the troops and officers were provided instruction in army administration, motor pool operation and vehicle mechanics, and supply management.

All of this was accomplished in the middle of Texas, in midsummer. At this point, the dangerous and difficult tasks of the war lay over the horizon, unfocused in the distance for these green yet eager troops.[87]

CAMP BOWIE

Such was the situation on August 17, 1942, when the regiment welcomed the arrival of its next and, finally, permanent commanding officer, Colonel H. Wallis Anderson. Anderson characterized the state of the 51st as "amusing had it not been serious."[88] Surely Anderson was being somewhat uncharitable, not taking into account the difficulties of raising a regiment so quickly and from scratch, and unfairly comparing the nascent 51st and its challenges with his Pennsylvania National Guard, which was able to handle reorganizations, expansions, and contractions with an experienced cadre of leaders and an organizational structure that had vast experience in dealing with decades of such adjustments.

Nonetheless, Anderson had a point. He wrote,

> The 51st "Regiment" it developed was a mere cadre of somewhat less than the allocated enlisted strength—and so much below quality that its composition had been the subject of an I.G. [Inspector General] investigation. Further, the officer complement consisted of one R.A. [Regular Army] Captain, of some 3 years' experience, one U.S.R. [United States Reserve] Lieut., whose civilian experience was in the Petro-Chemical field; one R.A. 2nd Lt. just two months out of West Point [the United States Military Academy]—and 64 brand new 2nd Lts. fresh from O.C.S.; plus a Med. Capt., a Dental Lt. and a Chaplain. 2nd Lts. were in command of battalions. It is believed certain that Ed Ketchum went to Bill Heavy's desk at Corps without tears.[89]

Anderson was faced with the challenge of building an entirely new regiment and transforming it into a military formation capable of handling the diverse missions of combat engineers. To assist this effort, he would have to initially rely on an officer cadre of seventy officers, none of whom (save one) had any relevant military experience as an engineer; Anderson alone had seen combat.

The officer cadre did not include even a handful of somewhat-experienced mid-grade officers (lieutenant colonels, majors, captains), who are usually at hand to assist. The lone exception was Captain Albert McCollum, who had served with the 11th Engineer Combat Regiment in the Panama Canal Zone. Anderson assigned McCollum as his executive officer, keeping close by his only experienced junior officer.

As the situation was somewhat unusual, Anderson employed an unorthodox method: he revamped the 51st, separating it into an "enlisted platoon" and an "officer platoon," with each platoon carrying out "an improvised training schedule including physical training for half the day and some housekeeping details for the remainder. This consisted largely of preparing the camp and processing equipment in anticipation of the expected 'fillers.'"[90] The regiment was still far below its allotted strength (with about seventy officers and a similar number of enlisted, at this point) and so expected a continued influx of personnel, as well as the allotted heavy equipment.

The new commanding officer demonstrated early on his own leadership style, which "laid the foundation for the development of teamwork and *esprit de corps* that bound the 51st together for any task."[91] With much construction still underway to transform open desert into a viable training facility, Anderson showed that he was unlike most conventional full colonels by "putting on his fatigues, grabbing a paint brush or hammer, and jumping in to work with the lieutenants and enlisted men."[92]

Training and expansion continued throughout the fall, as officers and enlisted arrived to somewhat fill out the unit. Even before the arrival of heavy engineering equipment, the long list of fundamental skills required meant for long training days. Anderson "arranged for all officers to attend classes every Tuesday and Thursday evening between 1900 and 2100 hours. The subjects ranged from first aid to map reading, and included the functions of S-1 [personnel], S-2 [intelligence], S-3 [operations], and S-4 [supply]."[93]

Knowing that combat tested one's ability to endure extreme environments and ordeals, Anderson instituted a somewhat unusual physical training regime: barefoot marches in the hot Texas summer sand. Lest one think that Anderson's passion for physical fitness had slipped past "intense" and into "cruel," apparently this was considered "standard cure for athlete's foot that was prevalent in those days."[94] With greater concerns than podiatry fungal infections, Anderson marched them in this manner "whether he had athlete's foot or not."[95] After seeing so much death in WWI "due in good measure to poor training, Colonel Anderson was a firm believer in a somewhat unappreciated, severe regimen of training. He believed in 'taking advantage of all inclement weather to toughen troops.'"[96] Central Texas in midsummer could certainly be considered "inclement weather."

LEADERSHIP CHALLENGES

The situation faced by Anderson in the fall of 1942 at Camp Bowie in Texas, as he sought to train and prepare the 51st Engineer Regiment for its combat role, deserves examination. Indeed, these same conditions were being experienced by other commanders at all levels, across the nation, as the US emerged from its prewar posture of near isolation to prepare for a global war. The vast American war machine had been switched on, and experienced leaders like Anderson were expected to take a collection of widely diverse, undisciplined individual civilians and forge them into effective military units. In the case of combat engineers, this meant the unit would have to become proficient in myriad highly specialized mission areas.

In the initial phase that fall at Camp Bowie, the regiment had received most of its officer complement, while being woefully deficient in the assignment of its actual troops. The all-important engineering equipment was not yet on hand; because of both these deficiencies—troops and equipment—the actual combat engineering training would have to wait.

Perhaps even more important than these hard skills, however, were the social and cultural challenges placed before Anderson. The Army needed an officer cadre that fully embraced the duties and responsibilities expected of them. Although the young lieutenants had all passed through basic officer training, they were referred to as "ninety-day wonders," a mocking nickname that reflects the skepticism that such dramatic changes—converting a civilian into an effective military officer—could be accomplished in a school environment, in such a short time. Anderson would have to pick up where OCS left off and teach the complex and abstract principles of leadership where they mattered most: the field environment.

The ethos Anderson sought to instill was a culture of hard work, teamwork, discipline, responsibility, determination, group identity, and selflessness. Like many commanders in positions of responsibility at the time, he had to rapidly synthesize aspects that he himself had learned gradually and innately. His own military indoctrination was very much community based. He had grown up in an environment of Pennsylvanian military kinship. His first exposure was with neighborhood friends who joined local National Guard units. When he joined, his enlistment was a natural and familiar act, quite different from being drafted by a remote federal government.

Anderson was raised to the ranks of commissioned officer by election, after demonstrating to his cohorts his proven traits of responsibility, work ethic, and organizational and leadership skills; this again reflects the community focus of his early service. His junior officers at Camp Bowie were selected and trained in a distant school by officials not present in Texas, and no real army work had yet been performed to prove out their judgment.

The culture of hard work, steadfastness, group loyalty, and fidelity to mission that had become such an integral part of Anderson's personality had been amply provided for and reinforced by the entire National Guard system, of which Pennsylvania was a strong component. This culture extended back more than 150 years and provided a powerful force that bonded individuals and groups to expectations. No one wanted to let down their community or state or, indeed, heritage; the rich history of service and sacrifice was well known by Guardsmen. Anderson in Texas would rely upon national pride—still strong, but a more abstract psychological lever by comparison.

Instilling a sense of duty is a complicated process. The troops and officers were young and eager, infused with a high degree of patriotic determination. Nevertheless, they were humans with normal motivations and nature. Anderson gave his charges a sense of purpose by focusing on duties and responsibilities. He worked them for long hours, and conducted group activities, including organized competitive recreation.

Duty in the military rests on a foundation of belonging to a group, and knowing one's place (and responsibilities, including sacrifices) within that group, even as the group shares risks. Although the military is a hierarchy, the uninitiated sometimes mistakenly consider it to be rigid and socially unequal. In fact, in some important social areas, the military is exceptionally egalitarian, far more than civilian counterparts. Group responsibilities for failure are shared far more equally—and severely—in the military than in the business world. When a ship sinks, the captain is as much at risk as the crew. Not so for a typical corporation, where the term "golden parachute" is used to show that in the event of a business tragedy, the senior managers will survive; the term implies that the more junior members will crash, unassisted: while all air passengers ascend together, parachutes are individually issued.

Anderson's history demonstrates this lethally brutal point of shared outcomes. On August 17, 1918, one German shell blast instantly killed two Franks of the 103rd Engineers: executive officer Lieutenant Colonel Frank Duffy and his motorcycle driver, Private First Class Frank Fiore. In that horrific, violent moment, Duffy's much more senior rank mattered not. When Anderson endured explosive and gas shelling, machine-gun and rifle fire, and airplane strafing while occupying the shallow trenches for three days outside St. Agnan, he was no more protected than his most junior private. At Camp Bowie, Anderson's challenge was how best to instill this concept into his troops quickly, in manufactured fashion—and how to do this without the all-encompassing embrace of Pennsylvania's rich military heritage.

Any good leader knows that sincerity is a key to success. One must impart lessons in one's own style, without artifices. Troops are notoriously expert at seeing through and immediately calling fraud on any aspect of a leader deemed inauthentic. Leaders must develop their own style to address timeless concepts, rather than simply repeating them by rote; failure to do so results in disrespect, dereliction, individualism, and contempt.

In Anderson's case, his personality traits were unmistakable: mild personality, soft-spokenness, humility, and an even temper. He was also hardworking, and possessed unnatural determination and dedication to duty. From the examples listed above, it is evident Anderson embraced one primary methodology above all others: leadership by example. He determined that the best way to demonstrate the principles that were so important was to join in.

And so, the fifty-two-year-old colonel, three ranks and twenty-five years senior to even the next in line, joined in as a common laborer. He would have done so without fanfare. It would not have been a mere symbolic gesture of ten minutes hammering or painting, and then back to executive work. The fact is, he made no mention of such behavior in his memoirs. (He omits many other examples that demonstrated his character as well.) The authors of *The 51st Again!* and *Unbroken Line* made mention of this aspect of Anderson's behavior precisely because it resonated across the fifty years that transpired between the events and the books.

Anderson's mild demeanor and absence of pretension would have sent powerful nonverbal messages to his impressionable young junior officers. The fact that he wore a uniform displaying his World War I Victory Medal with five battle clasps while remaining humble and self-effacing would only have underscored these traits and influenced others to emulate. Young men of the early 1940s would have been well acquainted with stories of the horrors and brutality of the previous war's campaigns and trench fighting. While confidence and exuberance were expected by groups of young men, one doubts that boastfulness was much in evidence—not when the old man in the front of the room, wearing five battle stars, was so modest and unassuming.

Anderson employed such methods over and over; it was as natural for him to lead by example as it was to put on a uniform. The lesson would have compelling: "If WE have to do it, you can bet the colonel will be there too." This behavior eliminates the justification for malingering, complaints of hard work, or perception of unequal treatment. It provides a sense of pride in the unit, right up to the commanding officer. It demonstrates to young officers what is expected of them far more effectively than a classroom lesson. Without shot and shell and danger, it underscores the sense of community that is so critical to newly formed military units.

From the start, the 51st Engineers enjoyed a high morale and *esprit de corps* primarily because of the example set by their leader. As will be seen, this condition is fragile, not to be taken for granted, and is vulnerable to even a singular change in leadership.

PLATTSBURGH BARRACKS

Throughout the fall of 1942, although the bulk of the troop contingent had not yet arrived, the regiment's equipment began to be delivered. These included scores of trucks (cargo, dump, and prime movers), bulldozers, road graders, air compressors, gasoline hammers and saws, steam shovels, and welding equipment. In total, when loaded onto a train for rail movement to its follow-on posting, the regiment's equipment was carried by a staggering "46 flatcars and boxcars."[97]

Having spent weeks building and preparing their training facilities in Texas to receive their full allotment of men and equipment, the 51st Engineers suddenly "became fully acquainted with the Military Version of 'loves labor lost.' We received orders for a permanent change of station to Plattsburgh Barracks."[98] Plattsburgh, in Upstate New York on Lake Champlain, twenty-five miles from the Canadian border, could not have been more different from Camp Bowie in Central Texas.

One might speculate what perversely diabolical scheme some War Department planner had in mind for Anderson's regiment, first establishing it in Central Texas in the summer and then, as winter approached, transferring it to Upstate New York. The contrast extended beyond mere climate. Whereas in Texas the regiment lived and worked in new facilities of their own construct, Plattsburgh Barracks had been a military base for more than 100 years and had extensive facilities. In the space of a few months, the regiment had been exposed to extremes; this could only have helped their ability to cope and adjust, even before combat service.

Upon receipt of the travel orders, the regiment dutifully loaded all its equipment onto trains and prepared to move cross-country. Anderson sent about fifty officers by car, and the remaining twenty-five officers and seventy-five enlisted boarded the train, accompanying the equipment. The regiment still only comprised about 10 percent of its designated complement of troops. The train departed on October 15 for its more than 2,000-mile journey.

Plattsburgh Barracks had originally been established as an Army post for the War of 1812. Situated on Lake Champlain, it guarded a natural invasion route by British forces moving into the US from Canada. In 1814, the Battle of Plattsburgh was fought, in which naval and land forces of the Americans decisively defeated the invading British. The US Army had maintained the post subsequently, although the missions shifted to fit the nation's needs. In 1914 the very first Reserve Officer Training Corps (ROTC) camp had been established at Plattsburgh, "and such training was known as the Plattsburg Idea for many years."[99]

Just prior to the arrival of the 51st Engineer Regiment, another engineering unit, the 180th Heavy Ponton Battalion, had been posted there. According to Anderson, "This unit reportedly had been moved south owing to the difficulties of training in the winter in upper NY."[100] In mid-October 1942, the camp, located about a mile south of the town, was comfortable and modern; all buildings were two- and three-story brick buildings, with steam heating.

The train hauling the 51st arrived at the barracks in midafternoon of October 17, amid snow flurries. Immediately upon arrival the regiment, approximately 150 men, half of them officers, set about the task of unloading the vast array of heavy equipment:

All of the officers were in fatigues unloading equipment when Colonel Chapin, the Post Commander, resplendent in his boots and breeches and accompanied by his staff in their pinks and greens, came by to visit the unit. He asked one of the men, diligently engaged in removing the wire tie-downs on a truck, where the commanding officer was. The man in fatigues replied, "I am he. I am Colonel Anderson."[101]

Settling into their new posting, Anderson and his staff devised a training regime. According to the authors of *The 51st Again!*, "Among other things the program included specialized training for officers and enlisted men in supply, motor maintenance and administration."[102] Although some training facilities existed, additional ones had to be constructed, a now-familiar circumstance for the engineers.

More important than building rifle ranges, garage bays, and classrooms, however, was the task of finding an appropriate expanse for combat engineers to learn their trade. Learning to build and destroy roads and bridges requires an expanse with a variety of terrain features. Anderson sought a place apart from the cozy and civilized post, with its amenities and luxuries.

He wrote, "The Post at Plattsburgh was a very nice residence area but with very limited and inappropriate field training terrain for combat troops." He went on:

Plattsburgh Barracks was really [a] very comfortable little post—and the station personnel can therefore probably be excused for treating it very much like a personal country club and somewhat resenting the intrusion of a gaggle of rookies. Troops counting cadence in their reveille exercises in the dark of a winter morning disturbed the slumbers of the "Establishment" much too early to make us popular among the permanent complement. However, that was not the object of our presence.[103]

He needed his troops to be "strong enough to survive the hardships of war."[104] As winter approached, he sought to use the pending inclement weather to induce hardship: "In my own book, it is always better to train under adverse conditions and then accept more favorable circumstances as a bonus."[105]

He sent his S-3 (an important position in any military organization is the chief of operations; *S* designates a staff officer for Army units below a general staff level), Second Lieutenant Fred Oberdorf, to search the area for a place where he could conduct appropriate field training while simultaneously removing his troops from the seductive lure of the "country club" and its "establishment" personnel. Oberdorf found such a place in Macomb Reservation,[106] an ancillary facility about twelve miles west of the main barracks.

Macomb was "uninhabited, rugged and quite well suited for our purpose."[107] Anderson found exactly what he was looking for: "ridges, hills, bogs, streams, lakes, forests, scrub, open flats, relief [about 1,000 feet], and space for maneuvers. All could be used effectively for combat engineer training."[108]

Personnel continued to trickle in. November brought new arrivals, including one Captain Robert Yates; Yates would play a significant part in the regiment's future, and was to become one of the strongest leaders under Anderson. For the time, Yates was given command of 1st Battalion. Major James Kirkland also arrived and was assigned as Anderson's executive officer, a position he held throughout Anderson's tenure. Anderson reassigned Captain Albert McCollum as his S-3, demonstrating the continued confidence he had in the captain. McCollum played a key role in developing the training for the regiment. Rounding out the top positions, Lieutenant Martin Massoglia (the original regimental commander) was assigned to lead 2nd Battalion. Other officers arrived as the regiment continued to fill out.

On November 24, Anderson began a new phase of training, that of combat engineer skills. On that Tuesday, he ordered a regimental march to Macomb Reservation, the first of many. After an overnight bivouac, they returned to the barracks, having covered twenty-four miles total. The colonel, twice the age of almost all the soldiers, led to and from the site. The 51st had found its training home and, as importantly, began to find its identity. Having earned it, the regiment was able to enjoy a warm indoor Thanksgiving the next day.

In the ensuing weeks, the remaining officers continued to arrive. Most of the enlisted, though, were still absent. Finally, in a two-and-a-half-week period ending January 10, 1943, the regiment increased in size from about 150 to more than 1,600. The trainload of recruits that started this deluge arrived on Christmas morning. Per Anderson:

> Our faith was finally rewarded—about 0500 Xmas morning. By some odd chance we were aroused by the fact that a train had stopped on the main track of the D&H [Delaware and Hudson] just east of the barracks. Investigation developed that it was a load of chilled and rather bewildered young men, mostly from the deep south. Only a few had ever been far from home, many had never seen snow, etc. And at Plattsburgh we had a couple feet of it and it was then 30° below zero.[109]

These new draftees came from all over the country, and had been "inducted into the Army, issued uniforms, and sent by rail to Plattsburg without any training. The majority were from the south, southwest and mid-Atlantic regions of the country."[110] A high percentage were from Pennsylvania and North Carolina, and Anderson noted that "some were of Mexican descent and could speak only broken English."[111]

New arrivals were assigned to the companies, with an attempt to spread evenly the recruits' experience, education, and specialized skills. Processing consisted of a complete medical and dental physical examination, briefings and administration, and further assignment to platoon, squad, and section.

Due to the manner in which the Army had filled out the table of organization (T/O), the 51st was flush with second lieutenants, but lacking in lieutenant colonels, majors, captains, and first lieutenants; and from the noncommissioned (NCO) ranks, it lacked adequate numbers of corporals, sergeants, and staff sergeants. The regiment had to make do, with many positions filled by those in an acting capacity. But having finally filled its ranks to somewhat near full capacity, at last training could begin in earnest.

As the recruits had been shipped directly to Plattsburgh without any kind of "boot camp," the regiment undertook a training regime for individual and basic training, which began January 11, 1943. Anderson's overall training plan guided the battalions, companies, and platoons from basic to more advanced skills. The most elemental organizational unit was the platoon, consisting of about forty-four men, led by a first or second lieutenant and assisted by a staff sergeant. Training was conducted and administered by that platoon's officers and NCOs. For the 51st, they began with the most fundamental of military basics: close-order drill and left- and right-hand facing movements, the most elemental form of discipline and instruction.

Anderson's training regime then progressed into more advanced skills and applications of engineering concepts. Infantry skills were combined with engineering activities. The close-order drills in turn became route marches and tactical maneuvers. Although many activities focused on skills at the platoon level, gradually the training involved coordination with other units and higher elements of the regimental echelon.

The array of engineering feats Anderson required of them was vast, with much of it performed amid the harsh winter. The extreme weather persisted throughout the basic training period and made routine training exceptionally challenging. With Lake Champlain frozen over to a depth of three feet, the training adjusted but did not cease.

In fact, the Plattsburgh weather was a factor that Anderson embraced rather than avoided. One soldier wrote home describing the initial basic training in January 1943: "Our day starts at 5 A.M. that is Reveille, then roll call, chow, about two hours of drilling in the snow, then a two- or three-hour march through the woods with a light pack and rifle."[112]

Anderson kept the focus on tactical realism as much as possible, by avoiding the trappings of the convenient, comfortable, and civilized Plattsburgh Barracks. As noted above, from their arrival, there were cultural differences between the permanent base personnel and the engineers: "With much less than the approval of the distaff contingent we began going out to the Reservation practically every Monday, spending the week in bivouac, field training, etc., and returning to the Barracks about Friday for cleanup and 'rest and recuperation.'"[113] These weekly marches to and from the location of their primary training established an essential experience of shared ordeal for all the men of the regiment.

Combat engineering techniques received the most emphasis, with bridge-building as one of the bread-and-butter skills. Anderson's novices learned to construct a variety of these. They learned to assemble the standard Army Model 1940 twenty-five-ton ponton bridge with pneumatic floats, with the bridge components being constructed onshore and then dragged onto the ice. After completion, it was dragged back for complete disassembly, which completed the task.

Although they used prefabricated material for some of the fixed and floating bridges, they also learned to construct spans using their own material, cutting trees to be used as lumber for bridge-building. This self-sufficiency extended to all aspects of combat engineering. For example, the engineers learned to build and maintain roads that would lead to their own bridge sites.

As ever, the training was conducted under increasingly realistic and challenging conditions:

> To complete basic training, the men had to qualify in fixed bridging. Each company was given two tactical bridges to be constructed under blackout conditions during the hours of darkness. The temperature during this exercise ranged down

to 40 degrees below zero. The first bridge was a standard double bent timber trestle bridge. These bridges were usually constructed with 8x8 or 10x10-inch timbers, depending on the design.[114]

Beyond merely enduring the weather, the training was designed to simulate realistic army-combat field conditions, including the following:

Assembling heavy pontoon units on the ice of Lake Champlain, building an H10-wooden trestle bridge over the Salmon River in the dark with a wind chill many degrees below zero that seemingly separated body from soul, camping out in pup tents on the "tundra" at Macomb Reservation near Plattsburg in 10 below zero weather, digging foxholes in solid frozen ground, running night compass courses through deep snow of the forest and icy bogs of the Reservation.[115]

The individual skills involved in these tasks were extensive. To ensure adequate coverage of those skills, no matter what organizational confusion might be encountered, cross-training of individual specialties was extensive. At the squad level, the skills required were those of carpenter, rigger, demolitions, electrician, driver, and basic construction (hammer, pick, shovel, mallet, rope, machete, block and tackle, adze, axe, saw, construction equipment operation, etc.).

One skills test provides a good example of the standard for self-sufficiency all the platoons were expected to demonstrate: "Each platoon was deemed capable of moving into any wooded area with only their own hand tools and cutting down trees for a vehicular bridge."[116] These bridges then became the object to defend in an infantry training exercise.

Tests such as these were designed as competitions with squads, platoons, and companies, all engaged in friendly contests to determine the relative proficiency. The competitions included infantry skills and capabilities as well. Despite the miserable conditions, the success of Anderson's methodology was reflected in the high morale enjoyed by the 51st. The men genuinely believed they were fast becoming "maybe the best outfit in the Army."[117] Even with the extreme cold and outdoor training regime he had established, medical absences and lost training time were low, a traditional measure of high morale for military units. One explanation for this had to have been the culture of stoic endurance he had successfully established, despite the extreme conditions. According to the authors of *Unbroken Line*, "By his [Anderson's] actions, he exemplified his beliefs. For instance, he slept in a pup tent in sub-zero weather just like everyone else and he did his push-ups every morning also (50 at age 50)."[118]

Other schools were designed and run for additional specialties. As always, the regiment provided for its own training, as the officers and NCOs were expected to conduct training as well as to prepare for the next day and phase; topics included intelligence, gunnery, chemical warfare, camouflage, supply, and various levels of leadership and management.

The only training that Anderson deferred to the spring for more mild weather was that for demolitions and range weapons. Due to shortages in military explosives such as TNT, the Army had substituted dynamite for training purposes. Unfortunately, dynamite is unsuitable for some aspects of military use, as it is much more sensitive to shock than TNT, especially in cold weather.

Range weapons firing for qualification was also postponed. While weapons use in tactical situations could be conducted at Macomb in bad weather, the objective on the range was to achieve as high a score as possible, to demonstrate marksmanship under ideal conditions. Shivering and manipulating a frozen rifle with cold-stiffened fingers would have adversely affected the scores and misrepresented the soldiers' actual skills.

Once spring arrived, engineers learned explosives, munitions, and demolitions, and how to apply these to both defensive and offensive operations. The various methods to destroy bridges, crater roads, destroy tunnels, and knock over trees (with the trunk still partially attached—this obstacle is known as an abatis, and is more difficult to remove) all required extensive knowledge of the practical application of explosives. Engineers learned to lay and remove minefields, build fortifications (and to destroy them), and to lay other obstacles such as barbed wire.

Training as combat infantry was an important secondary mission of the engineers', and Anderson, whose first five years of military service were spent as an infantryman, made sure this was not a neglected skill. Soldiers learned to operate crew-served weapons such as ".30-caliber machine gun and the .50-caliber machine gun that were assigned to all combat engineer companies."[119] They were also taught to use the 2.36-inch anti-armor rocket launcher (known as the "bazooka"), the 37 mm antitank gun, the grenade launcher (which attached to a rifle barrel muzzle), and the flamethrower.

In addition to learning the weapons systems, the engineers learned and exercised fundamentals of combat infantry tactics— patrolling, defensive techniques, reconnaissance, and even bayonet assault. They rehearsed such infantry maneuvers in larger assemblies up to the battalion level.

1111TH ENGINEER COMBAT GROUP

With the spring thaw in early April, Anderson moved to maximize the benefit afforded by the 5,000-acre Macomb Reservation. He shifted the entire regiment there, establishing a tent city for semipermanent residence. The troops could still commute to and from the barracks for post amenities or other luxuries, but Macomb became a more permanent staff headquarters. The troops (including all the officers) still slept in pup tents on the ground; staff and service activities were now conducted from the larger pyramidal tents.

Additional facilities were constructed on the reservation, including shower facilities, an outdoor theater with stage and seating for 2,000 persons (local civilians were occasionally invited to join the group for outdoor movie viewing), three buildings for the group and its two battalions' headquarters, and a post exchange. All these facilities were lit by electric lighting from portable generators. The construction provided valuable training for the engineers—not just for the buildings, but for project planning and organizing as well, conducted by the regiment's own officers.

Training could now be conducted for those requirements deferred during the winter months. Water had replaced ice throughout the area, so bridge-building became a common training focus. The H-10 and Bailey bridges[120] were built, deconstructed, and rebuilt over and over. Improvised bridges of all sizes and types were fashioned, with ponton and treadway bridges launched and floated.

Spring 1943 brought another round of reorganization. The Army, seeking to make the use of engineer units more flexible, redesignated engineer regiments as independent groups, and removed them from the permanent attachment to divisions. In WWI, the 103rd Engineer Regiment was organizationally a permanent part of the 28th Division. Had an engineering requirement emerged not requiring the 28th itself, wasteful administrative untangling would have been required. Under the new system, engineer groups would manage two to four engineer battalions, depending on the requirement. Engineer battalions were now independent entities, and could be assigned to infantry divisions, or to groups, as required.

The new administrative orders established the 1111th Engineer Combat Group on April 1, 1943, replacing the 51st Engineer Regiment (Combat). Virtually all personnel and positions were retained. Anderson's group staff basically became an independent management unit, with battalions assigned on an as-needed basis. For the time being, the 1111th retained the two formerly 51st Engineer Regiment battalions, which had been renumbered as well, with the 1st Battalion becoming the 51st Engineer Combat Battalion, and the 2nd Battalion redesignated as the 238th Engineer Combat

Battalion. Yates and Massoglia were initially retained to command the 51st and 238th, respectively.

Personnel changes continued as spring gave way to summer, including detaching sixty-four officers and men from the now 51st Battalion, who left to form a cadre for the creation of another engineer battalion in Mississippi. A new commander for the 51st Engineer Battalion arrived on June 4, Major Victor Reafsnyder, replacing Yates, who was retained as executive officer.

Training continued, with ever greater complexity and coordination between subordinate units. Pillboxes were constructed, then destroyed, using flamethrowers and TNT satchel charges. More and more complex tactical problems were created for the combat engineers. In one instance, the two battalions were pitted against each other in an infantry setting, with the 238th acting as the defender of a hilltop; the 51st was assigned the assault role, from its base ten miles distant.

Such exercises were enhanced due in part to realistic combat infantryman training, for which an "infiltration course" was constructed:

Designed to test troop reaction to simulated battlefield conditions, it was a most harrowing and unforgettable experience, even for the most stout-hearted; the course at Macomb Reservation was about half the length and width of a football field. At one end an open seven-foot trench crossed the width of the field and at the other were two emplaced .30 caliber machine guns. Between the trench and the guns were low barbed wire entanglements, craters, and trip wires attached to charges that would explode if the wires were touched. A platoon or similar sized group would be sent into the trench, then while the machine guns were sweeping the entire field with live ammunition about 30 inches above the ground, the men were ordered out. Crawling with their rifles cradled in their arms, they inched forward on their bellies, trying to avoid the craters and trip wires, keeping their heads and butts down. When they reached barbed wire, they had to flip over on their backs and wriggle under while holding up the wire with their hands [until safely past the machine-gun fire].[121]

One cannot help but notice the similarity between the 1111th's Macomb infiltration course, and the actual WWI battlefields of Meuse-Argonne and the Marne.

Colonel Anderson traveled to Louisiana to observe large-scale army maneuvers, as well as throughout New York to supervise various training efforts. One such trip by Anderson and his executive officer, now Lieutenant Colonel James Kirkland, took him across Lake Champlain, southeast from Plattsburgh, to Fort Ethan Allen, Vermont. Two officers from battalions there joined his group in September: Captain Henderson O. Webb Jr., who became Anderson's S-3, and Captain Thomas J. C. Williams, assigned as the first S-4 (logistics) for the group.

The 238th Engineer Combat Battalion received orders to detach from Plattsburgh and to report to the West Virginia Maneuver Area. Although in the middle of a joint training exercise with the 51st, the 238th was pulled from the field and on July 25 departed Plattsburgh by rail for West Virginia.

As the summer in Plattsburgh continued, additional capabilities were added to the 1111th with the assignment of a light equipment company, a light ponton company, and a heavy maintenance company. Other units were assigned for various ancillary temporary tasks or training throughout the summer, then subsequently detached.

As August 1943 wound down, so too did the 1111th's time in Plattsburgh. The US Army was increasingly involved in ground operations in the North African and the Southwest Pacific theaters, with future planning and additional preparation in England and India, generating overseas requirements for the engineers. Large-scale training lay ahead, followed by deployment to combat zones.

While it is altogether accurate to say the foundation for Anderson's regiment was laid in Texas at Camp Bowie, it is undeniably true that the structure itself—a resilient, sturdy castle—was built on the bleak wintery landscape at Plattsburgh Barracks and Macomb Reservation.

WEST VIRGINIA MANEUVER AREA

In early September, the 1111th Engineer Combat Group and the 51st Engineer Combat Battalion received orders to report to the West Virginia Maneuver Area, a permanent change of station. The group embarked by rail and passed through Philadelphia on September 6, Labor Day, arriving in Elkins, WV, the next day. The 1111th, with the 51st as its troop travel companion, moved to its bivouac area thirteen miles east of Elkins, in the Monongahela National Forest. The area was used by the Army for extensive advanced training, including live artillery and mortar firing, and mountain-terrain maneuvers.

In addition to the 51st Engineers, the 150th Engineer C Battalion (as it was often referred—C for "combat"; often abbreviated ECB) was also assigned to the 1111th, as were other ancillary units: the 628th Engineer Light Equipment Company, the 762nd Engineer Topographic Company (for map, graphic, and photographic support), and part of the 467th Engineer Water Supply Battalion. As usual by this time, the engineers not only conducted training in "the art of living in rugged terrain"[122] but were also called upon to construct training facilities for other Army units to use: rifle-firing and combat-maneuver ranges, infiltration and transition courses, road construction and maintenance, and even airstrips for the Army's light aircraft (Piper Cub, designated L-4 for the Army).

Anderson wrote that the primary benefit to his group of this period in West Virginia was "the frequent displacement of our headquarters—and the transition from permanent station to a mobile operation in the field."[123] With the bivouac sites being changed frequently, and new units being assigned and reassigned, the group learned its role as a mobile headquarters unit in the Army's new fluid command structure.

Anderson's engineers' time in the Elkins zone was relatively brief. On September 16, the 51st ECB was detached and sent to Fort Belvoir, Virginia, for a special assignment, as demonstration troops for the Engineer School. This would be an indication of the battalion's reputation and professional stature. Although it was briefly reattached to the 1111th again in New Jersey in October as it staged for being shipped overseas, the 51st was to embark on a long and circuitous journey before finding its way back under Colonel Anderson's care.

During this period, when the 51st was separated and began to operate more independently, a concern began to emerge: lower morale and a feeling among the troops that its commanding officer, Major Reafsnyder, was not turning out to be an effective commander. With combat looming, there is nothing more serious.

Meanwhile, the 1111th was shipped to Camp Dix, New Jersey, a staging point in preparation for service overseas. Arriving on October 6, the group conducted standard pre-deployment administration and preparation:

> Equipment was put in best condition possible, crated, and marked for shipment. Showdown inspections of individual clothing and equipment, and of organizational equipment was conducted. Shortages were filled and overages were turned in. . . . Physical examinations of all group personnel were made . . . and the necessary inoculations were administrated. Necessary transfers of personnel were made to eliminate those found physically unfit, and to attain T/O [table of organization] strength. Requisite films on security and personal hygiene were shown and lectures pertinent to overseas movement were given to all personnel.[124]

With receipt of their official Army travel orders (5-192 of September 3, 1943) the group moved out of Camp Dix to Fort Hamilton, NY, on November 17 for final overseas preparations. Anderson's group was destined for transport aboard the British passenger liner RMS *Queen Mary*. Flagship of the luxury Cunard-White Star Line, which first sailed between Southampton, Cherbourg, and New York in 1936, the liner saw service as a troopship during the war. *Queen Mary* was divided for administrative and control purposes into three areas, Red, White, and Blue. Under the British section chief, Colonel Anderson was placed in charge of all the Americans in the Blue Area. On December 3, 1943, the *Queen Mary* "sailed from New York Harbor at 1120 hours, destination unknown."[125] The 1111th Engineer Combat Group was going to war.

ENDNOTES

75   Blanche D. Coll, Jean E. Keith, and Herbert H. Rosenthal, *United States Army in World War II, The Technical Services, The Corps of Engineers: Troops and Equipment* (Washington, DC: Center of Military History, United States Army, 1958), 18.

76   Ibid, 16.

77   Ibid, 27.

78   HWAMil, 21.

79   Coll, Keith, and Rosenthal, *United States Army in World War II*, 3. H. Wallis Anderson was a charter member of SAME, which began in 1920.

80   Ibid, 116.

81   Ibid, 4.

82   Ibid.

83   Barry W. Fowle and Floyd D. Wright, *The 51st Again!* (Shippensburg, PA: White Mane Publishing, 1992), 2.

84   Albert E. Radford and Laurie S. Radford, *Unbroken Line* (Woodside, CA: Cross Mountain Publishing, 2002), 19.

85   Ibid, 3.

86   Ibid.

87   Demonstrating the high morale and specialized self-regard of the Corps of Engineers, in July 1942 at Camp Bowie, Lieutenant Roy W. Barnes became the first unit member to marry following the activation of the regiment. As he and his new bride exited the church, they passed under an archway of raised long-handled shovels instead of the traditional swords. The subsequent ceremonial ride through the camp was conducted by an Army half-track towing a ponton on a trailer, atop which rode the bride and groom.

88   HWAMil, 29.

89   Ibid.

90   Ibid.

91   Fowle and Wright, *The 51st Again!*, 4.

92   Ibid.

93   Ibid.

94   Ibid.

95   Ibid.

96   Radford and Radford, *Unbroken Line*, 15.

97   Fowle and Wright, *The 51st Again!*, 5.

98   HWAMil, 30.

99   Ibid, 7.

100   HWAMil, 30.

101   Radford and Radford, *Unbroken Line*, 22.

102   Fowle and Wright, *The 51st Again!*, 7.

103   HWAMil, 30.

104   Fowle and Wright, *The 51st Again!*, 7.

105   HWAMil, 31.

106   Named for Alexander Macomb, a war hero during the War of 1812 at the Battle of Plattsburgh. Macomb went on to be the commanding general of the US Army, rare for an engineer officer. Under Macomb, the Corps of Engineers adopted the distinctive three-turreted castle as its insignia.

107   HWAMil, 31.

108   Radford and Radford, *Unbroken Line*, 22.

109   HWAMil, 30. Anderson's two younger children, Helen (then attending Oberlin College in Ohio) and Audrey, traveled to Plattsburgh to spend Christmas with their father and Marietta. Anderson and his wife met the girls at the train station in a horse-drawn troika sleigh.

110   Fowle and Wright, *The 51st Again!*, 8.

111   HWAMil, 30.

112   Radford and Radford, *Unbroken Line*, 24. Private Frank H. Lee's letters home provide source material for *Unbroken Line*. Lee was inducted into the US Army on December 21 and boarded the train for Plattsburgh on the twenty-sixth.

113   Fowle and Wright, *The 51st Again!*, 16. A favorite bar was the Fife and Drum in Plattsburgh, where the regiment's favorite cocktail was determined to be Canadian Club and ginger ale.

114   Fowle and Wright, *The 51st Again!*, 11.

115   Radford and Radford, *Unbroken Line*, 15. Per Technical Manual TM 5-273 of July 1, 1942, the Army 25-ton ponton bridge consisted of four trestles with trestle bracing, twelve 12-ton pneumatic floats, and the floor-system material. In its basic configuration, the bridge had a span of 210 feet and was rated to handle vehicles weighing 25 tons. Other bridging material and reinforcements could be added on to extend the span and increase the weight capacity. Usage of "ponton," of French origin, was gradually replaced by the more familiar "pontoon" in spelling and pronunciation.

116   Fowle and Wright, *The 51st Again!*, 13.

117   Radford and Radford, *Unbroken Line*, 15.

118 Ibid, 28. In fact, Anderson was fifty-two during the period in Plattsburgh.

119 Fowle and Wright, *The 51st Again!*, 9.

120 The Bailey bridge is a portable, prefabricated, truss-type bridge, used by the Western Allies in WWII. It was designed by Briton Donald Bailey in the 1930s. With the onset of WWII, the British Army adopted and further developed the design. The basic idea was for modular box sections to be assembled in various configurations, depending on the load and length requirements. In this manner, the components were portable and could be applied to solve various bridging requirements.

121 Radford and Radford, *Unbroken Line*, 31.

122 HWAMil, 32.

123 Ibid.

124 Unit History, 1111th Engineer Combat Group, US Army, 1 November 1943–30 November 1943.

125 Ibid, 1 December–31 December 1943.

CHAPTER SIX

THE CALM

The RMS *Queen Mary*'s convoy took six days to transit the North Atlantic, including a daylong detour to avoid a reported U-boat wolfpack. The cargo of 16,000 American soldiers exceeded the available berthing, requiring a rotation: two nights sleeping in a bunk followed by a night sleeping on deck. The mess-deck galleys served food virtually around the clock. Anderson's duties as "CO Blue" kept him busy, although he continued, as always, to build his network of future colleagues among the other senior officers embarked as passengers.

U-boat wolfpacks notwithstanding, the crossing was uneventful, and the passengers awoke on December 9 to find the ship riding at anchor in the Firth of Clyde at Greenock Harbor, near Glasgow, Scotland. Debarking the *Queen Mary*, the 1111th Group boarded a train the same day, eventually arriving at the Engineer Bridge School at Howbery Park, Wallingford, in Oxfordshire, thirty miles northwest from London.

Initially, the 1111th was assigned "station complement" duties for this school, which was very much *not* to Anderson's preferences. As he was much more senior to the school's commanding officer, Anderson soon managed to detach his group from this assignment and instead perform operational-readiness activities. By December 17, he had the group engaged in more training, which included minefield laying and removal, booby-trap removal, and building and dismantling Bailey bridges, even during blackout conditions, at training sites along the Thames River.

Even though the group was ostensibly a headquarters unit, it still retained the capacity to conduct limited engineer field activities. At this point, the 1111th Engineer Combat Group consisted of a headquarters element and a headquarters company, with thirteen officers and sixty-five enlisted assigned in total.

For their first Christmas abroad, group personnel joined engineer-school colleagues to host a party for about fifty English children, orphans from the Blitz in 1940 to 1941. The celebration was a poignant reminder of the purpose of their being sent overseas; the festivities helped somewhat to ease the difficulty of being away from loved ones during the holiday season.

During December 27 to 28, Colonel Anderson and his S-3, Major Webb, traveled to Southern England to seek more gainful employment than being tied to a training school in Oxfordshire. After a meeting with the Army Service Forces district engineer (then in Falmouth), Anderson managed to secure an assignment to take his group to Yelverton, ten miles north of Plymouth, there to assist the British Royal Engineers with port-area preparations for the upcoming invasion of France. Specifically, the group was to supervise a construction program for arriving troops as they staged in Southern England for the invasion, Plymouth being one of the principal embarkation ports for the invasion fleet.

Anderson sent his advance party to Yelverton, Devonshire, on January 5, 1944, while the rest of the group followed January 6. Anderson's 1111th was designated as "Construction Group E," and tasked with building two camps in the Plymouth area. Each camp would contain facilities for approximately 750 men, which would accommodate an engineer battalion; in essence, the group was building facilities for two engineer battalions it would be receiving under assignment. The two camps were designated Ragland Barracks and Devonport Park.

The 1111th Group began work directly; while the troops lived in tents,

> Nissen huts were constructed for use as latrines, showers, mess halls, operations headquarters, etc. Other engineer work consisted of construction for new roads and widening and improving existing roads for use as main routes of traffic to embarkation points on the coast; repair and classification of existing roads and bridges; reconnaissance for possible bivouac areas, water points, etc., for troops en route for embarkation, charting same, etc.[126]

An important aspect of this activity was for the 1111th to interact with their British hosts. The British Royal Engineers were overall in charge of invasion ports, requiring the group to conduct all its activities in coordination with the British. Anderson established a close relationship with the deputy commander of the Royal Engineers in the area, Major Peter Scratchly, a friendship that continued after the war. Anderson assigned his S-2 (intelligence), Captain Richard Carville, as primary liaison officer with the British in Plymouth.

Anderson wrote that some of their work during this period included widening the notorious English streets: "The narrow and winding streets and highways were an invitation to accidents and blockades and in numerous cases it was even necessary to demolish buildings in order to ease corners, improve view and expedite the anticipated heavy traffic and over-sized vehicles—which would probably be driving 'black out.'"[127]

On January 26, 1944, the 296th Engineer Combat Battalion became the first operational unit to be attached to Anderson's group. This event was the first of a series of assignment/reassignment actions that are characteristic of army units in an environment of constant organizing. With the massive influx of American army units arriving in England during the months leading up to the invasion, organizational adjustments were continuous, and sometimes appeared random. For example, the 296th was attached, detached, and then reattached to the 1111th, all within a two-week period.

On February 4, the 291st Engineer Combat Battalion, under the command of Major David E. Pergrin, arrived for assignment to Anderson's group; by war's end, the 291st could lay claim to having the most distinguished service of any engineer outfit during the entire war. And on March 1, the 51st Engineer Combat Battalion somehow found its way back to Colonel Anderson, once again being assigned to the 1111th Group. To complete this Devonshire hoedown, also on March 1, the 1111th Group was withdrawn from Yelverton, reassigned to the First US Army operational control, in preparation for active involvement in the invasion. The 150-mile move to the northeast brought the 1111th to the final training area for its pre-invasion phase.

291ST ENGINEER COMBAT BATTALION
Laboramus Ad Muniendum
("We Work To Fortify")

Originally the 2nd Battalion of the 82nd Engineer Combat Regiment, the 291st ECB formed in early February 1943 at Camp Swift, twenty miles east of downtown Austin, Texas. The same Army Adjutant General's Office order that redesignated and reorganized the 1111th Engineer Combat Group also transformed the 82nd Engineer C Regiment. Accordingly, on March 15, 1943, the former regiment was designated as the 1115th Engineer Combat Group, while its 2nd

Battalion was redesignated as the 291st Engineer Combat Battalion. Major John Hayes commanded the battalion, which conducted training in Texas, Colorado, and Louisiana, following a similar program to that of the 1111th Group and its 51st Battalion.

David E. Pergrin's path to command of the 291st bears some striking similarities with Anderson's own early development, albeit a generation removed. Another Pennsylvanian, Pergrin was born in Elizabeth, ten miles southeast of Pittsburgh. Like Anderson, he studied civil engineering, although at Pennsylvania State University (PSU), the cross-state rival of Anderson's alma mater, Penn. Working his way through school, Pergrin was employed by the Pennsylvania Railroad (PRR), and performed railroad tasks very similar to Anderson's own early work history: surveying and work-party labor along the various lines.

Pergrin joined PSU's Reserve Officer Training Corps (ROTC) in college, which provided tuition and a path toward duty as a reserve Army officer. Graduating in 1940, Pergrin was commissioned a second lieutenant in the Corps of Engineers and sent to the Army's Engineering School at Fort Belvoir in Virginia, as were so many of Anderson's junior officers. A reservist, he was deactivated at the completion of this training, and obtained a full-time job with the PRR, in the maintenance department. In April 1941, however, he was recalled to active service, and reported once again to Fort Belvoir. After a series of recruit and training assignments in Virginia, Pergrin was finally sent to Camp Swift in April 1943 as the executive officer for the newly redesignated 291st Engineer Combat Battalion.

When he arrived in Texas, Pergrin was the only battalion officer above the rank of a second lieutenant, excepting the battalion commander, Major Hayes. The primary challenge they faced mirrored what Anderson had addressed a year earlier: an almost complete lack of experienced officers. In the latter phase of training, Hayes suffered a severe back injury, and on August 26, 1943, the twenty-six-year-old, now Major David Pergrin, was given command of the battalion. He was younger than many of his senior enlisted men, and most of the 291st's officers did not have college degrees; none had army experience beyond initial schooling. His first assignment was to prepare the battalion for immediate overseas assignment.

Despite these challenges, the 291st passed its pre-deployment tests and inspections, and in the fall of 1943 qualified for service overseas. The battalion was sent via rail from Texas to Camp Miles Standish in Boston, and there boarded the troop-carrying merchant vessel SS *Santa Elena*[128] for transit to England. The ship departed Boston Harbor on October 9, and dropped anchor in Liverpool, England, on October 19.

As with the 1111th Group, the 291st was sent to a training camp and assigned construction duties in preparation for the arrival of tens of thousands of American troops. Pergrin and his battalion were sent to Camp Stapely, in Taunton, Somerset, fifty miles northeast of Plymouth. The 291st constructed Nissen huts, hardstands (thick foundations for more permanent structures), and bases for large troop tents. The only operational activity came on November 19, when Company B of the battalion was transferred farther west, to Truro in Cornwall, to participate in rehearsals for amphibious landing assistance. This included demolition of beach obstacles, mine-clearing, pillbox destruction, and other assault infantry support. Otherwise, the battalion was engaged for another two and a half months in its construction duties as the new year brought the invasion closer.

Finally, on February 4, 1944, the 291st lost its "orphan status"[129] and was attached to the 1111th Engineer Combat Group and sent to Highnam Court, Gloucester. Pergrin considered his new commander, Colonel Anderson, to be "the most picturesque character [he] had met in the Army until then" and marveled at how much they "had in common—except for [Anderson's] age and combat experience."[130]

THE ODYSSEY OF THE 51ST ENGINEER COMBAT BATTALION

"Stopped By Nothing"

The 51st Engineers had departed the operational control of the 1111th Group in the US in September 1943, destined for service in the "CBI" Theater—China-Burma-India. The Army somehow determined it to be logistically advantageous to ship the battalion's almost 700 personnel from the eastern seaboard, while its equipment was sent *westward* by rail and thence to Asia by Pacific sealift. Commanding officer Major Victor Reafsnyder assigned Chief Warrant Officer (CWO) Walter Keesing and Technician Marcus Howard on detached service to accompany the equipment. As events transpired, the battalion and its equipment (including escorts Keesing and Howard) were never reunited.

Dividing into two halves, the battalion embarked on Liberty ships for the Atlantic crossing to Algeria. On November 12, the first component under Major Reafsnyder embarked aboard Liberty Ship HR 650, SS *Calvin Coolidge*. The remainder of the battalion followed the next day aboard Liberty Ship HR 656, SS *Richard Rush*. The intended route would take the battalion via convoy for North Africa, where it was to proceed across the continent to Asia via the Suez Canal, the Middle East, and thence to India. Their convoy of seventy-four Liberty ships and seventeen escort vessels departed Hampton Roads, Virginia, on November 14, 1943.

While the 51st was at sea, decisions as to the direction of the war effort were realigned as a result of the Tehran Conference (November 28 to December 1, 1943), during which President Franklin Roosevelt and Prime Minister Winston Churchill formally committed to General Secretary Josef Stalin the proposition that the Western Allies would invade Nazi-held northern France during the first half of 1944. The effects of this decision rippled through the Army, and the 51st had its orders changed while en route to Algeria.

Disembarking in Oran on December 5, the battalion's ensuing change of direction and destination added frustration and misery to the troops who had just endured an uncomfortable ocean passage. After a period of waiting for its new onward travel, on January 6, 1944, the battalion was moved via rail to the port of Casablanca, Morocco, for the voyage to England.

Other circumstances deepened the battalion's plight: the continued worsening of the relationship between the commander and his troops. While the uncertainty and confusion surrounding the unit's mission and destination could not have helped Reafsnyder during this period, more evidence emerged to highlight the troops' growing lack of confidence in their commander's leadership.

In a notable episode, during their rail transit from Oran to Casablanca, the train made periodic stops for the troops to take a break and stretch their legs. During one of these breaks, Major Reafsnyder and his adjutant were left behind. Although blamed at the time on an uncooperative and inattentive French train engineer, in fact it was prompted by some of the battalion's officers. Reafsnyder caught up "many hours later"[131] via a rail handcar. Commanders who have their men's respect and admiration simply do not become the victims of such humiliating and mean-spirited pranks. One cannot conceive of this happening under Anderson's watch.

Travail followed. The 51st and four other engineer battalions were assigned to be carried to England from Morocco aboard a British steamer, HMS *Andes*. The *Andes* was fast enough to sail unescorted, and normally Casablanca to Liverpool would have taken three days; however, several suspected U-boats were detected, so the *Andes* zigzagged and detoured well to the west, then north, before reaching its destination, after a nine-day journey, on January 21. The *Andes* and its passengers had to endure the misery of North Atlantic winter storms throughout the extended voyage.

The battalion was immediately moved to Llanelly on the south coast of Wales, and assigned to the First US Army (FUSA) under

General Omar Bradley. The 51st's training was limited, as it possessed no major engineering equipment and none of the authorities in England had any record of the 51st's assignment there. This dilemma was eventually resolved, but only after the involvement of US Army headquarters in Washington, which confirmed that the 51st was in fact where it was supposed to be (England), and was thus authorized to have all its required equipment.

Finally, on March 1, the 51st was assigned once again to Colonel Anderson and the 1111th Group. (On May 15, eight months after they departed, accompanying all of the battalion's engineering equipment as it was sent westward, CWO Keesing and T/5 Howard were dropped from the battalion's roles, as they were being absorbed into the Headquarters US Armed Forces in China-Burma-India.)

HIGHNAM COURT

Arriving in Highnam Court, Gloucestershire, on March 1, the 1111th and its operational units established themselves throughout the region, with most of the personnel billeted in commercial and private residences. The 1111th itself set up headquarters in Stroud, eight miles south of Gloucester. By March 3, the three engineer combat battalions assigned to Anderson's 1111th Group were in place in Highnam Court, Gloucester: the 296th, the 291st, and the just-arrived 51st. Other various units were temporarily assigned to the 1111th for training activities, including the 86th Heavy Ponton Battalion.

A good deal of effort was made by 1111th staff to establish relationships with the various First Army and British units in the area; there were many exchanges of liaison officers for various training coordination and staff exercises. As a headquarters element, the 1111th's main functions were to plan, schedule, and coordinate training for its operational units. On March 18, the 1111th Group and its assigned battalions celebrated the one-year anniversary of their formal redesignation. The day was set aside for various celebrations and ceremonies, including medals, awards, and promotions. Anderson held a sports tournament with competitions in football, boxing, volleyball, track-and-field events, and softball.

March through May 1944 was filled with inspections, rehearsals, the usual swirling personnel changes and adjustments, and various other preparatory activities. On April 15, the group was alerted for departure; although not scheduled to take part in the actual D-Day invasion, it was scheduled to land in France at some point soon thereafter. Anderson was not yet aware of the specific location for the invasion, such was the tight security in place at the time. However, a visit from a senior officer to the group headquarters provided a clue: he was noticed staring intently at a group status map, specifically at the Normandy beaches. Shortly after, Anderson and his staff were read into the "bigot list" and briefed on the D-Day sites.

The commander used this period to test and train his staff of officers, making frequent reassignments within his group and throughout the assigned battalions. The purpose of this was twofold: first, to cross-train his staff officers so that they would be able to step into jobs with some background expertise, should the combat situation require; perhaps as important, Anderson could observe and evaluate his men, assessing their strengths and weaknesses, in order to make better personnel assignments.

First Army provided instructions for Anderson and the 1111th Group as to how the movement to France would proceed: first the group would land, to be followed by the operational battalions a day later. In this way all planning and coordination would allow for a smooth, organized deployment of the units. The First Army engineer was Colonel Bill Carter,[132] with whom Anderson would have a close relationship throughout the upcoming months.

Although specific movement plans were not yet scheduled, Anderson prepared his group, holding two "dry run" movement exercises in May:

The entire Hqs and Hq Co. assembled their vehicles at a prescribed rendezvous and were given the orders to pack up for movement; all equipment, both organizational and individual then being loaded into assigned vehicles. After an inspection by the Group Commander [Anderson] and Executive Officer [Kirkland], the trucks were unloaded, and equipment returned to normal locations.[133]

Even in this simple exercise one can see important aspects of Anderson's sound leadership. Knowing the destination his group would take, but not the date, and anticipating the chaos that would almost certainly ensue when travel orders did arrive, he understood that by practicing procedures until they become routine, men and units are then able to adjust to the inevitable last-minute changes and ensuing confusion. He was demonstrating yet again to his junior officers how leadership works—preparation and planning are as important a responsibility as personally leading a route march.

Anderson now had responsibility for around 3,000 men, as final training and preparation for the invasion of France reached its peak. None except himself had any war experience, yet they were eager and ready to do their part in the invasion, to bring the war to an end.

ENDNOTES

126   Unit History, 1111th Engineer Combat Group, US Army, 1 January 1944–31 January 1944.

127   HWAMil, 34.

128   SS *Santa Elena*. Three weeks after delivering the 291st to England, the *Santa Elena* was attacked by German torpedo planes on November 6 and sunk off Philippeville (present-day Skikda), Algeria.

129   David E. Pergrin and Eric Hammel, *First Across the Rhine* (New York: Macmillan Publishing Company, 1989), 15.

130   Ibid.

131   Radford and Radford, *Unbroken Line*, 37.

132   Colonel William A. Carter, General Omar Bradley's chief engineer for First US Army, was a West Point graduate, 1930. He took part in the American army invasions of Tunisia and Sicily, then accompanied Bradley to England for Operation Overlord and subsequent FUSA campaigns through the invasion of Germany. He and Anderson corresponded in retirement. After the Army (service included the Panama Canal Zone in the early 1960s), Carter worked for the Inter-American Development Bank. He died in 1996.

133   Unit History, 1111th Engineer Combat Group, 1 May 1944–31 May 1944.

CHAPTER SEVEN

INTO THE STORM

Operation Overlord unleashed the combined Western Allied armies onto the coast of France, opening a front to drive the German forces out of Western Europe. The operation fulfilled the commitment made to Stalin in December 1943 in Tehran, forcing Germany to engage forces on yet another front in addition to the fighting already taking place in Italy and Germany's eastern front. The overall command of Overlord rested with General Dwight Eisenhower from the US; under his direction, the Allied air, sea, and ground forces were to strike the Normandy coast, as more than 150,000 troops were to be landed on the first day, overwhelming the defenders.

ENGINEERS AT NORMANDY

The use of combat engineers for beach clearance on D-Day was addressed somewhat late in the invasion planning because "during 1943 reconnaissance had uncovered no obstacles along the Normandy coast. Indeed, an early engineer plan assumed that there would be no obstacles or that, if the Germans attempted to install any at the last minute, naval gunfire and aerial bombardment would take care of them."[134] However, in late January 1944, aerial reconnaissance revealed beach obstacles on what would become Utah Beach, on the Cotentin.[135] By late March, the German defenders were observed emplacing obstacles along Omaha Beach as well. The obstacles appeared to be arranged in three belts in the tidal zone and consisted of various types of construction. Some of these wood or iron devices were mined.

Thus, a scant ten weeks before the most elaborate and complex joint-arms amphibious operation in history, substantial adjustments were made to the most critical aspect of the entire operation: how to destroy beach obstacles before the main body of assault infantry landed. Joint army and navy teams were sent to Fort Pierce, Florida, to observe the US Navy's new underwater-demolition team training school, in order to learn how tidal-zone beach obstacles could be demolished.

This unique and highly specialized capability was brand new, and with so little time available, by D-Day no real combined training or coordination between the various landing elements—infantry, landing craft, and naval forces—had been conducted. The resulting confusion, and limited success, is not surprising.

On D-Day, virtually nothing went according to plan for the various US Army and Navy (and combined) demolition teams. Some made it to shore ahead of the infantry, while some came well after; many were intermixed. Of the planned eighteen 50-yard-wide gaps these courageous troops were assigned to on Omaha, less than half were cleared. The beach-demolition units took horrendous casualties, with both the Navy and Army teams taking between 30 and 50 percent losses.

Heroic efforts by individuals and small groups of engineers and demolitions men achieved just enough success to allow following waves to gradually establish a foothold on the beach. With the midmorning incoming tide, Navy destroyers were able to close within a half mile of the beach due to the steep shoreline gradient, allowing point-blank naval gunfire over open sights in support of the pinned infantry. In this manner, individual German machine-gun positions were targeted by shipboard five-inch guns and eliminated, providing substantial assistance to the infantry. Omaha Beach was taken—barely.

At Utah Beach, the amphibious assault encountered far less resistance, and benefited from a lucky break. Two Navy control vessels navigated erroneously, hindered by smoke from the prelanding bombardment, which obscured the beach to the landing craft. As a result, the entire first wave landed more than a mile south (left, facing the beaches) of the intended beach; this stretch of sand turned out to be far less heavily defended by either German troops or beach obstacles. The combined Navy and Army beach-obstacle teams had a far easier experience than their Omaha colleagues, as did the corresponding infantry. Deciding to "start the war from here,"[136] the Army and Navy adjusted the follow-on landing waves to exploit the new Utah Beach, rather than trying to use the original, planned beaches. By nightfall of D-Day, engineers had cleared obstacles, established and maintained beach exits, built and improved roads, created storage areas for both ammunition and medical supplies, and sent out reconnaissance efforts. Casualties were light, in comparison to Omaha.

Although Hitler's Atlantic Wall had been breached in a matter of hours, the German defenders reacted with characteristic vigor, limiting Allied assault objectives in the early days of the invasion. By D-Day+22 (June 28), when Colonel Wallis Anderson landed with his 1111th Engineer Combat Group, the Americans on Utah and Omaha Beaches had consolidated their beach head into one contiguous zone.

THUMBING A RIDE TO FRANCE

Despite the First Army instructions, planning, and rehearsing, the actual movement to France for Anderson's group had a somewhat

"Keystone Kops" air about it, as the careful sequencing went awry from the start. Instead of the planned movement twenty-four hours in advance of its battalions, which would have enabled the group to prepare for its following units, on the morning of June 18 (twelve days after D-Day), Anderson was notified by the 51st ECB that it had already received movement orders and was en route to embarkation at Southampton. The 291st Engineers received similar orders shortly after the 51st received theirs.

Anderson finally received orders for movement of the 1111th Group an hour later, and "we just took off like a scared rabbit to regain the lost ground."[137] Reaching the bivouac area outside Southampton that Sunday night, Anderson learned that no embarkation preparations for the 1111th Group had been made, and so made arrangements to bed down his unit and resolve the issue in the morning.

However, shortly after, in the early hours of June 19, Anderson was informed that the 51st had already begun boarding its assigned transports, three Liberty ships. Still determined to arrive in France in advance of his assigned component engineers, and despite the failure of the logistical planning, Anderson sought ad hoc transportation for his small group, which numbered around thirteen officers and sixty-five enlisted men.

Hustling his troops from their bivouac to the port in the middle of the night, Anderson took his case to a succession of Transportation Corps officers, none of whom had ever heard of the 1111th Group, which wasn't listed on any of their embarkation schedules. Persisting, Anderson engaged a sergeant "who was actively engaged in putting troops on a partly loaded Liberty ship—the SS *Charles M. Hall*—a ship on the opposite side of the pier from [the ship loading] the 51st."[138] The sergeant indicated the ship, which was almost fully loaded, was being held from departure because none of the embarked officers were willing to accept assignment as "commander of troops."

Seizing the opportunity, Anderson volunteered on the spot to take this responsibility in exchange for space on the ship for his small group. In his words, "We traded our command duties for a lift across the channel and thus thumbed our way to France and got to the beachhead in advance of any of our battalions after all—and to that extent in accordance with the advance planning."[139]

Anderson's tongue-in-cheek comment notwithstanding, his timely arrival in France had nothing to do with "advance planning" and everything to do with his determination, experience (especially in dealing with army logistics), savvy, and mission focus. The *Charles M. Hall* sailed at 0730 on Tuesday, June 20, and waited for its convoy to make for the French coast.

The actual landing in France on the Normandy beachhead was delayed by an unforeseen storm, which struck on June 19 and lasted three days. The storm was violent enough to wreck significant portions of the Allied infrastructure on the invasion beaches, causing disruption and delays. On June 27, the *Hall* finally departed its anchorage in England and headed for France. Arriving off Omaha Beach (the original planned destination for the 1111th) at 2300 hours, the ship anchored and waited for dawn. Early on Wednesday, June 28, the ship was shifted to an anchorage off Utah Beach (the westernmost of the five invasion beaches, and the only one on the Cotentin Peninsula in Normandy), and the 1111th Group began to disembark, with the advance echelon arriving in the afternoon.

Anderson moved to Hébert, a crossroads hamlet[140] about two miles inland from Utah Beach and a mile northeast of the nearest village, Saint-Marie-du-Mont. Here he organized his headquarters for field operations and established communication links to higher headquarters and subordinate units. The 1111th Engineer Combat Group was staffed thus:

Group Headquarters

Commanding Officer	Colonel H. W. Anderson
Executive Officer	Lieutenant Colonel James A. Kirkland
S-3 (Operations)	Major Henderson O. Webb
Assistant S-3	1st Lieutenant Robert N. Jewett
S-2 (Intelligence)	Captain Richard O. Carville
Assistant S-2	Captain Ira S. Barzilay
S-4 (Logistics)	Captain Thomas J. C. Williams
Assistant S-4 (Motor)	2nd Lieutenant J. D. Folck
S-1, Adjutant (Admin., Pers.)	1st Lieutenant Ray L. Bailey
Assistant S-1	2nd Lieutenant C. B. Buckley
Group Surgeon	Major Edgar W. Weir
Group Dental Surgeon	Captain Gerard J. Casey
Group Chaplain (P–Protestant)	Captain Harold E. Berger
Group Chaplain (C–Catholic)	Captain Luke J. Ouska.

Headquarters Company

Commanding Officer, HQS Company	Captain J. C. Messenger
Communications Officer	2nd Lieutenant G. R. Donelson
SSO (Special Services)	1st Lieutenant G. M. Long

The 51st Engineer Combat Battalion (ECB), commanded by (now) Lieutenant Colonel Victor Reafsnyder, sailed to France aboard three Liberty ships, set up in Hébert as well, and received its first orders from the 1111th on June 29. The 291st ECB, under Lieutenant Colonel David Pergrin, had a more scattered experience, beginning at the marshaling area at Southampton. Its various elements were loaded onto two Liberty ships and an LST (large amphibious landing ship: "Landing Ship, Tank"). Landing on both Omaha and Utah Beaches over a four-day period, the 291st was finally able to consolidate in Vierville, France, one mile southwest of Saint-Marie-du-Mont, by the twenty-ninth. By July 1, the last of the 1111th's assigned engineer battalions, the 296th, arrived and began operation, having collected its scattered companies.

As mentioned previously, the 1111th Engineer C Group was a First Army asset under the new flexible scheme for organizing the engineers. The fundamental unit for the Army when an engineering mission arose was the battalion, usually commanded by a lieutenant colonel (or major), and consisted of around 650 men, organized into three letter companies (A, B, C), plus a headquarters and service (H&S) company. These engineer C (combat) battalions were generally assigned at one of three levels in the Army hierarchy: division, corps, or army.

Most Army infantry and armored divisions were assigned an engineer combat battalion to support their operations. These engineer units did not belong to the division permanently, as in WWI; the engineers were often reassigned as new tasks emerged.

At the next two upper levels, engineer groups were engaged as corps and army assets, to manage the activities of multiple engineer battalions. Groups, like the 1111th, were usually commanded by a full colonel, like Anderson. Thus, Anderson guided the activities of his three battalions under the direction of First Army.

The Normandy campaign provides a useful example of this organizational principle in action. On D-Day, the US landed two corps—VII Corps at Utah and V Corps at Omaha—with a total of five infantry divisions. ECBs attached to the infantry divisions took part in the beach landings, and ECGs (with their own attached ECBs) landed as well, under corps control. By the time Anderson's group had arrived on D+22, more corps had landed, and the First US Army (FUSA) had been established, under General Omar Bradley; the 1111th ECG was duly attached as the engineer component at the army level.

Other engineer units were mixed in as well, in addition to the ECBs. Specialty units at the company and battalion level existed, and were assigned in various ways, usually under ECG control. Light and heavy ponton, light equipment, treadway bridge, maintenance, and even dump truck units were part of the Army's elaborate table of organization (T/O). All of these had specific capabilities and were applied wherever they were needed.

When Anderson established his headquarters in France, then, he was under FUSA, in the VIII Corps zone. Actual orders were usually informally given to Anderson to provide additional support to an Army corps. He would then give the mission to the nearest or most appropriate engineer battalion to handle the task.

The 1111th Engineer Combat Group began operations, having been assigned its initial mission: "maintain and repair roads within the area assigned."[141] This mission was soon expanded to include "operation of water points, opening and running of rock quarries and gravel pits, lifting of minefields and in some instances, the neutralizing of booby traps."[142]

On June 29, Colonel Anderson made a personal reconnaissance of the group's operational area, visiting his battalion commanders. By this date, the French Route Nationale 13 ("N13") had been established as the critical part of the main supply route (MSR), the road network that linked all the army units in Normandy. This small highway was especially vital in that the N13 was the main connection between Utah and Omaha Beaches.[143] Maintaining this link was a mission of critical importance to the Allied armies, ensuring effective communications, command, and supply. Conversely, severing this road and rendering it unusable became a prime task for the German defenders in the region.

By June 29, the German lines had been pushed back only as far as Carentan's southern suburbs. The N13 MSR at Carentan was well within German artillery range, notably the infamous 88 mm guns. At the time, the most fearsome and determined German troops in the area belonged to the Waffen-SS. This was the first encounter between 1111th Engineers and German SS units; it would not be the last.

Anderson met with Pergrin and assigned his 291st ECB to maintain the MSR along N13 from Carentan north toward Sainte-Mère-Église, a ten-mile stretch that was under frequent German artillery fire as well as occasional aircraft bombing raids. For Pergrin and his 291st, this meant continuous road and bridge repair, as well as mine-clearing operations; gravel from the quarries provided most of the fill material. One site of vital importance in this zone was the so-called "Tucker Bridge,"[144] an Army-built Bailey bridge over La Taute River along Carentan's eastern boundary. Tucker Bridge linked Carentan to the north, alongside the Carentan Canal, to Omaha Beach, where vast amounts of supplies to sustain the Army were being delivered daily. Because of this role, Tucker Bridge was a frequent target of German shelling. The bridge was named for Major John Tucker, commanding officer of the 300th ECB, who was killed during bridge-repair operations under fire on June 27. In addition to the continuous road maintenance, minefields were swept and neutralized throughout the zone. Pergrin set his men to work around the clock, in three 8-hour shifts.

Also on June 29, Anderson met with the 51st commander, Lieutenant Colonel Reafsnyder, to discuss 51st ECB operations. Anderson assigned Reafsnyder road maintenance, minefield clearing, and other assorted tasks, mainly in the areas and roads surrounding Sainte-Mère-Église, north from Carentan about ten miles along the N13. Maintaining the road network was the top priority.

One can only speculate as to why Anderson placed his battalions in the arrangement described. He placed Pergrin in Vierville just behind the MSR he was assigned to cover, and three miles forward from Anderson's own 1111th headquarters. Conversely, Anderson kept Reafsnyder close at hand, even though the 51st areas of responsibility were centered on Sainte-Mère-Église, six miles from Hébert. Perhaps there was nothing more to it than a matter of logistics. Nevertheless, with an eye to the future, one must consider the possibility that Anderson wanted to keep a closer eye on the commander of the 51st ECB. Certainly, by comparison, Anderson gave Pergrin more independence than was afforded Reafsnyder.

For the next several days, Anderson roamed the area between FUSA headquarters on Omaha Beach, VIII Corps headquarters (under Major General Troy Middleton), and throughout the 1111th operational area. By July 2, the area covered by the 1111th straddled the corps boundaries, with the 51st operating in the vicinity of Sainte-Mère-Église (VIII Corps), and 291st in the VII Corps (Major General Lawton Collins) zone.

During one visit to Pergrin shortly after one of many artillery shellings at Tucker Bridge, Anderson told Pergrin of the death of Colonel Daniel Spengler, a Pennsylvanian like Anderson and Pergrin. Spengler had commanded the 1110th ECG, located immediately to the west of Anderson's group; he was killed by a German machine gun as his engineers supported infantry attacks in the vicinity of La Haye Du Puits, west of Carentan.[145]

In addition to the aforementioned tasks, the engineers were called upon to conduct explosive ordnance disposal, as needed. Duds and misfired munitions were commonplace, requiring the specialized skills of the engineers to render areas safe. As the requirements for this type of work increased, Anderson established a training school for mine-clearing, to expand the number of qualified personnel.

On July 12, around 4:30 in the afternoon (1630, using military terminology), a large fire erupted in a nearby munitions dump at Audouville-la-Hubert, about two miles northwest of Anderson's headquarters in Hébert.

Anderson immediately drove to assess the emergency, taking his S-3, Major Webb, with him. Seeing the size and scope of the conflagration, Anderson took charge and ordered "all available men, vehicles, and equipment in the Bn [51st ECB] . . . mobilized and sent to the scene to assist in fighting the fire. The bulk of [backfilling] and covering was done by bulldozers and tankdozers."[146] Personnel from 1111th and 51st—including Anderson—exposed themselves to exploding ammunition, artillery shells, and other munitions while fighting the blaze for hours. Of special note was the heroic effort by Master Sergeant Lee Raper, who drove a D-7 bulldozer,[147] replacing the usual operator, who was injured. Raper used the bulldozer to smother flaming munitions even as they were cooking off.

The blaze was finally controlled and extinguished after an eight-hour fight, ending after midnight. A number of 1111th and 51st soldiers were singled out for heroism: Colonel Anderson, Major Webb, Major Robert Yates (executive officer of the 51st), Captain John Barnes (51st headquarters element, assistant division engineer), First Lieutenant David Henry (51st motor officer), Second Lieutenant J. A. Murphy, Master Sergeant Lee Raper, and Private First Class G. M. Cash all received Soldier's Medals.

The 1111th and its assigned units operated from the same base locations for several weeks, reflecting the difficulty the Allies were having pushing the Germans back. Several reasons account for this, both expected and unforeseen. The ability of the German Army to react, adapt, and adjust was well known by this point in the war. Although caught somewhat wrong-footed by both the precise timing and location of the invasion, German commanders were able to marshal their forces quickly to establish a cohesive defense. None of the Allied forces accomplished all their objectives on D-Day, although they all succeeded in their main goal, that of establishing a supportable beachhead in France.

The other factor slowing the American advance in the western Normandy enclave was the principal terrain feature in the region: the Norman *bocage*. Whereas in England the smaller and thinner hedgerows were not considered to be major obstacles, the large, thick French counterparts were quite different, having been developed very differently by landowners over centuries.

The French bocage imposed obstacles for advancing troops: twelve or more feet tall, and eight to ten feet thick, they encompassed an average of around fifty to seventy-five acres. Each field was serviced by (often sunken) roads and only a couple entrances/exits. While Allied planners noted these terrain features, they did not fully appreciate the difference between English and French versions.

The resulting fight in Normandy's farmland was a grueling struggle. In bocage country, fighting was reduced to an acre-by-acre, small-unit combat arena, where the skillful Germans could use the terrain to pick and choose where and how to fight, reducing the Allies' advantages in numbers and firepower. By turning every action into an ambush-and-retreat scenario, German forces slowly gave ground while extracting the maximum price—in men, material, and time— from the larger and better equipped and supplied Allied armies.

Army combat engineers were essential to the Allied effort. They cleared minefields, blasted holes in the bocage to bring more firepower to bear, and applied inventive solutions to difficult problems, proving their worth throughout.

Two remarkable examples of resourcefulness and initiative were the Carentan Bypass and armored bulldozers. The slow advance by the Americans kept the vital MSR within German artillery range for weeks. This threat resulted in damage and delays along the vital supply line for vehicles traveling in both directions. Personnel from the 291st proposed an idea to build a road bypass to alleviate traffic congestion in southern Carentan and allow for a more circular, dual one-way traffic flow, greatly reducing risk and increasing the delivery of supplies. Anderson and Carter (FUSA engineer) approved the idea, and the two-mile track in south Carentan was constructed between July 7 and 11.

Another 291st idea involved rigging bulldozers with armor plating, enabling their use in bocage combat; much of the material used for this was salvaged from destroyed beach obstacles.[148] The 291st, under the command of Lieutenant Colonel David Pergrin, was proving to be a well-led and first-rate unit that Anderson could rely upon.

BREAKOUT

On July 17, after spending almost three weeks at Hébert in bivouac, Anderson received orders to shift the 1111th with First Army as it prepared a major offensive designed to crack German lines and break out from bocage country. Accordingly, Anderson's group headquarters and two of its attendant battalions (the 51st and 291st ECBs; the 296th ECB was detached from the 1111th and sent to VII Corps) headed south past Carentan, along a three-mile axis running between Le Haut, Vernay, and Saint-Jean-de-Daye. The 1111th's units were positioned behind the US 3rd Armored and 30th Infantry Divisions; the engineers provided support by clearing, widening, and improving all routes leading up to the front.

On July 25, First Army launched its offensive, Operation Cobra, which commenced a week after the British launched Operation Goodwood, to finally take Caen. The Americans thus benefitted from German preoccupation with and concentration around that city. Operation Cobra kicked off when the weather finally cleared enough for the opening: a massive aerial bombing effort intended to obliterate the German defensive positions. Three thousand Allied light, medium, and heavy bombers hit an area just south of the Saint-Lô—Periers road, only 6,000 yards wide by 2,200 yards deep, west of Saint-Lô, a major hub city.

The bombers, attacking in three waves for ninety minutes, "flew over the area in an endless stream from 0945 to 1100, immediately followed by an artillery barrage."[149] Anderson's engineers from the 51st, who were just two miles north of that demarcation boundary, reported "the ground shook, and shock waves fluttered the legs and sleeves of the men's fatigue clothing as though they stood in a gale-force wind."[150] The defending German SS Panzer Lehr Division took the full brunt of this aerial assault and suffered heavily. The breakthrough was accomplished, as American armored units exploited the gap and raced deeper into France.

Operation Cobra and the breakout west of Saint-Lô initiated a new phase in the Normandy campaign, and for the 1111th and its subordinate units. Engineer units raced along with and just behind their frontline army counterparts, repairing and constructing roads, culverts, and bridges to assist and enhance the ground forces' mobility.

Ancillary tasks, such as quarrying (which provided rocks and gravel for the roads), unexploded ordnance disposal, and minefield clearance were also important assignments for the engineers. Anderson shifted his headquarters frequently; the 291st and 51st kept pace accordingly. Anderson established bivouacs at Le Dézert on July 26; then to Dupard, six miles west of Saint-Lô, on the twenty-ninth. He moved his 51st and 291st to nearby La Chapelle-en-Juger and just north of Saint Gilles, respectively.

Although German artillery barrages lessened as their artillery was given little opportunity to set up and fire, German air attacks occurred. Anderson's headquarters element was subjected to one in late July, which fortunately only resulted in a minor casualty thanks to Anderson's preparations: "The value of dispersion and slit trenches was effectively proven to all personnel, and from this time on, it was never necessary for the Commanding Officer [Anderson] to order such digging."[151] In such manner, veterans impart wisdom and knowledge that saves lives. The 51st was attacked and strafed by German aircraft fighters as well and suffered five nonlethal casualties.

During this period, Anderson was responsible for the following units, under his 1111th Engineer Combat Group:

- 51st Engineer Combat Battalion
- 291st Engineer Combat Battalion
- 296th Engineer Combat Battalion (having returned from temporary attachment to VII Corps)
- 508th Light Ponton Company
- 629th Light Equipment Company
- 767th Dump Truck Company
- 962nd Engineer Maintenance Company

As the Germans retreated, they left behind equipment and vehicles, some of which were repaired and subsequently put into use by the industrious Americans; engineers excelled in this regard, for obvious reasons, having been specifically selected and trained for this. The engineers' table of equipment was enhanced by an assortment of "liberated" German (and French and American) material, all of which improved their standard of living (or was intended to). Many items were "repurposed" as improvisation became the watchword: "German soup kitchens as asphalt mixers . . . gas mask canisters as toilet article cases . . . German gas capes for water proofing mattresses."[152]

Vehicles too were recovered and refurbished—some put to more usefulness than others: while in the vicinity of Saint Gilles, Technician 4th Grade Jeff Elliott, of the 291st's Company A, discovered he had a knack for getting German armored vehicles running. He managed to repair several, including a *Panzerkampfwagen* V Panther tank (a medium tank, at just under fifty tons), which he took on joy rides, including showing off for his commanding officer, Lieutenant Colonel Pergrin, who tolerated such high-spirited mischief. Elliott also added a German half-track to the battalion's inventory.

Coincidently, the positioning of Anderson's troops within the now vast American army brought some contact with old friends— in one instance, the 238th Engineer Combat Battalion, formerly the 2nd Battalion of the old 51st Regiment, which Anderson had commanded in Plattsburgh. The 51st ECB found itself within a half mile of the 238th while in the vicinity of Le Guislain.

Another dynamic of which Anderson was surely aware was the continued, beneath-the-surface concern regarding the 51st's leadership. An officer in the 51st wrote home, "Reafsnyder gets more nervous every day. If we ever come under any great pressure, he will crack."[153] Certainly, commanding troops in combat is an extreme circumstance, one requiring extraordinary and uncommon personal characteristics. That some are not emotionally able to meet this challenge, despite training and selection efforts, is not surprising. As this situation had been extant for months, and the people involved were Plattsburgh-trained personnel with whom Anderson enjoyed a close bond, it would be extremely unlikely the group commander was unaware. However, apparently Anderson was not yet ready for such drastic action as replacing a battalion commander.

COUNTERATTACK AT MORTAIN

On August 7, the Germans struck the Americans with a surprise counterattack, one directed by Hitler himself. As American forces poured into Normandy, another numbered army had been established, the Third US Army, activated on August 1, 1944, under the command of Lieutenant General George Patton. With two armies operating in Normandy, Bradley had been elevated to command the Twelfth Army Group, consisting of First and Third US Armies, Lieutenant General Courtney Hodges having taken command of First Army. Patton's forces occupied the western segment of the American lines, with

Hodges aligned on Patton's left; Hodges held territory running east until the British-Canadian armies took over, near Vire.

By the end of the first week of August, Hitler saw that due to Patton's rapid advancement past Avranches, an opportunity presented itself: driving west from Mortain, if the Germans could reach the sea (Golfe de Saint Malo) at Avranches, potentially three infantry and two armored divisions of Third Army could be cut off, driving a wedge between Third and First Army, creating a crisis of major proportions. Accordingly, Operation *Lüttich* was drafted and launched.

Senior German commanders were opposed to the idea, citing lack of sufficient forces and their vulnerability should the initial thrust not be successful. They favored a fighting withdrawal, to better conserve their strength in the face of increasing imbalance between their battered forces and the growing Allied might. This mentality was logical and practical but would do nothing to reverse the tide of Allied success. Hitler, on the other hand, always sought a path that would lead to victory, however improbable or even illogical. The ensuing Germans offensive got off to an "exceptionally poor start," where "nothing went right in the German attack."[154]

Although initially surprised, the Americans reacted quickly, their troops aided substantially by the overwhelming Allied airpower, and benefited from a well-established supply and logistical infrastructure. (At this point the Allies' logistical chain was still half the distance of that of the Germans, who were fighting far from their border.) Lüttich failed within five days, as the Germans had insufficient forces to accomplish their goals, or even to make much headway at all. This operation, unsuccessful though it was, revealed Hitler's mindset: He sought to upend the Allies' advantages, and reverse the German fortunes with a bold, surprise counterstroke. But unless he wanted a repeat of Lüttich's failure, he would need to increase the German strike forces, shorten his supply lines, and ensure strategic surprise, while somehow negating Allied airpower. The seed of his boldest idea yet had been planted.

As feared by the German generals, when their offensive stalled, the Allies subsequently thrust forward, forcing the Germans—outnumbered and increasingly outmaneuvered—back.

On August 12, the 1111th Group moved again to the southeast from Guislain, about eight miles from La Bourdonnière. Here Anderson had the 296th construct a prisoner-of-war enclosure to hold Germans collected from Lüttich. More rapid movement followed, as Anderson's troops shifted three times, covering about thirty-four miles in a five-day period. His engineer battalions kept pace as the American armies rolled out of Normandy, turning east toward Paris.

The race continued, although the supply lines, extending back to the Overlord beaches, were now stretched thin. Engineer units were being stripped of vehicles in order to haul supplies, as well as to provide additional transportation for bridging equipment. As the First and Third Armies turned east following the Mortain battle, the Americans hurried to encircle the rapidly collapsing German forces in what became known as the Falaise Pocket. A significant portion of the German *Wehrmacht* ("army") still in France was either killed, captured, or driven east by August 22.

Reflecting this hectic pursuit, Anderson's 1111th Group moved again on August 26, turning east to Ancinnes, a small town five miles southeast of Alençon. Bridging became a top priority, and all engineer units were ordered to contribute vehicles to get this material into position as the American armies approached the Seine River. On August 25, Paris officially fell to First Army units, including a French armored division, which was given the honor of liberating the capital.

The 1111th's units sent all available trucks and carriers to support this effort. Heading east now, the 1111th and its battalions joined the rapidly surging US forces pursuing the fleeing Germans. At this point Anderson and his engineers were around 120 miles west of Paris, and the front had collapsed completely; German forces were streaming back through Belgium and to Germany. Some units maintained a front, backpedaling in front of the British lines, with some semblance of a fighting withdrawal.

Shifting location once again on August 29, Anderson reestablished his headquarters at Écrosnes, ten miles northeast of Chartres. This 100-mile, twelve-hour overnight motor march, which included all Anderson's subordinate units, provides another insight into how this commander was always thinking ahead, to prepare his troops for the next crisis. With the tactical situation such that there were no Germans anywhere nearby, Anderson reverted to a familiar theme: training, to best prepare his units for difficulties and dangers that might lie before them. He once again saw the opportunity to benefit his men by "taking advantage of all inclement weather to toughen troops."

Accordingly, Anderson directed the move to take place "as a unit[,] and strict blackout precautions were observed. Although not intended as such, this movement proved to be an excellent night problem, the night being extremely dark and accompanied by a constant downpour of rain."[155]

The excellent training nevertheless resulted in an accidental casualty, with serious consequences, involving the 51st ECB's free-spirited executive officer, Major Robert "Bull" Yates. The tall, lanky Texan, "easygoing in nature but determined in spirit,"[156] was one of the "Plattsburgh winter" members of the old 51st Engineer Regiment, who Anderson had placed in command throughout much of their arduous training. Respected and admired by his troops, Yates always seemed to be in the thick of things with his oversized personality.

On this night, however, Yates's exuberance got the best of him—perhaps aided by some liquid impairment, as "Yates had a bottle of whiskey at his side to make the evening a little more pleasant."[157] Eschewing his place in the command car, he took over the operation of one of the battalion's Harley-Davidson motorcycles, which were used as route guides to scout along the intended course. Racing past the lead jeep at the head of the convoy, he took a wrong turn in the darkness and heavy rain, and crashed into a ditch, while the battalion's almost 100 vehicles carried on to their destination.

Eventually, Yates was found, with a crushed right foot that required his medical evacuation to England for treatment and recovery. This was quite a blow to the 51st, as Yates was very much the glue that held the battalion together. Captain Richard Huxmann was assigned as executive officer, replacing Yates.

Despite the mishap, the 1111th units arrived in their destinations intact and continued their work. Anderson leapfrogged his battalions forward, toward the Seine River, and Paris. The 1111th moved to Vert-le-Grand on the thirtieth, twenty-five miles to the east, while directing the 291st to Melun on La Seine, to survey road and bridge sites. The 291st built yet another prisoner-of-war cage, in addition to their bridge and road activities. Near Paris the group paused, allowing recreational time off for some of the troops.

This pause was brief, however, as the Allied armies continued to roll forward. Anderson was directed to take his group east of Paris, to the area where he had been with the 28th Division in hard fighting in 1918. Establishing his command post (CP) on September 4, he noted,

> We crossed the Marne a bit west of Château-Thierry, then headed northeast—which by coincidence took us through exactly the same area where the writer [Anderson] had been involved with the 103rd Engineers in W.W.I. Our Hdqtrs. bivouaced at Fismes on the Vesle River where our 28th Div. had such bitter fighting in 1918 and we then headed for the crossing of the Meuse near Sedan which had also been an objective in the Meuse-Argonne Offensive in W.W.I.[158]

The 1111th's path took them from Fismes on September 4, to Châtelet-sur-Sormonne on the tenth, about twenty miles northwest of Sedan, and less than ten miles south of the France-Belgium border.

Along the way, trailing behind the advancing frontline units, the 1111th and its battalions worked to remove and replace the temporary bridges thrown up by the engineer units accompanying the infantry and armored divisions. These were generally the floating treadway or Bailey bridges, which tended to have lower load capacities.

Using locally-sourced materials, the group's engineers replaced one-way forty-ton bridges with two-way class 40 and one-way class 70 timber trestle bridges, to further enhance the Army's mobility. ("Class" refers to the weight capacity for vehicular travel over the bridge. Although it involves complex factors to calculate, basically a "two-way class 40" bridge allows for two forty-ton vehicles to use the bridge, traveling in opposite directions.) All three 1111th battalions got into the act, with larger bridges being erected at Sedan (la Meuse River), Montmédy, Longwe, and Florenville and Bouillon (Belgium).

On September 16, the 1111th Engineer Combat Group was directed to continue forward into Belgium, to establish a base in the vicinity of Bastogne, about fifty miles to the northeast. This shift caused an adjustment to the security posture of all units:

> Up to this time, First Army had been functioning in friendly territory and little attention to security of installations or transportation was therefore required. However, since operations were approaching enemy territory, it was becoming necessary that all vital installations and transportation be securely guarded. Security of bivouac areas was reinforced, and the convoy system was used to the maximum extent possible.[159]

The group's units repaired, maintained, and upgraded roads, culverts, and bridges as the Allied armies rolled forward into Belgium. Personnel and subordinate units were transferred and reassigned continuously and routinely. Into October, "normal field functions and job construction work was being carried out by all units of the Group."[160]

OPERATION MARKET GARDEN

As the Allies rolled across France and into Belgium, the four armies—First Canadian, Second British, First and Third American—seemed unstoppable. Eisenhower pressed all his forces forward on a broad front, while the Germans struggled to find troops strong or organized enough to hold defensive positions. Individual Wehrmacht units conducted fighting withdrawals as best they could all along the line, but any unit that stood and fought was likely to be bypassed, encircled, and destroyed. More often they pulled back as quickly as they could, blowing bridges and roads behind them.

By September 4, British troops entered Antwerp, Belgium's major port city. The capture of Antwerp would provide a solution to the only truly serious problem Eisenhower faced: logistics. The German Army before them was a shattered remnant of its strength even two months' prior. The German West Wall protecting their border was a shell, incomplete and largely unmanned. The main factor holding back the Allies as they surged into Belgium was the difficulty of supplying their huge, powerful, highly mechanized armies. Even in September, supplies were still coming over the Normandy invasion beaches, then trucked 350 miles to the advancing units. Antwerp would potentially provide Eisenhower with a logistics base large enough to feed his armies.

Even with the capture of the port city, though, the supplies were not yet flowing. Under German general Kurt Student, the Wehrmacht had managed to organize a skillful, tough defense of the estuaries leading from the sea, rendering Antwerp incapable of handling the supplies Eisenhower so eagerly wanted delivered close to the front.

Despite the severe supply difficulties, Eisenhower had two massive advantages, neither of which the Germans could match. First, he had four field armies along a broad front, all of which were hammering the Germans, forcing the Wehrmacht to burn resources—men and matériel—they simply could not replace. Even with a slowdown (or even a pause) due to an increasingly overstretched supply chain, Eisenhower was grinding the Wehrmacht in the West into dust. By forcing the Germans to spread their defensive efforts across the 300-mile front, nowhere could they truly halt the Allies for long; Eisenhower could range up and down any part of the broad front, and pick and choose where to attack, then do it again elsewhere. The only mistake would be to stop, giving Germans time to recover.

The second advantage was the brutally effective methodology enjoyed by the Allies, ironically developed by the Germans with their blitzkrieg tactics. The bocage fighting in Normandy had accelerated the integration of combat arms in the Allied armies; by September, these skills and capabilities had been honed to a peak. The air-ground team of artillery, mechanized infantry, and armor, supported by close air support, was unbeatable. Wherever and whenever the Allies chose to assault in open ground, they could do so with irresistible power.

By approving Montgomery's proposal for Operation Market Garden, Eisenhower allowed both advantages to be neutralized. He stopped other major advances and concentrated logistical support to Montgomery. The operation called for a narrow advance primarily along a single road, through three air-landing zones, one for each of three airborne divisions. By the evening of the first day, the Germans knew exactly where the Allies were heading; the mobile broad-front strategy had been replaced with a too-narrow thrust in terrain that favored defenders—exactly the conditions the Germans desperately needed.

Neither could the Allies utilize the full weight of their air-ground team to probe for weaknesses and to exploit and overwhelm the defenders. Instead, the British-American mix of armored and airborne forces were strung out in a narrow corridor that never allowed the attackers to fully bring their combined arms advantages to bear.

Market Garden began on Sunday, September 17. The fighting developed into a wide-ranging battle all along the thin, sixty-four-mile-long ribbon of Holland, ending in Arnhem, on the Dutch Rhine.

By the twenty-fifth, the Allies had given up on the operation without reaching their goal, Arnhem Bridge. A stalemate ensued, giving the Wehrmacht enough breathing space to prepare the West Wall for the anticipated Allied assault on Germany itself.

And yet, Hitler wanted more than to merely adequately prepare to defend the Fatherland. The respite provided after Market Garden and the overall Allied pause due to logistics gave him the opportunity for one last chance, a final roll of the die.

ENDNOTES

134 Alfred M. Beck, Abe Bortz, Charles W. Lynch, Lydia Mayo, and Ralph F. Weld, *The Technical Services, The Corps of Engineers: The War Against Germany* (Washington, DC: Center of Military History, 1985), 304.

135 Allied planners added the fifth and final beach, Utah, to the western flank of the invasion zone in late January in order to facilitate the taking of the port city of Cherbourg.

136 Brigadier General Theodore Roosevelt Jr., assistant division commander of the 4th Infantry Division, landed with the first waves on Utah, and made the decision to change the beachhead for the following waves. He told an engineer officer, Colonel Eugene Caffey, to communicate with the Navy regarding where to land the supporting waves. "I'm going ahead with the troops. You get the word to the Navy to bring them in. We're going to start the war from here." The fifty-six-year-old Roosevelt, afflicted with a heart condition and arthritis, was the oldest man to land on D-Day, and the only general to land with the first waves. He died of a heart attack on July 12 and was posthumously awarded the Medal of Honor for his gallantry on Utah Beach on June 6. Beck, Bortz, Lynch, Mayo, and Weld, *The Technical Services, The Corps of Engineers: The War Against Germany*, 337.

137 HWAMil, 35.

138 Ibid.

139 Ibid.

140 Present day, this location is close by memorials and tributes to events, people, and units involved in the Normandy campaign. Sainte-Marie-Du-Mont has memorials to the 101st Airborne Division and the 4th US Infantry Division, and has a "Rue de la 101e Airborne" just south of the city square. Roughly 1,000 feet northeast of the Hébert crossroads on the GC-70 local road (leading toward Utah Beach from Hébert) stands the Richard D. Winters Leadership Monument, in tribute to the American 101st Airborne Division paratroop officer made famous by the *Band of Brothers* TV series. Further, approximately 400 yards west of the Hébert crossroads was the Brécourt Manor Gun Battery, the German artillery position attacked and destroyed on D-Day by Winters and the small band of paratroops he led.

141 Unit History, 1111th Engineer Combat Group, 1 June 1944–30 June 1944.

142 Ibid, 1 July 1944–31 July 1944.

143 Part of France's national road network established by Napoleon early in the nineteenth century, the N13 ran from Paris into Normandy at Caen, then west, paralleling the beaches, finally turning north at Carentan to Cherbourg.

144 *Tucker Bridge*. This 100-foot long "double-double" Bailey bridge, two panels wide and two panels high, *is still in use today*, although it has been fortified by French civilian bridge construction.

145 Spengler, like Major Tucker, was a veteran of the Pacific War in WWII. Both had served with Army engineer units in Guadalcanal when the US wrested the island from the Japanese in a hard-fought campaign in 1942 to 1943.

146 Organizational Diary, 51st Engineer Combat Battalion, 4 December 1943–15 October 1944. National Archives.

147 The D7 bulldozer, manufactured by Caterpillar Inc., was first introduced in 1938, and adopted by the Army shortly thereafter. Modern versions are still in use. Tankdozers were M4A1 Sherman tanks modified and fitted with a D7 bulldozer blade.

148 A number of engineer units claimed to be first with this idea; in any case, it was widely practiced in Normandy.

149 Organizational Diary, 51st Engineer Combat Battalion.

150 Fowle and Wright, *The 51st Again!*, 55.

151 Unit History, 1111th Engineer Combat Group, 1 July 1944–31 July 1944.

152 Radford and Radford, *Unbroken Line*, 52.

153 Ibid, 54.

154 Rick Atkinson, *The Guns at Last Light* (New York: Henry Holt and Company, 2013), 155–156.

155 Unit History, 1111th Engineer Combat Group, 1 August 1944–31 August 1944.

156 Radford and Radford, *Unbroken Line*, 13.

157 Fowle and Wright, *The 51st Again!*, 56.

158 HWAMil, 39.

159 Unit History, 1111th Engineer Combat Group, 1 September 1944–30 September 1944.

160 Ibid, 1 October 1944–31 October 1944.

CHAPTER EIGHT

WINTER

As Market Garden in Holland evolved into a grinding slog, the American units in Belgium slowed and virtually stopped; that operation to their north had received priority for supplies, which were slowing to a trickle in any case. As they approached the German border, more caution was exerted. Anderson and his 1111th Engineer Group managed to remain in one area for a period of weeks in the vicinity of Bastogne, while his subordinate units carried out rear-echelon tasks in support of the First Army. For their part, the Germans had pulled back inside their border as they fortified their West Wall defenses.

The Army began a winterization program to provide field troops with large wood-frame tents with flooring, which were far more comfortable and more effectively heated. Wood was also used to "corduroy" roads, and for the inevitable bridge-building. As lumber was needed for all these activities, Anderson's battalions started running wood-cutting and milling operations.

Throughout September and October, Anderson's far-flung engineers were engaged all across southern Belgium. During the last two weeks of September, Pergrin established his 291st CP in the Hockai Woods north of Malmedy, while he had work parties building, replacing, or upgrading bridges in Jemelle, Berledang, Willerzie, and Steinfort (Luxembourg); these work sites covered an area eighty miles by sixty miles, in three countries. The 51st ECB was engaged similarly, building bridges and maintaining roads throughout the same area in southern Belgium.

Although the group's activities more and more resembled a large-scale forestry operation, there were still ample reminders of being in a war zone, even miles removed from the front. Germany launched V-1 flying bombs (or "buzz bombs") into the region, attempting to disrupt the Allied advance. These revolutionary weapons were unguided, low-flying missiles, each carrying an 1,870-lb warhead. They were relatively slow (about 400 mph)—about as fast as propeller-driven fighter planes. Notoriously inaccurate, V-1s aiming for targets such as the Allied supply hub at Liège were likely to land anywhere in the area. The engineers noted numerous V-1 impacts during this period and reported how unnerving it was to be anywhere near such large explosions.

Another disturbing event took place in mid-October, a mystery that remained unsolved for months. In the region of the juncture of three borders—Germany, Luxembourg, and Belgium—the front was only loosely guarded, due to a combination of rugged terrain and the fact that both sides considered it a quiet zone:

> The situation along the line of contact at this time was uncertain and "fluid"—neither side had much continuity in their "line of resistance" and strong points were scattered, irregular and seldom held continuously. The main highway which was parallel to and perhaps a mile west of the so-called "front" was not absolutely controlled by either side—and sometimes hazardous.[161]

Anderson's S-4 (logistics) officer, Captain Thomas Williams, used the highway (dubbed "Skyline Drive" by the American soldiers in defensive positions along the front) to travel between the 1111th units. On October 10, while running an errand to pay local lumber providers for the wood being fed to the Army wood-mill operations, Williams went missing.

Another incident occurred the same day in the same area, wherein a US officer was killed in a shoot-out with a suspicious patrol wearing American uniforms. One of the enemy patrol members was killed and discovered to be a German wearing Williams's overcoat. The patrol had also used his jeep. According to Anderson, "From the fact that the coat was neither bloody nor damaged we felt sure Tom had been captured 'intact.'"[162]

Interspersed with their bridge jobs, during this period Anderson had the battalions pull engineer companies from construction projects to undergo infantry training as a refresher. Given their routine, mundane work behind the lines at the time, there was no compelling reason for this. As events unfolded, this would highlight Anderson's particular foresight.

TROIS-PONTS

Anderson was ordered to shift his command to eastern Belgium, farther north. He selected Trois-Ponts, a road-and-rail crossroads, as his new headquarters location, moving into the town November 1. Anderson divided his group for operation and billeting by function, not by rank; in each building, officers and enlisted men shared the same billeting. According to the unit history, "This occupation of buildings was the first for the group since its arrival on the European Continent 27 June 1944";[163] since landing in Normandy, Anderson and his group had been continuously bivouacking in tents (or open air) during the entire campaign. Especially as the Central European weather changed, being billeted in civilian houses was surely a welcome, comfortable development.

The buildings Anderson chose were fortuitous, as events would play out. As he describes the area, "Our headquarters at the time was on a hillside nearby—so with apparently little chance of movement and the inclement weather of early winter it was decided to 'move indoors' in the little town of Trois Pont [sic], west of Malmedy. Here we established a building which had evidently once been a hotel."[164] This provided for a panoramic view of the town and environs, including N23, the road leading east toward Stavelot and Malmedy. The group's headquarters company stayed in another former hotel down the hill from the group headquarters, close to the main intersection in town, and near the bridge over the Salm River, alongside the N23 as it continued west to Basse-Bodeux, and then on to Werbomont. The 1111th's attached battalions, 51st, 291st, and 296th, were shifted into the area as well.

About thirty miles southwest of Trois-Ponts, Anderson placed the 51st headquarters in Marche-en-Famenne. There it began operation running sawmills, cutting and hauling logs to provide the raw materials; at "peak production, with three companies operating 32 sawmills, the 51st produced a total of 80,000 board feet of lumber each day."[165] By the time sawmill operations were suspended to deal with the upcoming emergency, the battalion had produced 2.6 million board feet of lumber. The battalion's sawmill operations were scattered throughout a wide area, around "Marche, Dinant, Rochefort, Ciney, Hotton, and Érezée,"[166] a rough triangle with legs of twenty, twenty, and thirty-five miles.

Of his three battalions, Anderson placed the 51st farthest from the front, possibly because of his continued concern with the commander's state of mind; the battalion's Headquarters and Service Company commander referred to Lieutenant Colonel Reafsnyder during this period as "overly nervous."[167] With the continued absence of Major Yates's leadership, Anderson may have felt a need to place the 51st in the safest location possible.

Dave Pergrin's 291st ECB, meanwhile, was positioned closer to the front, with the battalion headquarters element in Basse-Bodeux, only three miles west of Trois-Ponts on the N23. Pergrin's battalion was similarly scattered throughout the area. As with the 51st, sawmills and road improvements provided the bulk of its activities.

The third 1111th battalion, the 296th ECB, had its headquarters at Sourbrodt, six miles northeast of Malmedy, in the Eupen area. It too was given an area of responsibility for wood-cutting and sawmill operations. The 296th suffered casualties while building a bridge over the Roer River, at Monshau on the German-Belgium border. Three men from the 296th were wounded by a V-1 flying bomb on the night of November 22, when it landed near their bivouac area.

In all, as "many as 41 sawmills were in operation at one time producing a maximum daily output of 103,832 board feet."[168] Another 1111th unit, the 629th Engineer Light Equipment Company, opened a quarry at Walheim, actually inside Germany, eighteen miles north of Sourbrodt. Being so far forward, it was subjected to occasional enemy artillery barrages.

On November 19, the First Army engineer from FUSA headquarters in Spa, Colonel William Carter, presented Soldier's Medals to 1111th unit personnel for their July 12 ammunition dump–fire heroics in Normandy. Anderson and six other officers and enlisted men received their awards. In other ceremonies, six enlisted soldiers from 1111th units received direct commissions to second lieutenant.[169]

With the weather turning to winter, "rock on roads and cinders on the snow and ice lessoned the impediment of traffic and allowed supplies and travel to pass to forward battle areas."[170] By mid-November the weather had turned ugly. One 51st soldier wrote home, "The area we just vacated must have nearly 3 ft. of snow on the ground by now. Some of the roads have at least 1 foot that we've got to clear. We have some winter pictures of these roads with snow piled 10 to 12 feet high. Our Plattsburgh training will come in handy now."[171]

Despite the weather, difficult terrain, supply situation, and German resistance, Eisenhower pressed ahead with some offensive operations. The Allies followed the capture of Aachen with an attack in the Hürtgen Forest in November, southeast of Aachen. Although the First Army had conducted offensive operations in the region beginning in September, a more sustained effort was made beginning mid-November.

The Germans had time to prepare the rugged terrain, and although outnumbered and outgunned, they put up a stubborn defense. In action reminiscent of the fighting in the Argonne Forest in 1918, the Germans were pushed back but ultimately repelled the Americans with heavy losses. One of the American divisions that took part and suffered heavy casualties, the 28th Infantry Division (Anderson's former unit), was sent to rest and recuperate in the quiet area of the Ardennes, southeast of Trois-Ponts. Here it occupied a quiet sector in southern Belgium and Luxembourg, along the German border.

In December, Eisenhower launched other offensive efforts against the German lines around the Roer River. Intent on not giving the Germans any respite, these attacks did not gain much ground but nevertheless forced the Germans to commit men and matériel to stave off the Allies. First, Third, and Ninth Armies were thus engaged, although into mid-December 1111th units were not directly involved.

Taking stock, in early December 1944 Colonel H. Wallis Anderson's 1111th Engineering Combat Group consisted of the following (headquarters location listed):

- Group Headquarters and Headquarters Company (Trois-Ponts)
- 51st Engineer Combat Battalion (Marche)
- 291st Engineer Combat Battalion (Haute-Bodeux)
- 296th Engineer Combat Battalion (Sourbrodt)
- 629th Engineer Light Equipment Company (Butgenbach)
- 962nd Engineer Maintenance Company (Malmedy)
- 767th Engineer Dump Truck Company (one platoon) (Butgenbach)

In all, Anderson had around 2,500 officers and men under his command. They were a First Army (Hodges) resource, operating in the V Corps (Major General Leonard T. Gerow) area. The group was responsible for maintaining the rear-area road and bridge network in a twelve-mile-wide, sixty-mile-long swath, with the southern base of the southwest-to-northeast axis running from Rochefort through Marche, Hotton, Érezée, then continuing to Basse-Bodeux, Trois-Pont, Stavelot, Malmedy, and finally Sourbrodt.

The front, although not a continuous line, ran roughly along the German borders with Belgium, then Luxembourg. The combat units in the area were strung along the front; none were based in the 1111th's zone. Although elements of the 1111th conducted security patrols, no defensive constructions were ordered.

According to the unit history, the 1111th was "maintaining a total of two hundred and seventeen (217) miles of the Army Road Net in addition to roads in the (V) Corps area from Monschau to Kalterherberg, Monschau to Eupen, and Eupen to Rötgen; constructing an airstrip for liaison planes, and conducting continuous engineer reconnaissance." In early December, "severe snow and ice storms caused extremely hazardous traffic conditions, necessitating the organization of road maintenance patrols."[172]

Anderson, who as a Pennsylvania Railroad operations manager had walked his assigned fifteen miles of track at least weekly, and who had led weekly twenty-four-mile round-trip route marches in wintery Plattsburgh, ensured that he and his staff were intimately familiar with the entirety of his road net. With his well-established habit of continuously ranging around and visiting elements throughout his area of responsibility, he would have been exceptionally knowledgeable of the road, river, bridge, and rail network.

The group had been in the Ardennes for more than five weeks, with more than forty sawmills and log-cutting operations throughout the entire area. Thorough knowledge of the region's terrain would play a decisive factor in the coming campaign.

With his headquarters in Trois-Ponts, Anderson had placed himself in a key location. Two rivers met in the town. The Amblève River ran into Trois-Ponts from Stavelot, four miles to the northeast. At Trois-Ponts, the Amblève curved to the north and was joined by the Salm River from the south; it continued its meandering path northwest to merge with the Ourthe River, which flowed to the Meuse. Together, the Salm and Amblève formed an effective barrier to road traffic.

Trois-Ponts was a road junction as well, sitting astride the N23 highway, which ran roughly east-west between Malmedy and Werbomont. North-south road traffic passed through Trois-Ponts on the N33/N28 (N33 leading to the north, N28 as it continued south from the town). Further, rail lines merged at Trois-Ponts Station, with a north-south track passing through the town and a line branching east to Stavelot.

Trois-Ponts, French for "Three Bridges," in fact had a total of ten road, rail, and foot bridges, overpasses, and viaducts in December 1944. The three most significant were the road bridges, as the rail line ran atop a steep, raised embankment, inaccessible to road traffic. On the north edge of the town, the N33 crossed a bridge over the Amblève after joining the N23, coming from Stavelot to the east. The second important road bridge was in the town center itself, crossing the Salm on the N23, leading west to Werbomont. Finally, south of town, a bridge allowed the N28 to cross back over the Salm and then south to Vielsalm. The other spans provided various foot, road, or rail access within the area, but traffic from the east traveling west must pass through Trois-Ponts using some combination of those three bridges.

The Ardennes around Trois-Ponts was characterized by a jumble of crisscrossing ridges and valleys. It had a minimally developed road network, forest tracks, a few rail lines, narrow but deep rivers and streams, and was serviced by only a few bridges with the capacity to handle large heavy vehicles. A transportation engineer with more than twenty years of experience would have appraised the road, bridge, tunnel, and rail network and deduced that if a handful of bridges were dropped, all heavy vehicular travel in the region could be stopped cold.

ENDNOTES

161   HWAMil, 38.

162   Ibid.

163   Unit History, 1111th Engineer Combat Group, 1 November 1944–30 November 1944.

164   HWAMil, 37. Present day, this is the Hôtel Le Beau Site, a tourist accommodation.

165   Fowle and Wright, *The 51st Again!*, 68.

166   Ken Hechler, *Holding the Line* (Honolulu: University Press of the Pacific, 2005), 10.

167   Radford and Radford, *Unbroken Line*, 72.

168   Unit History, 1111th Engineer Combat Group, 1 November 1944–30 November 1944.

169   One of these outstanding soldiers, Second Lieutenant Virgil Rothra, received his commission on November 9, and was killed just three days later, while participating in infantry operations with the 104th Infantry Division, crossing the Roer River. Fowle and Wright, *The 51st Again!*, 64.

170   Unit History, 1111th Engineer Combat Group, 1 November 1944–30 November 1944.

171   Radford and Radford, *Unbroken Line*, 67.

172   Unit History, 1111th Engineer Combat Group, 1 December 1944–31 December 1944.

CHAPTER NINE

THE ARDENNES

Even before the bomb went off, Adolph Hitler was in trouble. The July 20, 1944, assassination attempt failed for a number of reasons, not least of which was a mundane weather factor: the situation briefing Hitler was attending was shifted to an aboveground converted barracks room with windows, better suited for the summer heat. Had the regular underground enclosed bunker been used, the blast would have been much more contained—and deadly. Hitler survived with only modest injuries, and even met with the ousted Italian leader, Benito Mussolini, later that day, providing *Il Duce* a tour of the destroyed conference room.[173]

By July, Hitler and Germany were in serious peril. On the Eastern Front, the Red Army's Operation Bagration was hammering the Wehrmacht with 500 divisions, pushing German forces back through Eastern Europe—Hungary, East Prussia, Slovakia, and Romania. The Soviets had retaken all of Ukraine, and Warsaw was being threatened. Against the seemingly endless reserves of Russian men and munitions, delay and causing the maximum amount of damage was the Wehrmacht's only desperate strategy.

In Italy, the Allies inched up the peninsula in heavy fighting. By midsummer, they had captured Rome and were driving the German defenders into the top of the Italian peninsula "boot." The Germans were not losing as quickly there as in the other theaters, but they were still losing, despite fighting a skillful retreat in the rugged terrain. Precious resources were being used to fend off the Allies. Italy had been knocked out of the war as Germany's main ally a year prior.

Finally, with the Western Allies' invasion of Normandy in June, a second strategic front had been opened, one that threatened Germany directly. By July, the Americans had taken Saint-Lô, while the British had finally driven the stubborn German defenders from Caen. Poised to break out from the bocage terrain, the Allies would only become more mobile, powerful, and unstoppable.

His armies reeling, his allies almost all gone, his war-making industries under constant attack by day and by night from long-range heavy bombers, and his own strategic weapon (U-boats) losing the Battle of the Atlantic, Hitler had now been personally attacked.

After the near miss of the July 20 assassination attempt, a normal, rational leader might have considered his position unsustainable, and abdicated or otherwise quit, fled, or vanished. But being Hitler, instead he desperately sought something, anything, that would turn the tide in his favor. While his generals (some of whom were actively plotting against him) fought on in a rational manner, seeking military solutions to problems of resources and territory, Hitler alone looked for a way to reverse the entire situation.

At a staff conference on July 31, Hitler declared that the war's final decision would take place in the West and not on the Eastern Front. He thereupon ordered the Mortain offensive (Operation Lüttich, August 7 to 13), which failed badly for a litany of reasons: the Wehrmacht failed to achieve strategic surprise; Allied airpower and reserves were brought quickly to bear, without a German counter; the attacking forces involved were too few, compared to the Allied defenders; and German supplies were insufficient, with too-long supply lines. These factors combined to doom the German effort from the onset, after only minor gains.

Nonetheless, Hitler still believed that a truly decisive effort in the West could happen. He reasoned that the Italian front was not significant enough, and not yet an existential threat to the German homeland. Further, despite the massive Red Army in the East approaching German borders, Hitler assessed that any available resources would be insufficient to alter the situation unless he could first halt the British and Americans.

Accordingly, Hitler focused on the Western Front, which was rapidly closing in on the German borders following the battles in France. The Allies there had achieved an overwhelming force of mixed arms—infantry, armor, artillery, and airpower, all supplied to an extravagant degree. The Allies' matériel superiority was much greater than the imbalance of actual troops involved. Eisenhower had only a modest seventy-five total divisions as he crossed Belgium and prepared to breach Hitler's Siegfried Line.

To inflict a game-changing defeat on the Allies, completely altering the strategic situation, Hitler would have to wait for conditions that would offset the Allies' massive advantages. To carry out such a decisive action, Hitler needed additional resources, time to prepare, and a bold plan.

Estimating that he would be able to gather a new force of twenty-five divisions, Hitler sought a point where such a force might have the most impact. If he could launch a surprise attack at a weak point in the line, he could achieve a breakthrough sufficient to split the Allies in two, causing a crisis of major proportions.

Hitler remembered the campaign of 1940, when his panzers drove through the supposedly tank-prohibitive Ardennes to the sea *behind* the British forces that had advanced through Belgium, cutting them off from the French Army. In that instance, Germany's mobile forces *had* caused a crisis, as the Franco-British coalition had crumbled, handing the Germans a stunning, completely one-sided victory in six weeks, despite the numerical parity of the opposing sides.

Taking stock of the failure of the Mortain offensive, Hitler "began to clarify his plans and announced on August 19 that the offensive would begin in November when the Allied air forces would be hampered by bad weather. He ordered large quantities of war matériel to be prepared for the Western Front."[174] Thus, even as his armies were being rolled back, Hitler was planning a strategic reversal intended to throw the Western Allies into chaos.

To underscore how radical Hitler's thinking was, this announcement was issued just as his forces in France were being crushed in the vicinity of the Falaise Gap, which led to the survivors' mad flight back to Germany just ahead of the pursuing Allied armies.

On September 2, Hitler tasked Joseph Goebbels, appointed July 23 (shortly after the assassination attempt) as the *Reichbevollmächtigter für den totalen Kriegseinsatz* ("Reich Plenipotentiary for Total War"), with raising a new army to be used in this all-or-nothing offensive. In the fall of 1944, Goebbels managed to dredge up half a million more men, earmarked to conduct this grand offensive. However, after five years of heavy war losses and with frontline troops already engaged against enemies pressing in from three directions, the source and composition of these new troops reflected Germany's dire situation. Many of these new recruits came from the munitions industry and from supporting service components (which Hitler, a frontline combat soldier in WWI, called "rear area swine").[175] Additional troops were scoured from the *Kriegsmarine* and *Luftwaffe* (navy and air force).

Heinrich Himmler, head of the SS and now placed in charge of the "Home Army," was directed by Hitler to create new divisions with these "fresh" (though substandard) troops. They were rushed through what training could be had in order to fill out twenty-five new *volksgrenadiers* divisions, despite well-known qualitative limitations.[176]

Throughout the fall, Hitler ruthlessly hoarded war matériel—fuel, ammunition, weapons; all were held back from the active fronts in order to have enough to sustain the planned offensive. The

German war machine had suffered massive losses in all categories in the West during the lost Battle for France.

Yet in an effort equal to the unlikely raising of an army that could launch a large offensive, the Reich minister of armaments, Albert Speer, somehow managed to provide Hitler with the necessary matériel as well: "In the four critical months [September through December] nearly a million and a quarter tons of ammunition were manufactured [also a record], while no less than three quarters of a million rifles, one hundred thousand machine guns, nine thousand mortars and nine thousand heavy artillery pieces came out of Germany's bomb-shattered war industry."[177] In the critical industry of tank manufacture, however, no such miracles took place. Allied bombings "cut the production of Tiger tanks by two-thirds and only just over a hundred were delivered before the great Ardennes counter-attack."[178]

Hitler got the breathing space he needed to assemble and to prepare his new armies during the fall. The combination of the Allies' supply crisis and the ill-fated Operation Market Garden slowed the British, American, Canadian, and French armies from a rampage in France to a crawl through Belgium. The Allies slowed enough to allow the German defensive border fortifications to be manned and strengthened. As a result, by early December, the Allies were having a much rougher time of it along the entire front.

To begin planning for his war-turning operation, Hitler took extreme measures to ensure the security of this all-out effort. Aware that the assassination-attempt plotters came from within the Wehrmacht, he no longer trusted the army and excluded senior planning staffs from his preparations; only his own personal staff knew his intentions. By keeping the planning cell for the offensive small and under his control, Hitler hoped to catch the Allies as off guard as the Normandy landings had caught him.

Thus, in Nazi Germany military organizational terms, only Hitler's *Oberkommando der Wehrmacht* (OKW—"High Command of the Armed Forces") was involved; the army commands that would oversee the operation were excluded.

Further, while he had no specific knowledge of the Allies' code-breaking capabilities (which resulted in the famous "Ultra" intelligence), Hitler was well aware of the capabilities of Allied intelligence, including the vulnerability of radios to signals interception. As a result, "deliberate wireless silence, which Hitler imposed for security reasons along with a special oath on those he entrusted with planning it [the Ardennes offensive], was one reason why Ultra had no precise foreknowledge of the Ardennes offensive of December 1944."[179]

Working with only this small staff of trusted inner-circle confidants, Hitler pieced together his radical idea: launch a counteroffensive in the West that would split the Allied armies and shatter the British and American alliance, giving him time to develop the "wonder weapons" (V-2 ballistic missiles, jet fighters and bombers, and more-capable U-boats) that would provide a counterweight to the massive Soviet imbalance in conventional forces. In his view, if the strategic situation was reversed in the West, maybe he could even induce the Western Allies to join him in his fight against the Soviet tide.

Throughout September, October, and into November, Hitler prepared the West for his surprise offensive, only gradually briefing layers of senior German Army commanders of the offensive so that detailed planning could take place.[180] All of them seem to have tried to talk him out of it. They argued from the perspective of professionally trained army staff officers, which Hitler decidedly was *not*. All lobbied for a wiser, more rational expenditure of the severely limited resources—smaller, less ambitious attacks with more limited (and achievable) objectives.

All such rational strategies would have surely led to the Wehrmacht being eventually obliterated by the overwhelming power of the Western Allies, as was happening in the East. *None* of the ideas offered by these professionally trained generals offered a solution to the problem of how to win the war. Only Hitler's wild gamble offered such a possibility, however unlikely.

WACHT AM RHEIN

The concept was entirely Hitler's. The Führer was a devotee of nineteenth-century Prussian war theorist Carl von Clausewitz, who espoused that victory comes primarily from offensive action, and that concentrating one's forces on a key, critical point—*Absoluter Schwerpunkt*[181]—provides the best opportunity to prevail over an opponent.

Applying this Clausewitzian strategy, Hitler dictated his plan to the head of the OKW, *Generalfeldmarschall* Wilhelm Keitel, and his chief of staff, *Generaloberst* Alfred Jodl. They in turn laid out the details on September 25:

1. The attack should be launched sometime between November 20 and 30 when flying weather would be bad.
2. It should be made through the Ardennes in the Monshau-Eckternach sector.
3. The initial objective would be the seizure of bridgeheads over the River Meuse between Liege and Namur.
4. Thereafter Antwerp would be the objective.
5. A battle to annihilate the British and Canadians would be fought north of the line Antwerp-Liege-Bastogne.
6. A minimum of thirty divisions would be available, ten of which would be armoured.
7. Support would be given by an unprecedented concentration of artillery and rocket projector units.
8. Operational control would be vested in four armies—two panzer armies in the centre and two infantry armies to cover the flanks.
9. The Luftwaffe would be prepared to support the operation.
10. All planning would aim at securing tactical surprise, and speed.

11. Secrecy would be maintained at all costs and only a very
few individuals would be privy to the plan until the last
moment.[182]

The Germans selected *Wacht Am Rhein*[183] as the code name
for the operation that would disrupt the Western Allies and cause
a catastrophic crisis. The main offensive armies mentioned in
paragraph 8 above were aligned along the front, as follows:

15. Armee in the north, along the Aachen front, opposite First US
Army's VII Corps and the Ninth US Army. *15. Armee*, already engaged
defending the Roer River dams, was tasked with protecting the right
flank of *6. Panzerarmee* as it drove to the main objective, Antwerp.
15. Armee consisted of infantry divisions, and was to conduct its own
offensive attack, Operation *Spätlese* ("Late Harvest").

From around Bitburg south to Echternach, *7. Armee* in the
south was to *5. Panzerarmee*'s left flank. The *7. Armee*'s four infantry
divisions consisted mostly of the half-trained and lower-quality troops
raised in the fall. This modest army faced off across the front along
the southern Luxembourg border, opposing only one regiment each
from the US 4th and 28th Infantry Divisions, who were supported
by 9th Armored Division.

Success for the offensive lay with the two central formations,
6. and *5. Panzerarmees*. *5. Panzerarmee*, under *General der
Panzertruppe* Hasso von Manteuffel, was assigned the supporting
role of sweeping alongside the neighboring *6. Panzerarmee* as it cut
swiftly through the thin Allied lines to Antwerp. *5. Panzerarmee* was
given a powerful cast: four infantry, three panzer divisions (plus an
additional armored brigade), and support troops.

Opposite *5. Panzerarmee* were American lines thinly held by
green, newly arrived troops, and understrength units recuperating
from the savage November battle for Hürtgen Forest. Only four
US regiments plus a cavalry squadron held a twenty-mile front
in the rugged Ardennes opposite this German army. On the US

"HQ Twelfth Army Group Situation Map" for December 16, 1944, the eventual first day of the offensive, half the German forces are depicted with question marks, and the 5. *Panzerarmee* is not even identified, indicating the effectiveness of German security measures.

This left the final force, 6. *Panzerarmee*, to which Hitler specifically and personally assigned the key objectives for the entire offensive: take Antwerp and cut the Allied armies asunder, shattering the British-American alliance and ending the threat in the West.

German intelligence indicated only one US infantry division, the 99th, opposed 6. *Panzerarmee*. In fact, the veteran US 2nd Infantry Division was also present, moving to attack toward the Roer River dam complex, which caused a major problem when the offensive began.[184] These two divisions were in the V Corps sector of First US Army. In the rear of this section, behind the thinly held front lines, lay only a scattered force of engineers: Colonel H. Wallis Anderson's 1111th Engineer Combat Group.

6. PANZERARMEE

While 5. *Panzerarmee* had strong, even elite forces, the main prizes and attendant glory were to be reserved for 6. *Panzerarmee*. To accomplish the do-or-die task, the most powerful and loyal forces in the German armed forces were assigned: the Waffen-SS.[185]

Hitler personally selected the Waffen-SS units that would break the Allied lines and save the Reich. SS-*Oberstgruppenführer* Josef "Sepp" Dietrich,[186] a former street-gang member from the earliest days of the National Socialist party, was assigned to command and ordered to stand up his "Sixth Panzer Army between Monschau and St. Vith. As befitted the concept of *Absoluter Schwerpunkt*, the Sixth Panzer was by far the strongest of the three German armies."[187]

The 6. *Panzerarmee* consisted of five infantry-type divisions and four of the elite Waffen-SS panzer divisions, the cream of the German armed forces. Withheld from the recent bloody, bitter fighting with enemies on either front and the attrition that ensued, they were built up to near full strength (a rare luxury by late 1944), reinforced, rested, and prepared. According to Danny Parker, in *Battle of the Bulge*, "Including support elements, the army totaled over 140,000 men, 1,025 corps artillery guns and rocket launchers and some 642 tanks and assault guns. This powerful force planned to crush American resistance from Monschau to Krewinkel and then race across the Meuse on both sides of Liège, then turning north to capture Antwerp."[188]

Recognizing Dietrich's limitations as a commander of large-scale formations, Hitler assigned the highly skilled SS-*Brigadeführer* Fritz Krämer as chief of staff to manage the actual field operations for 6. *Panzerarmee*. Krämer had filled a similar role with Dietrich previously when the latter commanded the I SS-*Panzerkorps* in the Normandy campaign. Originally a regular Wehrmacht officer, Krämer had only been admitted into the Waffen-SS in August 1944. Beginning his assignment on November 16, Krämer set about to refine and provide specific details to the broad outline of *Wacht Am Rhein*.

Krämer "immediately made an extensive study of the terrain and composed the battlegroups and their suggested march routes . . . in some detail"; he noted that the attack plan was "dictated by the terrain, the lack of roads for full deployment and the need for a rapid breakthrough. He anticipated an echeloned assault where mobile units were to attack at many points in columns, hoping to break out in several places and speed forward in road formation."[189]

That is, rather than an offensive on a broad front, which the terrain and road network did not support, his battlegroups would be organized in columns, each of which would seek to break through as far and fast as possible. If enough columns were successful, the American front might collapse into chaos. Krämer stated, "The principle was to hold the reins loose and let the armies race. The main point was to reach the Meuse regardless of the flanks. This was the same principle we used in the French campaign of 1940."[190]

However, Krämer's estimations of the progress that could be made were exaggerated and overly optimistic: "We calculated that by noon of the 17th of December, we could reach the Hohes Venn mountains, which run northwest from Monschau to Stavelot. By 19 December, the panzer spearheads were to reach the Meuse."[191]

Although the panzers were to exploit the shattered American lines and race to the Meuse and beyond, the infantry units were to make the initial assault. Once the infantry punched holes in the American lines, the panzers would burst through. From Krämer: "The time of attack was scheduled for the early morning hours, because it was hoped, that the infantry would succeed in taking advantage of the early morning mist and succeed in breaking through the first positions. It was hoped that by midday they would win 5–8 km of ground."[192]

The rough terrain in front of 6. *Panzerarmee*, especially in the harsh winter conditions, was of major concern. Krämer carefully considered the existing roads and terrain and then "designated five roads, [and] of these the four southern ones were designated as the so-called Panzer rolling roads."[193] These rolling roads (*rollbahns*), designated A through E, were the paths that the panzers would use to race through the American lines to reach the Meuse.

From the left, or southern end, of 6. *Panzerarmee*'s front, 3rd *Fallshirmjäger* Division[194] was placed to clear the start point of rollbahn E by attacking the American 14th Cavalry Group at Krewinkle and clearing the way to Lanzerath and Manderfeld. A mile to the north, 12th *Volksgrenadier* Division was ordered to drive the Americans from the road between Losheim and Losheimergraben, held by the 394th Infantry Regiment of US 99th Infantry Division. The opening of rollbahn D would clear this path.

Moving a mile to the north, the next attack area up the line was assigned to 277th Volksgrenadier Division, which was to attack the American front lines in the Mürringen, Rocherath, and Krinkelt region. This was the start of rollbahn C. Rollbahns A and B began as a combined route leading from Hollerath to Rocherath, and split once

Sourbrodt was reached; two volksgrenadier divisions—272nd and 326th—were directed to clear this path for the following panzers.

I SS-PANZERKORPS

For the task of breaking through the US Army lines, shattering the defenses, crossing the Meuse River, and reaching Antwerp, Hitler chose the only two army units allowed to carry the Führer's name: 1st SS Panzer Division (*Leibstandarte* Adolph Hitler, abbreviated "LAH." *Leibstandarte* can be effectively translated as "bodyguard") and 12th SS Panzer Division (*Hitlerjugend*, "Hitler Youth"). These two powerful formations would be deployed "side by side of the Hohes Venn and Schnee-Eifel . . . in order to form a strong breakthrough wedge."[195] They were grouped into I SS-Panzerkorps, under SS-*Gruppenführer* Hermann Priess, a veteran of many campaigns who had been assigned to the post on October 24, specifically for the Ardennes offensive.

Behind this armored battering ram, II SS-Panzerkorps was positioned to exploit the gains made by the initial panzer thrust. II SS-Panzerkorps was yet another powerful and elite SS formation, consisting of 2nd SS Panzer Division (*Das Reich*, "The Empire") and 9th SS Panzer Division (*Hohenstaufen*; the Hohenstaufen were a dynasty of Germanic kings during the Middle Ages).

On December 12 to 13, Hitler presided over a meeting at OB West to brief the senior leadership on the final plans for the offensive. The attack had been postponed several times, from November 25 to December 10, and finally to December 16. In the process, another code name, *Herbstnebel* ("Autumn Mist"), was assigned.

The final plan was as follows: "I SS Panzer Corps, on X-day, assembles at 0600 hours, breaks through the enemy positions into the sector of Monschau-Udenbreth and Losheim, then with the 12 SS Panzer Division on the right and 1 SS Panzer Division on the left, pushes across the Maas [Meuse] into the sector of Lüttich [Liege]-Huy."[196]

The two panzer divisions in I SS-Panzerkorps received orders to move to a staging area on December 12—yet security was still so tight that no explanation for the move was given. The infantry units were moved quietly into position, with restrictions prohibiting patrolling their assigned front.

1ST SS PANZER DIVISION—LEIBSTANDARTE ADOLPH HITLER

Originally formed by Sepp Dietrich as a 118-man personal bodyguard to Hitler upon his ascension in 1933 as chancellor of Germany, Leibstandarte Adolph Hitler (LAH) grew into the premier division of the entire German armed forces. Beginning the war as a regiment, it had expanded into a full-fledged division by 1941. Never a parade ground ceremonial formation, it fought almost continuously in major campaigns on the Eastern and Western Fronts.

Although organizationally a part of the Waffen-SS, Leibstandarte remained separate and unique, enjoying the prestige and perquisites befitting its personal connection to the Führer. A combat veteran himself, Hitler had low regard for noncombatant units, and he was determined that his LAH would "earn the respect of the German people by serving at the front and suffering casualties."[197]

For the Ardennes offensive, under the command of SS-*Oberführer* Wilhelm Mohnke, LAH was given the most prized assignment and armed accordingly. Krämer's plan called for the northern three rollbahns, A, B, and C, to be used by 12th SS Panzer Division (Hitlerjugend) to take the Elsenborn Ridge (northeast of Malmedy) and hold the high ground against the expected Allied retaliation.[198] The Germans anticipated that the concentration of Allied armies in the north would react by turning south to threaten the north flank of 6. *Panzerarmee*.

That left the final two southern rollbahns, D and E, for Mohnke's LAH. With the 12th SS Panzer Division on his right, blocking the presumed American forces turning to cut off an advance toward the Meuse, Mohnke's panzers would sweep west and then northwest to cross the Meuse between Liège and Huy, and then on to Antwerp.

To accomplish this task, the primary assignment of the entire offensive, Mohnke was given more firepower than any other division in the campaign, German or Allied. Organizing his forces to align with Krämer's column-based rollbahn plan, Mohnke assigned *kampfgruppes*, or battle groups, to the two roads laid out by 6. *Panzerarmee*.

THE LAH KAMPFGRUPPES

The standard organization for an SS panzer division by late 1944 included a panzer regiment of two panzer battalions, two *panzergrenadier* (mechanized infantry) regiments, and an artillery regiment consisting of both self-propelled and towed guns and rockets; additional supporting arms, such as reconnaissance, engineer ("pioneers" in the German armed forces), and tank-destroyer forces were also attached.

Mohnke configured his division appropriate for the rollbahn scheme. With two routes to work with, he divided most of his force into four main groups, with one group following another along each of the two rollbahns, D and E. Rather than dividing them equally, instead he put his most powerful column on rollbahn D, with the rollbahn E units providing flank support. The four groups were designated as three kampfgruppes, plus a *schnellgruppe* ("fast group"). Each group was named for its commander: Kampfgruppe Peiper, Kampfgruppe Sandig, Kampfgruppe Hansen, and Schnellgruppe Knittel.

To lead LAH division's charge through the southernmost route, along rollbahn E, Kampfgruppe Hansen (KG Hansen) was selected. His battle group was provisioned with a powerful force of three battalions of Waffen-SS panzergrenadiers—mechanized infantry traveling in half-track armored vehicles, usually variants of the

Sonderkraftfahrzeug 251, or Sd.Kfz 251. These ubiquitous vehicles were referred to by German officers as *Schützenpanzerwagon* (SPW), "armored infantry vehicle."

To support his thrust behind the American lines, Hansen was provided an SS-Panzer-*Jäger* battalion, with twenty-one late-model tank destroyers, the JagdPanzer IV (JgPz IV). These "hunting tank" armored vehicles were turretless chassis mounted with powerful 75 mm cannons. Although effective against tanks when placed in defensive positions, such as lying in ambush, the JgPz IVs were not designed for nor particularly effective in an infantry-support role, nor as main battle tanks. Hansen was provided mobile and towed artillery, including cannon and rockets (*Werfer*). He was given mobile antiaircraft batteries and a company of pioneers. In total, Hansen commanded a powerful force of more than 4,500 SS men with 750 vehicles.

Following KG Hansen along rollbahn E was Schnellgruppe Knittel. This mobile unit consisted mostly of light reconnaissance vehicles with supporting artillery, so "Knittel had the option of switching routes so that he could, if the opportunity presented itself, race ahead and seize a bridge over the Meuse."[199] Knittel's force consisted of 1,500 men and 150 vehicles.

Hansen and Knittel's rollbahn E began at Krewinkel, passed west through Manderfeld, then dipped southwest through woods, valleys, and hills, then up through more rugged terrain to Amel (alternatively known and labeled as Amblève, after that area's largest and most important river). From there rollbahn E continued southwest to Born, west to Recht, Vielsalm, Lierneux, then northwest to Werbomont, where rollbahns D and E merged. The combined rollbahn carried on northwest to the Meuse, reaching the river at Huy and Ombret-Rawsa, roughly seventeen miles southwest of Liège.

KG Hansen with Knittel trailing were positioned to provide flank protection for the main effort to their right, several miles to the north. The Hansel/Knittel forces were built for speed and intended to find a route quickly through the scattered and lightly defended rear area. The tandem column possessed no tanks, only tank destroyers and light armored vehicles, with supporting arms. Their route covered approximately seventy-one miles; on modern roads this path is estimated to take just under two hours.

Hansel and Knittel's planned route would generally skirt to the south of Wallis Anderson's troop placements, although the back-end loop traveling northwest through Werbomont would just pass through the gap between the western boundary for the 291st ECB's operations and the 51st ECB's easternmost positions.

KAMPFGRUPPE PEIPER AND ROLLBAHN D

Kampfgruppe Peiper was the lead column on rollbahn D, and could be considered as the spearpoint, the vanguard, for the entire German offensive. Built around an SS panzer regiment, the kampfgruppe was provided the most and best of the late-model German tanks available; KG Peiper was the most powerful regiment-sized force in the entire German Army.

At the heart of Peiper's column were the medium tanks, the workhorses of SS panzer forces. The *Panzerkampfwagen* IV (known as "Mk IV" or "PzKw IV" or combinations thereof) had been in production since before the war began and had undergone continual improvements and upgrades. It was the most-produced German main battle tank during the war, with more than 8,500 built between 1937 and 1945. KG Peiper was provisioned with two companies of PzKw IVs, thirty-four in total.

Peiper was also given two companies of PzKw V Panther tanks, thirty-eight in all. The Panther is considered by many armaments historians as the overall finest medium tank of the war. Introduced in 1943, around 6,000 were produced, with many variations and improvements developed throughout its service life. Its high-velocity 75 mm main gun could defeat any Allied main battle tank, while its forward armor provided ample protection against most Allied opponents.

The final German tank Peiper had in his arsenal was the heaviest: the much-feared Tiger tank. Officially designated as *"Panzerkampfwagen Tiger Ausführung B,"* this heavy tank was known by several formal and informal titles, including *Königstiger* (the German word for Bengal tiger), King Tiger, Tiger II, and Royal Tiger. A successor to the original Tiger I, the Königstiger was an entirely different design, despite the similar name.

Suffering from the usual German manufacturing problem of being rushed into production with multiple variations before serious design flaws were resolved, the sixty-nine-ton Königstiger was still considered a formidable field presence. Its 88 mm cannon dominated the battlefield, while thick armor provided some of the best protection of any tank in WWII.

For Peiper's charge through the Ardennes, however, the Königstiger's size and lack of mobility severely restricted the heavy tank's value during a dash through wooded terrain. Nevertheless, a battalion of Tiger IIs, the 501st SS *Schwere Panzer Abteilung* ("SS Heavy Panzer Battalion"), with forty-five of these battlefield monsters, was assigned to Peiper's column.

Peiper was given substantial infantry, pioneers, antiaircraft, and artillery to support his dash to the Meuse. Some units were integral to the LAH division, while others were attached specifically to bolster Peiper's column. His battle group was given a battalion of panzergrenadiers riding in SPW half-tracks and trucks. Two companies of pioneers accompanied his drive. For artillery support, Peiper was provided an array of towed guns, a combined total of twenty-four 105 mm and 150 mm howitzers.

Finally, KG Peiper received two companies of 20 mm and 37 mm–armed *"flakpanzers"* ("antiaircraft tanks"), which provided some measure of protection against the dreaded Allied fighter-bomber aircraft, which had proved so devastating to German armored units since the Normandy campaign.

In all, Peiper was given "an extremely powerful Kampfgruppe, comprising some 4,800 men and 800 vehicles including 117 tanks,

149 SPWs, twenty-four artillery pieces and nearly forty AA guns."[200]

Trailing behind Peiper along rollbahn D would be KG Sandig in support. Sandig followed with the remainder of the motorized 1st SS Panzergrenadier Regiment (less one battalion, assigned to Peiper). Other LAH divisional units not assigned to the KGs followed Sandig.

The route assigned to Peiper led first to Huy on the Meuse, seventy miles, then another seventy-five miles to the major port city of Antwerp. Intending to start east of Losheim along the N32 main road, the rollbahn ran northwest to Losheimergraben, then westerly to Hünningen, Honsfeld, Hepscheid (skirting south of Büllingen), and Mödersheid. Weaving west across minor tracks to Schoppen and Ondenval, the route continued south of larger towns (Faymonville and Weimes), which were on the 12th SS Panzer Division's route. Proceeding west along small roads to Thirimont, then Ligneuville, the rollbahn cut across mountainous terrain before descending to cross north over the Amblève River at Stavelot. Rollbahn D continued along the N23 highway southwest to Trois-Ponts. At this confluence of two rivers, three roads, and two rail lines, rollbahn D turned west through Basse-Bodeux, across a small but deeply cut stream, La Lienne (so small it isn't labeled on contemporary and modern maps), at Habiémont. Proceeding west to Werbomont, the route was thenceforth merged with rollbahn E, and continued northwest to the Meuse at Huy.

Although the rollbahn assignments were precise and specific, they were never intended to be rigidly followed. Regarding the routes, 6. *Panzerarmee*'s chief of staff Krämer stated in an after-war interview, "I selected the five routes . . . on the map. These roads were to be directional only. If division commanders wanted to take others, they were at liberty to do so."[201] As will be seen, this situation occurred several times during KG Peiper's westward dash.

The routes assigned to all the rollbahns were far from ideal. This was the trade-off for accomplishing surprise by choosing to conduct a panzer assault through terrain not deemed appropriate for armored vehicles. These debilitating factors were well known, and indeed were central aspects of Hitler's plan; he considered them essential in order to achieve surprise and to counter the Allies' ability to defeat panzers with airpower.

To overcome the severe weather and terrain difficulties and achieve success, Hitler realized the main offensive units would have to be supremely motivated, skillfully led, and ruthless. His selection of the Waffen-SS panzer troops as the key offensive weapon reflect this thinking. And to lead the most important column of the entire offensive, Hitler selected an SS panzer officer well known to him. The most important column with the most critical mission was to be led by an officer who has been called "the 'Siegfried' of the Waffen-SS":[202] SS-*Obersturmbannführer* Joachim Peiper.

THE DEVIL'S ADJUTANT:[203] JOACHIM PEIPER

The honor of leading the Waffen-SS panzers on their desperate charge to turn the tables in the West fell to a man seemingly picked by Hollywood central casting to play the role. Tall, dashing, and with the classic looks of a cinematic leading man, Peiper appeared to be exactly what he was: a ruthless panzer leader.[204]

Peiper's photographs show unmistakably the features of a military officer. Serious, tense, focused, he routinely looks determined, as if he is about to carry out some dangerous task. When he allows a smile, it is controlled, confident, and chilling.

Joachim Peiper was born in Berlin on January 30, 1915, into a military family during World War I, which unsurprisingly led him into a system devised by the Nazi Party to groom young men for combat. His father, *Hauptmann* (military rank captain) Woldemar Peiper, served with the Imperial German Army in Turkey and the East African campaign in the 1914 to 1918 war. Joachim (who preferred the less formal "Jochen" name variant) had two older brothers, Hans Hasso and Horst. Jochen's father raised his sons in strict German military traditions of extreme patriotism, sacrifice, and discipline.

Even before the Nazi Party's ascension in Germany, Jochen and his brother Horst joined the German Boy Scouts, with the intention of following their father into the military. After Hitler was appointed chancellor of Germany on January 30, 1933 (Peiper's eighteenth birthday; one cannot help but suspect Peiper considered this an omen), the Nazi Party's *Hitlerjugend* absorbed the German national scout organization. Jochen was assigned to the *Deutsches Jungvolk* as a leader for the youths, an early indication of his evident leadership abilities.

Later in 1933, Peiper formally began his military career by enlisting in the 7th SS *Reiterstandarte* on October 12, about the same time Major Wallis Anderson was reappointed as a battalion commander with the National Guard of Pennsylvania, following a four-and-a-half-year break in service. Promoted to the rank of SS-*Mann* ("trooper," the lowest-grade enlisted rank) on January 23, 1934, Peiper was issued the SS registration number 132496.

Nineteen-year-old Jochen attended the momentous annual Nuremberg Rally in September 1934[205] and gained the attention of Heinrich Himmler, the head of the SS (*Reichsführer*-SS) and a member of Hitler's inner circle. At Himmler's urging (and very possibly his support), Peiper was selected to attend the SS *Junkerschule* in Braunschweig, entering in April 1935.

Graduating near the top of his class in January 1936 (16 out of 240), Jochen Peiper attended a platoon leader course, then was assigned to Leibstandarte (then a regiment) in April 1936, as the leader of the 3rd Platoon, 11th Company, with the rank of *untersturmführer* (second lieutenant equivalent). Peiper remained on the rolls of the Leibstandarte his entire military career. By then the Leibstandarte had already been used as a showcase formation for high-profile actions, such as leading the military's reoccupation of the Saarland, which since the Versailles Treaty had been governed by Britain and France. Peiper's first commanding officer was Sepp Dietrich, who had formed that unit.

After Peiper served for about two years as platoon leader and battalion adjutant, Himmler arranged for Peiper to be assigned to his staff as an adjutant. Peiper was promoted to SS-obersturmführer (lieutenant) on his birthday, 1939 (the sixth anniversary of Hitler's appointment as chancellor, which led to his designation as führer in 1934). Peiper's social standing benefitted as well. He met Sigurd Hinrichsen, a secretary on Himmler's staff; they were wed on June 26, 1939, in a formal SS ceremony.

Peiper accompanied Himmler in the early stages of World War II, for travel to Poland following the fall 1939 campaign that began the war. Peiper was still on Himmler's staff when the attacks on France, Belgium, and Holland took place, May 1940.

Peiper briefly returned to his Leibstandarte Adolph Hitler (LAH) for combat service during this campaign. Commanding the 3rd Battalion's 11th Company, Peiper led an assault on French artillery positions at Wattenberg, a hill near Valenciennes, France. His unit took part in the drive toward Paris following the British evacuation at Dunkirk. Just prior to France's surrender, Peiper returned to his assignment on Himmler's staff. For his actions during this five-week spree, Peiper was awarded the *Eisernes Kreuz* (Iron Cross) for valor and promoted to SS-*hauptsturmführer* (captain).

Taking up his adjutant duties, Peiper accompanied SS-Himmler during this period of maximum German expansion. Nazi Germany had beaten and occupied France, Belgium, the Netherlands, Norway, Poland, the Balkans, and Greece; Himmler began his grim work of subjugating these conquered populations.

With the massive invasion of the Soviet Union in June 1941, Nazi Germany embarked on its greatest military adventure, and one that ultimately brought about its demise. Peiper again sought to take part as an active service officer, rather than on a rear-echelon staff. He returned to combat in August, initially taking up an assignment on the staff of Leibstandarte SS Adolph Hitler (LSSAH).[206]

When the 3rd Battalion commander was wounded in action around the southern Dnieper River, the 11th Company commanding officer took his place, opening the way for Peiper's assignment as company commander, beginning October 11, 1941. Peiper took part in the division's heavy fighting from 1941 to 1942. In early summer 1942, LSSAH was transferred to the Normandy, France, area for refit, reorganization, and rest. Peiper was elevated to command of 3rd Battalion, and on January 30, 1943, Peiper was promoted to SS-*sturmbannführer* (major).[207]

Leibstandarte—now a panzergrenadier unit, with more mechanized weaponry—returned to the Eastern Front in early 1943, following the Stalingrad disaster and subsequent crisis; Germany was now losing ground to the Soviets. LAH, with Peiper commanding 3rd Battalion, was assigned near Kharkov.

In what may have been the signal action that led to his future Ardennes assignment, Peiper led a daring rescue operation to extricate the German 320th Infantry Division, which had been surrounded in the vicinity of the Donetz River, near Kharkov. Peiper's column drove through Soviet lines, contacted the 320th, then led the entire combined force back to German lines. Peiper had to fight fierce enemy resistance along the entire route, in both directions. The three-day ordeal was conducted amid the Russian winter, in February 1943. Because of this and other exploits, Peiper gained renown as a bold and aggressive commander.[208]

Peiper and his battalion also acquired a reputation for brutality, and a nickname to match: Blowtorch Battalion; the battalion's vehicles were painted with small images of a blowtorch. Although he later claimed the nickname was conferred because his troops "used this highly practical tool in the winter to pre-heat the engines in our vehicles, to heat the water quickly for cooking and many other things,"[209] this is very likely a postwar rationalization, disingenuous at best. A combat unit is unlikely to choose a rather ordinary piece of garage hardware to promote a fearsome self-image.

A much more likely explanation would be that the SS troops adopted an emblem that symbolized the battalion's ability to cut through Soviet forces. After all, what better way to intimidate Soviet soldiers, who revered their leader, than by emblazoning their war machines with a device designed to cut through steel? The name "Stalin" is derived from the Russian word for steel.[210]

Further enhancing this likely explanation, the SS way of war on the Eastern Front often included brutal atrocities—burned villages, massacred civilians, and executed prisoners. Both sides engaged in such acts throughout the long eastern war. Peiper and his men most certainly participated in such barbarity.

Throughout the first half of 1943 on the Eastern Front, Peiper and his battalion were heavily engaged, including the massive Battle of Kursk (Operation Citadel). Peiper received several personal citations for valor and combat skill, including the *Deutsches Kreuz* ("German Cross"; in gold, for repeated acts of bravery in combat), and the *Ritterkreuz des Eisernen Kreuzes* ("Knight's Cross of the Iron Cross"), the German military's highest award. Peiper received recognition in SS publications, further bolstering his growing reputation.

With the failure of the German attempt to break through the Soviets at Kursk, the Leibstandarte was transferred to Northern Italy in July 1943. This was a complicated and confusing time on the Italian Front. The Allies had invaded Sicily in July, provoking the collapse of Mussolini's regime. Mainland Italy was next, with British and American landings in September; the new Italian government wasted no time arranging an armistice with the Allies. The Italian Army was disarmed by both sides, and German units quickly established a front line. For Peiper and his fellow SS troops, Italy was a short interlude; LAH returned to the Eastern Front in early November 1943.[211]

With the situation in the East worsening, German military actions grew more desperate as they sought to stave off the increasingly powerful Soviet forces. Deployed in northwest Ukraine, Peiper replaced the commander of LAH's 1st SS Panzer Regiment, Georg Schönberger, who was killed in action. Peiper and his panzer regiment fought throughout the winter of 1943 to 1944, seeing heavy action and suffering grievous losses against the overwhelming numbers of Soviets.

In January 1944, Peiper was recalled, receiving his second Knight's Cross (oak leaves denoting the second award), the award this time being presented by Hitler himself. Peiper was by now a nationally known figure, a hero in the tradition of the Teutonic Knights. His promotion to SS-obersturmbannführer (lieutenant colonel) followed; naturally, it was bestowed on his twenty-ninth birthday, January 30, 1944 (and the eleventh anniversary of Hitler's regime).

However, the strain and stress of prolonged combat action, exacerbated by Peiper's aggressive style and tendency to lead from the front, had taken its toll. While in Germany to receive his honors, Peiper was diagnosed as being exhausted, physically and mentally. He convalesced in Bavaria, reuniting with his wife, Sigurd, until rejoining his unit in April 1944. Meanwhile, LAH was withdrawn from the Eastern Front and once again sent west, this time to Belgium.

The Allied invasion of Normandy activated LAH back into combat, this time in France, with Peiper again leading the 1st SS Panzer Regiment. Engaged primarily against the British and Canadians in the Caen area, LAH and the other elite SS panzer and panzergrenadier units, suffering from attrition wrought by five years of continual warfare on multiple fronts, were simply overwhelmed by the Allied juggernaut.

By early July, LAH was fighting defensive delaying actions, trying to hold off the advancing combined Allied armies. On August 2, Peiper was withdrawn from combat. His regiment had suffered significant casualties fighting the Canadians south of Caen; Peiper was either wounded or, more likely, again suffered from severe combat fatigue.[212] He was again sent to convalesce at a military hospital near his family in Bavaria, until early October.

LAH was virtually destroyed during the battles in Normandy. Hitler withdrew I SS-Panzerkorps (which contained his namesake divisions, LAH and HJ) in the fall of 1944 for rebuild; he withheld it from further action, saving it for his planned offensive, *Wacht Am Rhein*. From October to December, LAH was rearmed, and its roster filled out. On paper, by mid-December, LAH was again a full-strength and powerful force. However, despite its combat prowess and experience, the division showed signs of fragility.

Ironically, LAH's greatest strength also reflected its most vulnerable aspect: the leadership abilities of its combat commanders. While Peiper is a good example, he was by no means an isolated case. Normandy had shown that his experience was a huge advantage; he expertly led his troops to accomplish difficult tasks. However, this experience was brittle; his accumulated combat exposure meant that he was likely to be effective for only a short period. Combat fatigue can never be completely erased, no matter the rest and recuperation. The more intense and prolonged the exposure, the more likely it will reemerge, sooner and more debilitating.

The SS officers with Peiper for the Ardennes campaign were similarly impressive, with combat credentials that compared with Peiper's. All had served and survived in the harshest of combat conditions and were as vulnerable. Max Hansen, who would command KG Hansen on rollbahn E in the Ardennes, had been wounded for the *ninth* time in Normandy. Rudolf Sandig, whose KG would trail Peiper's on rollbahn D, lost two panzergrenadier battalion commanders killed in Normandy, putting extra strain on him, the regimental leader. Gustav Knittel (a Knight's Cross recipient as well), the reconnaissance column leader (Schnellgruppe Knittel), had been wounded four times by the Normandy campaign.

Thus, as the Ardennes offensive loomed, LAH was blessed with a vast amount of combat skill and experience in the commanders chosen to launch one final, desperate effort. The division was cursed, though, with having to rely on an officer corps brittle from combat exposure. Author Michael Reynolds perceptively compares the men of the SS to steel: malleable, hard, and strong, they were also susceptible to being broken when subjected to prolonged, unreasonable stress.[213]

THE ALLIED FRONT

On the Allied side, in mid-December 1944 Hitler's deception plan and Allied offensive focus aligned. Eisenhower received a constant stream of intelligence reporting that Nazi Germany was approaching the brink of collapse. On all fronts and at home, Germany was being hammered relentlessly, and was increasingly unable to effectively hold off the combined weight of Allied might. A few more weeks, Eisenhower was told, and the inevitable would occur; Hitler and Nazi Germany would break.

Accordingly, the Supreme Commander Allied Expeditionary Force (SHAEF) commander intended to keep hammering. Although American forces had been bloodied for little territorial gain in November in the Hürtgen Forest, Eisenhower was confident he was winning the war of attrition: Hitler was forced to fight to defend German soil, and could not readily replace losses.

Eisenhower felt assured enough to take risks, believing that Germany would be unable to discover and take advantage of some calculated gambles in troop disposition. Instead of pulling units that had suffered heavy casualties off the line, he instead placed them in sectors determined to be quiet, and unlikely to see any significant fighting. His wager was readily apparent: in some areas, Allied lines were stretched thin, with understrength units battered from recent fighting. Worse, inexperienced replacements were placed along the front without adequate preparation. In the Ardennes, all these factors converged: combat-reduced and inexperienced units were placed in thinly held positions along a line in an area where attack was not expected.

As winter approached, Eisenhower kept up the pressure, knowing Germany would struggle to fend off continual pounding. His focus was on the area south of Aachen. He sent First Army under Lieutenant General Courtney Hodges and Ninth Army under Lieutenant General William Simpson against the Roer River area, intending to capture the river dams and drive into the industrial heart of Germany. Hodges launched divisions of the VII and V Corps, attacking in increasingly bitter weather.

Despite efforts to hide and disguise the massive buildup of German forces opposite the Ardennes, Allied intelligence did notice and even identify some German units earmarked to take part in the offensive. However, leadership failed to discern the significance of these German moves due to a well-known danger, although the terminology was not used in 1944: confirmation bias.

The Allies were building up forces to assault the Roer River area. Hence, when the German units and preparations were noticed, the Allies interpreted German movements as a response to Allied actions. That is, as a *defensive* move. With a six-month string of victories since Normandy, the Allies had good reason to project that German assemblies were merely intended to stave off yet another Anglo-American assault.

The American and British planning and intelligence staffs assumed the German buildup was following the very logic that their German counterparts had used in approaching the problem of continuing the war: *How best to manage limited resources, in the most efficient and effective manner?* None of the senior military planners on either side approached the situation the way Hitler had: *What can I do to win the war, however remote the chances?*

Confident in their strategy, secure in their position of military advantage, and seemingly able to predict and counter any possible German action, the senior Allied leaders fell into the deadliest of military mindsets: complacency.

In mid-December 1944, then, the Western Allies were pressing a tottering Germany with two powerful, confident, and well-supplied army groups. However, Hitler had devised an extraordinary plan to surprise them; by secretly assembling and concentrating a powerful force of his own, he could achieve military superiority for a brief period in a limited area. Launching the assault during a period of inclement weather to nullify the Allied airpower, he would drive swiftly through unsuspecting and outgunned Allies along a thinly held portion of the front. Before the expected counterattacks could be mounted against them, German armored forces would race to Antwerp, splitting the Allies in two, surrounding the northern half and cutting it off from their main supply base. This would cause a crisis similar to 1940, shattering the British-American alliance.

Once through the thin and unsuspecting frontline defenses, all that stood between SS-Obersturmbannführer Joachim Peiper and a devastating setback for the Allies were two scattered, rear-echelon battalions of American army combat engineers, under the overall command of Colonel H. Wallis Anderson.

Before dawn on December 16, Hitler's last and boldest blitzkrieg loomed, one of the most desperate actions of the entire war. Although the wintry battle would rage for several weeks, the initial clash in the opening hours would largely determine the outcome. In eastern Belgium, the forces under two regimental-level commanders would meet, ultimately deciding victory, and defeat.

ENDNOTES

173   Hitler had ordered the rescue of Mussolini the previous September, after Mussolini was placed under arrest with the collapse of the Fascist government in summer 1943. Sending his commandos under Otto Skorzeny to rescue Mussolini wasn't so much a strategic or tactical move as it was a sentimental gesture to a fallen ally. The respite for the two dictators was temporary; they were to die within two days of each other, nine months later.

174   Winston G. Ramsey, editor, *After the Battle, Number 4* (London: Battle of Britain Prints International, 1974), 1.

175   Danny S. Parker, *Battle of the Bulge* (Cambridge: Da Capo Press, 2004), 6.

176   In addition to previously being considered too young or too old, some volksgrenadier soldiers were released from prisons, convicts formed into penal battalions. Others were organized into *magen* (stomach) battalions and *ohren* (ear) battalions, in which soldiers with those medical problems could be grouped together to salvage some military contribution.

177   Peter Elstob, *Hitler's Last Offensive* (South Yorkshire: Pen & Sword Books, 2003), 9.

178   Ibid.

179   Ralph Bennett, *Ultra in the West* (New York: Charles Scribner's Sons, 1979), 21.

180   *Generalfeldmarschall* Karl Rudolf Gerd von Rundstadt was brought out of retirement (for the second time, having been dismissed for urging Hitler to make peace after the Allies landed in Normandy) to command *Oberbefehlshaber* West (OB West/Army Command in the West), which would ostensibly conduct the offensive, although he had almost no hand in the planning and preparation for it. He was used as a public figurehead for the offensive, as his name and prestige were still held in high regard by the German public.

181   "Absolute focus." Literally, "absolute hard-point."

182   Ramsey, editor, *After the Battle, Number 4*, 1.

183   Literally, "Watch on the Rhine"; the name was selected to give the impression of defensive preparations along Germany's western river barrier. Readers will note a similar attempt at strategic deception in World War I, when the Germans named their final offensive in July 1918 "Marne Defense." "Die Wacht Am Rhein" is the name of a traditional patriotic German poem and song. In the famous nightclub scene in the film *Casablanca*, the German soldiers attempt to sing "Die Wacht Am Rhein" before being drowned out by French patriots singing the French national anthem, "La Marseillaise."

184   The curtailment of German reconnaissance in the region, a precaution taken to reduce the chance of alerting the Americans, also had the negative impact of denying for the German forces the opportunity to discover this entire US division in their attack path.

185   *Waffen-SS.* The military wing of the Nazi Party's *Schutzstaffel,* "Protection Squad," or SS. Considered elite, fanatical, and ruthless, they were determined, aggressive, and merciless foes. Numerous SS personnel were later convicted of committing war crimes. In the complex and elaborate organization of the German war machine, the Waffen-SS were an army separate and distinct from normal Wehrmacht units. They were favored with higher-quality troops and better equipment and supplies, and even had a separate rank hierarchy.

186   Michael Reynolds, *Men of Steel* (South Yorkshire: Pen & Sword Books, 1999), 19. Josef "Sepp" Dietrich, while not considered to be adept at senior levels of command, was nevertheless an active, brave, and experienced combat commander (he was also described as "brutal" and "cunning"). While his political patronage ensured his rise within the SS, he nonetheless took part in many battles and campaigns. Dietrich was greatly admired by his men, and enjoyed national popularity. Per Reynolds, "[I]t is not without significance that the badge of the Leibstandarte, later to be incorporated into that of both the Hitlerjugend Division and I SS Panzer Corps, was a skeleton key—'Dietrich' is German for skeleton key."

187   Danny S. Parker, *Battle of the Bulge*, 69. Parker is discounting *15. Armee*, which preexisted the surprise offensive and was already engaged in the Aachen region.

188 Danny S. Parker, *Battle of the Bulge*, 69.

189 Danny S. Parker, editor, *Hitler's Ardennes Offiensive* (London: Greenhill Books, 1997), 34.

190 Ibid.

191 Ibid, 35.

192 Ibid, 42.

193 Ibid, 43.

194 Danny S. Parker, editor, *Hitler's Ardennes Offiensive*, 42. 3rd *Fallshirmjäger* Division (FJD). Originally elite parachute infantry, by 1944 these troops had lost the élan and skill that marked their early battlefield prowess. Like so many German units, attrition and exhaustion greatly reduced their effectiveness. Krämer stated that the 3FJD "had no battle experience, and besides their Commander had very little understanding about infantry matters." For a unit assigned the task of breaking through American lines, this did not bode well for the Germans; this was borne out by events. Organizationally, they were part of the Luftwaffe.

195 Ibid, 40.

196 Ibid, 44.

197 Michael Reynolds, *Men of Steel*, 2.

198 Equipped with the second most powerful force after LAH's KG Peiper, Hitlerjugend's KG Kuhlmann consisted of forty-one PzKw Mk V Panthers, thirty-seven PzKw Mk IVs, twenty-eight JgPz IVs, and fourteen JgPz Vs; a battalion of SS-panzergrenadiers; an artillery battalion of eighteen 105 mm howitzers; an additional artillery company of six 150 mm guns; plus a company each of pioneers and antiaircraft guns.

199 Michael Reynolds, *Men of Steel*, 50.

200 Ibid, 49.

201 Danny S. Parker, editor, *Hitler's Ardennes Offiensive*, 34.

202 Michael Reynolds, *Men of Steel*, 19.

203 From the book by Michael Reynolds of the same title.

204   Other senior members of the SS didn't especially convey the appearance of that organization's fearsome martial reputation. Division commander Wilhelm Mohnke's photographs display a chinless, humorless face suggesting a high school science teacher. An even better (or worse) example is Sepp Dietrich. His nickname, "the Butcher," alludes to his brutish behavior during the early street-fighting days of the Nazi Party and, later, his remorseless SS warfare. However, in candid photographs, he is often smiling, and one gets the feeling that he would be perfectly at home behind the meat counter of a deli, wearing an apron, cheerfully filling his patrons' orders.

205   This was the Nuremberg Rally during which Leni Riefenstahl made the film *Triumph des Willens* (Triumph of the Will).

206   Leibstandarte went through a substantial number of name and organizational changes during its existence.

207   Apparently, the SS favored promotion ceremonies on recipients' birthdays, or, possibly, the anniversary of Hitler's rise to power. This instance happened on Peiper's twenty-eighth.

208   In one individual combat action, Peiper is alleged to have borrowed a rifle grenade-launcher ("*Schießbecher*"), and stalked a Soviet T-34 tank. He closed to within twenty meters before launching the grenade that set the tank afire; he returned the rifle to its owner, saying the act should qualify him for a close-combat badge. He was indeed awarded the Close Combat Clasp in silver, indicating he had been in such actions a minimum of thirty times.

209   Han Bouwmeester, *Beginning of the End: The Leadership of SS Obersturmbannführer Jochen Peiper* (Fort Leavenworth, Kansas: US Army Command and General Staff College, 2004), 56.

210   By 1943, Stalin had led the USSR about twice as long as Hitler had ruled Germany.

211   The short duration of his Italian posting notwithstanding, Peiper still managed to commit actions resulting in accusations of war crimes.

212   An alternative explanation is that Peiper may have contracted jaundice; German wartime medical records were heavily influenced by state propaganda efforts to shield the truth from the populace.

213   Michael Reynolds, *Men of Steel*, xi.

Along Mexican border. Anderson with Company K officers.

Company K, on the Mexican border, 1916-17.

Captain H.W. Anderson,
Infantry, 28th Division,
Augusta, Georgia, 1917.

Engineers in Front line, St Agnan
July 16-17 1918

Shallow trenches of St. Agnan, July 1918. Ed Shenton, sketch artist.

103rd Engineer officers, France. Col. F. Snyder, Commanding Officer, second from right. Capt. H.W. Anderson, far right.

Barbed Wire- N. of Toul

Anderson photograph of barbed wire, after Armistice, in France.

AEF Commander Gen. J. J. Pershing,
during 28th Division troop review, March 1919, France.

Between the wars.
Anderson with 103rd
Engineer Battalion
shoulder epaulette badge,
Mexican Border ribbon,
and WWI Victory ribbon
with five campaign stars.

Anderson at Camp
Bowie, Texas, 1942.

Anderson with
51st Engineer
Regiment symbol,
Plattsburgh,
New York.

1111th Engineer Combat Group officers, England, 1944 pre-invasion. Front row, Anderson with his executive officer and three battalion commanding officers: Pergrin (291st), Reafsnyder (51st), Anderson, Kirkland, and Jeffrey (296th). Note Anderson has blotched out unit identifier patches on officers' left shoulders.

Anderson in Normandy,
hedgerow country.
With VII Corps Engineer,
Colonel Mason Young (l).

Remagen bridge, from Erpeler Lay, March 1945

German artillery fire on floating bridge, March 10 1945.

Engineers preparing bridge floats.

Anderson at St. Agnan, 1971.

SS officer Jochen Peiper, prior to Ardennes Counteroffensive.

FIG. 38.   BATTLE DURING THE DRIVE ON THE MARNE
AND IN CHAMPAGNE, 1918

German Plan—Second Marne

(Source: The General Service School. "The German Offensive of July 15, 1918." Fort Leavenworth, KS: The General Service School Press, 1923.)

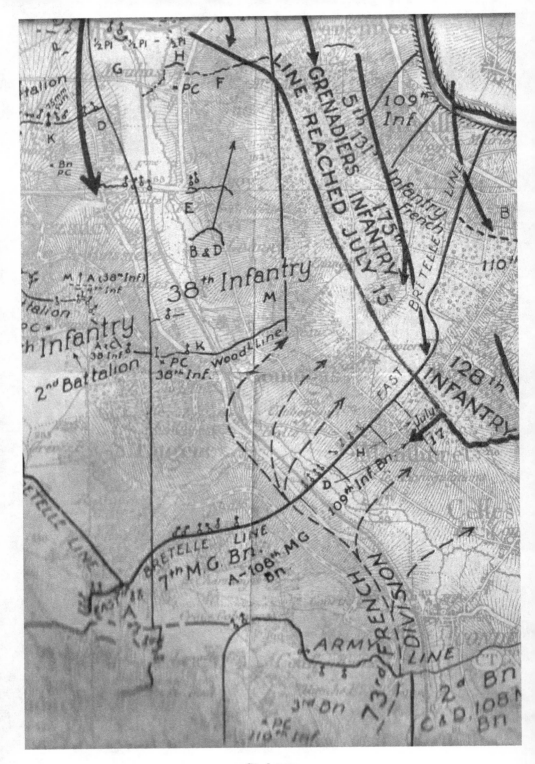

St. Agnan

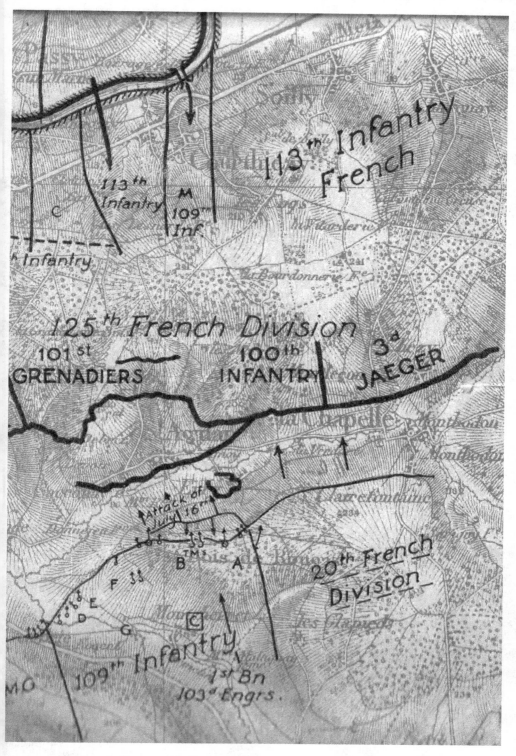

(Source: The General Service School. "The German Offensive of July 15, 1918." Fort Leavenworth, KS: The General Service School Press, 1923.)

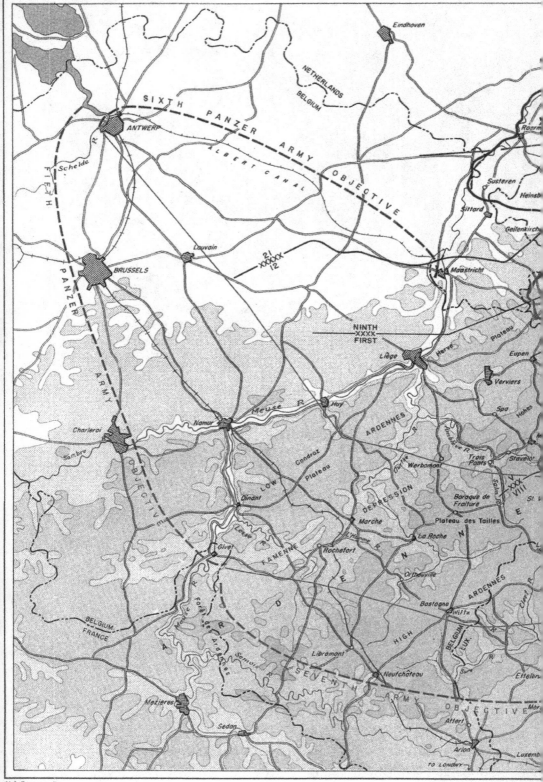

H.C. Brewer, Jr.

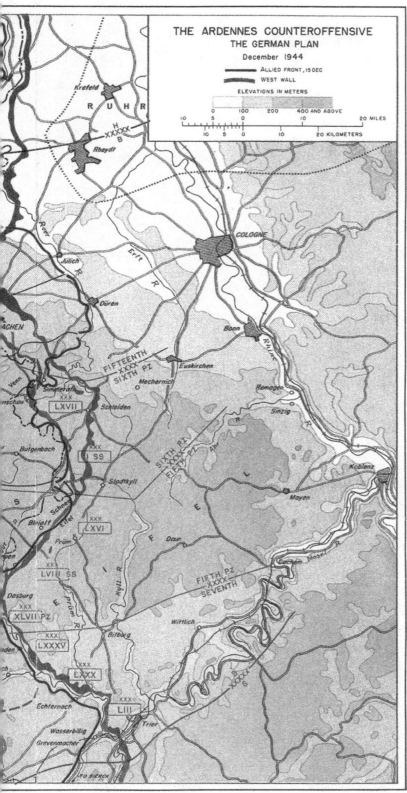

The Ardennes
Counteroffensive
—
The German Plan

(Source: Cole,
Hugh M., *United
States Army
in WWII—
Europe—
The Ardennes:
Battle of
the Bulge*.)

MAP I

1111th ECG Positions and Kaumpfgruppe Peiper Route

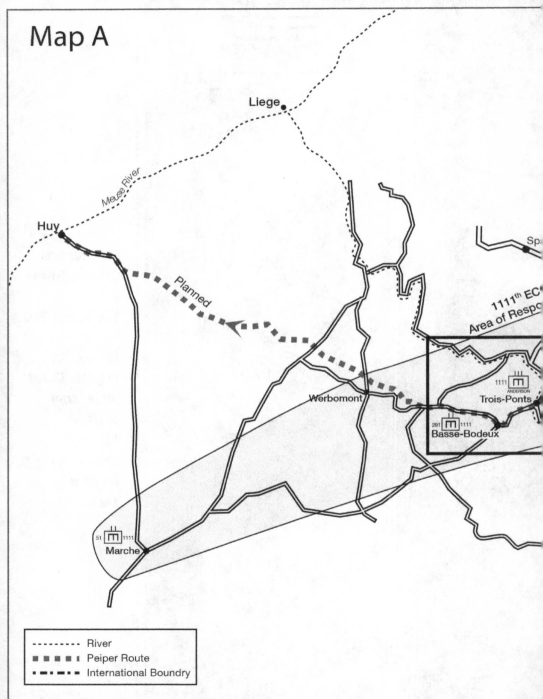

Map A

Liege

Meuse River

Huy

Planned

Sp...

1111th EC...
Area of Respo...

Werbomont

1111 [m] ANDERSON
Trois-Ponts

291 [m] 1111
Basse-Bodeux

51 [m] 1111
Marche

·········	River
■ ■ ■ ■ ■	Peiper Route
■-■-■-■	International Boundry

A. B. CHRISTOFFERSEN

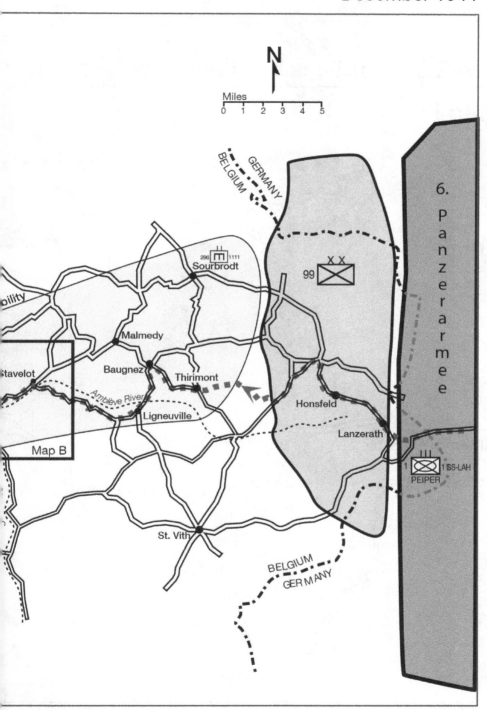

December 1944

1111th Ardennes—Map A

1111th ECG Positions and Kaumpfgruppe Peiper

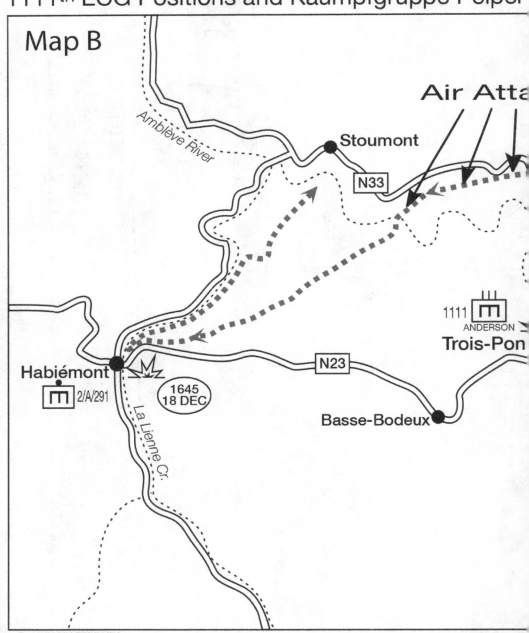

Map B

Amblève River

Stoumont

N33

Air Atta

1111 ANDERSON

Trois-Pon

Habiémont

2/A/291

1645
18 DEC

La Lienne Cr.

N23

Basse-Bodeux

A. B. CHRISTOFFERSEN

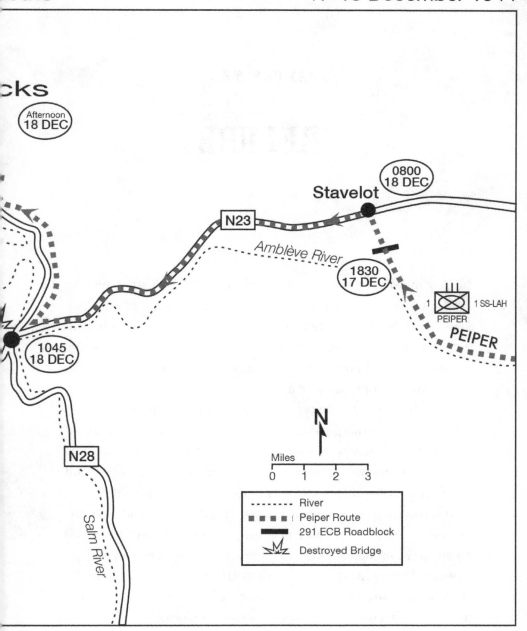

cks

Afternoon
18 DEC

0800
18 DEC

Stavelot

N23

Amblève River

1830
17 DEC

1 ⊠ 1 SS-LAH
PEIPER

PEIPER

1045
18 DEC

N28

Salm River

N

Miles
0   1   2   3

- - - - - - - River
▪▪▪▪▪ Peiper Route
▬▬▬ 291 ECB Roadblock
💥 Destroyed Bridge

1111th Ardennes – Map B

CHAPTER TEN

PRELUDE

B y mid-December, the engineers in the 1111th's sixty-mile arc of Belgium could be excused if they viewed life as not too bad, considering they were at war. They were located well behind the front lines and, after six months of bivouacking their way across Europe, were finally living in comfortable civilian quarters, remaining in one location for more than a month—this stability itself a luxury.

The troops were engaged in routine rear-echelon support activities, maintaining roads and bridges, while running quarries and sawmills. There were even local bars and restaurants available for off-hour entertainment; even *having* "off hours" was a new and enjoyable development. Life was considerably more comfortable than it was for most US Army troops. There were reminders of the ongoing combat—V-1 buzz bombs, primarily—but these posed no apparent immediate danger, as the V-1s were targeting the big cities, and the fighting was over the horizon to the east. And as the German offensive neared, even those aerial attacks were reduced in the Ardennes, adding to the Allies' sense of security.[214]

Anderson's command was active but had settled into a winter routine, miles to the rear of the V and VII Corps activity. Direct support for combat operations was handled by engineer units assigned directly to the divisions involved.[215]

On December 1, Anderson's 1111th Engineer Combat Group consisted of three engineer combat battalions (51st, 291st, 296th; with headquarters, respectively, in Marche, Basse-Bodeux,[216] and Sourbrodt); 629th Engineer Light Equipment Company (Butgenbach); 962nd Engineer Maintenance Company (Malmedy); and one platoon of the 767th Engineer Dump Truck Company (Butgenbach). All the units under Anderson's command were widely dispersed throughout the region. Unlike Anderson's WWI experiences, there was no fear of a German breakthrough; no defense-in-depth preparations had been made.

The weather turned bad, with worse expected. Managing and preparing for the deteriorating weather was as much a concern as the enemy front. Anderson was directed to move all the lumber being produced by 51st ECB to Werbomont, for use by FUSA units to winterize their quarters. Company C, 51st ECB, under the command of Captain Sam Scheuber, was selected for this assignment during the week of December 11.

Also on December 11, the 202nd Engineer Combat Battalion was assigned to Anderson's group, bringing his battalion total to four. The 202nd ECB, coming up from VIII Corps in the south, established its command post about ten miles northeast of Spa (First Army's headquarters) on December 13. With the V and VII Corps offensive against the German lines in the Roer Dam area, additional units were being sent to the area; the 202nd was one such unit.

December's relatively low-key routine provided Anderson the opportunity to finally resolve an ongoing concern: the problematic leader of the 51st ECB. Although Anderson had kept the 51st ECB well back from the front, he would have had no illusions about the potential for combat once First Army launched more large-scale efforts to invade Germany proper. Anderson would have realized the danger of sending that battalion into more direct combat operations under the command of a man who was held in such low regard by his troops, and liable to "crack."

Fortuitously, an alternative presented itself in the form of an eager young engineer officer—a West Pointer, which couldn't have hurt his chances. This officer, previously assigned to port-clearance duties in Brittany, had been petitioning for a more active assignment. Twenty-six-year-old Lieutenant Colonel Harvey Fraser was sent for reassignment to Colonel Bill Carter, First Army engineer, in Spa. Carter consulted Anderson, and they agreed that Fraser's arrival and eagerness for action provided an ideal opportunity: Fraser could replace Reafsnyder. This would presumably please both officers.[217]

It is no small thing to relieve a commanding officer while engaged in combat-support operations. Anderson and Carter weighed the balance of replacing a weak commanding officer with one who was new and somewhat unknown. But Fraser's eagerness and his record would have made the decision a straightforward one: he had won a Bronze Star for combat action in Normandy and had previously commanded engineer battalions in peacetime and war.

After meeting with and being briefed by Anderson in Trois-Ponts on December 12, Fraser was sent to Marche to take command of the 51st ECB. Fraser arrived in Marche on Thursday, December 14. His arrival was described by one of his junior officers, in a letter to home: "Our new C.O. is a West Pointer only 26 years old and a Lt.Col. He is a real live wire and seems very likable. He knows what he wants even though he has not had much troop experience. He has a lot to learn but I am sure all the officers will be behind him 100%. Reafsnyder is as happy as a lark."[218]

Despite the differences in their respective military service upbringing, Fraser was an officer very much of the same mold as Anderson. Decisive and energetic, Fraser made his presence immediately felt. On his third day on the job, Saturday, December

16, the new commander made the rounds of his scattered command, visiting the companies engaged in sawmill operations. Events would soon transpire to cut short this tour and give the young lieutenant colonel the action he craved.

The timing for this improvement in leadership was a stroke of very good fortune; the surprise German offensive was now just forty-eight hours off. The importance of sound leadership during a crisis cannot be overstated. At this critical moment, Anderson and, indeed, the US Army received another unexpected boost: the return of executive officer Major Robert "Bull" Yates to the 51st ECB.

Yates had been hospitalized since late August, following his unfortunate (and at least partly self-inflicted) motorcycle accident during a battalion movement in France. Overcome by restlessness during his three-month rehabilitation for a broken foot at a hospital in England, Yates had determined to rejoin his battalion. He discharged himself from hospital, without authorization, by walking out, painfully concealing his not-healed injury (and apparently removing the foot cast himself). Yates made his way across the English Channel, and then across France to Belgium, where he managed to locate the 51st ECB. Hobbled, he arrived in Marche on Friday, December 15.

Over the space of two days, then, due to two coincidental events, Anderson's concern over the command leadership of the 51st ECB was significantly and serendipitously resolved. With the strong leadership of Lieutenant Colonel David Pergrin guiding the 291st ECB, and with the 51st finally in capable hands, Anderson's area of responsibility—and the First US Army's last line of defense—now presented any encroaching enemy with the challenge of facing troops led by skilled and resolute commanders.

The second week of December 1944 was a busy time for Jochen Peiper and his SS men as well. Gradually, the plan and organization of *Wacht Am Rhein* was revealed to more junior echelons of the Wehrmacht and Waffen-SS. Sepp Dietrich, commander of 6. *Panzerarmee*, which was assigned the central objective for the campaign, was only briefed on November 29, such was operational security. Division commanders were briefed a week later. Hitler personally exhorted his senior commanders on December 12 to carry out the offensive with fanatical vigor, to again tilt the situation in the West to Germany's favor.

On Tuesday, December 12, I SS-Panzerkorps' two SS panzer divisions, 1st and 12th, were placed into position—without explanation—across the front line where they would attempt to break through. SS-Oberführer Wilhelm Mohnke, division commander of Leibstandarte, the 1st SS Panzer Division, only formally briefed his own senior unit commanders on December 14, less than forty-eight hours before the attack commenced.

Peiper, however, was given informal advanced notification, probably due to the importance of his assignment. On Monday, December 11, 6. *Panzerarmee* chief of staff Krämer visited Peiper and asked the panzer leader's opinion about "the possibilities of an attack in the Eifel region, and how much time it would take a tank Regiment to proceed 80 km in one night. Feeling that it was not a good idea to decide the answer to such a question merely by looking at a map," Peiper decided to make "a test run of 80 km with a Panther tank [himself], driving down the route Euskirchen-Meunstereifel-Blankenheim."[219] Peiper deduced that a major offensive was building, and that he would play a major part.

By midmorning Thursday, December 14, Leibstandarte was in position, hidden in woods several miles east of the American lines at Losheim. Peiper was provided detailed instructions for his assignment, including forces assigned, maps marked with routes, and timetable. Upon studying his rollbahn, Peiper objected that "these roads were not for tanks, but for bicycles." Peiper was nonetheless ordered to use the assigned route. The young yet experienced SS panzer leader was told of the importance of his role: "They said that my combat team [kampfgruppe] in the center was to have the decisive role in the Offensive. I was not to bother about my flanks but was to drive rapidly to the Meuse River, making full use of the element of surprise."[220]

With such priority on speed and surprise, Peiper planned the organization of his column. In general, he decided to place armored half-tracks in the lead, with his medium panzers (Mk IVs and Mk V Panthers) just behind. The SPW half-tracks would speed ahead until they encountered resistance. When this occurred, the panzers would be close at hand to come up and destroy whatever defensive positions had confronted the SPWs. Peiper anticipated that he would need only his medium panzers for the initial run up to the Meuse.

He therefore kept his slow, gas-guzzling Mk VI *Ausf.* B Tiger II heavy panzers well back in his column. For his dash to the Meuse, Peiper planned to defeat his foes by racing swiftly and forcefully through the lines and beyond, not with overwhelming firepower.

Peiper estimated that his column would stretch 25 km once all elements were in line and moving through Belgium. He spent the remaining time briefing and organizing his troops, and coordinating with 12th Volksgrenadier Division (12VGD), the infantry assigned to conduct the initial assault to open up the gaps in the front for Peiper's kampfgruppe to drive through.

The SS, rushed into position and provisioned and prepared as best as could be expected by this point in a lost war, waited for a final chance to drive into the heart of the enemy. Led by experienced, ruthless, and skilled commanders who suffered cumulative fragility from five years of physical and mental overuse and grueling stress, the SS men were now ready to conduct one final, desperate blitzkrieg.

ENDNOTES

214 Albert Radford, *Unbroken Line*, 69. Captain Albert Radford, 51st ECB's Headquarters and Service (H&S) Company commander, located in the vicinity of Marche, wrote home on December 8, "Seems like the Germans are running short of buzz bombs." On December 12, he wrote, "Everything has been peaceful and quiet the last 2 days. Either the Jerries have run out of V-1s or they are hoarding them for the big blast because none of them have come over lately." In fact, reduced V-1 use was part of the German deception plan.

215 Seven Army engineer battalions were assigned at various level in V Corps zone. The 1111th ECG and its battalions were under separate FUSA control.

216 Pergrin's 291st battalion headquarters and H&S Company are variously described as being in both Haute-Bodeux and Basse-Bodeux. The 100 or so Americans were likely spread throughout these two "high" and "low" elements of essentially the same small village, separated by less than a mile of Belgian countryside.

217 In a letter to his wife about two weeks later, while the Ardennes campaign still raged but the immediate crisis had passed, Anderson wrote, describing his pride in the performance of two of his outfits (the 51st and 291st), "However the less said about some of my immediate cohorts the better—and I guess the fates were most kind to me in another way—had a certain party not left the preceding week I am pretty <u>sure</u> that there would have been an entirely different tale in his outfit—and probably drastic action required—so his good luck was undoubtedly mine also. Strange how fate works things out for you sometimes in ways you least expect." In this passage, Anderson is almost certainly referring to Reafsnyder and his replacement by Fraser on December 14.

218 Albert Radford, *Unbroken Line*, 69.

219 Wilhelm Weiss, editor, *Standartenführer Joachim Peiper, The Interview* (2012), 38.

220 Ibid.

CHAPTER ELEVEN

DISTANT THUNDER

December 16, 1944
Saturday

A t 0530[221] on Saturday, December 16, German guns all along an eighty-five-mile front opened a massive barrage against the American front lines. The largest concentration of German might in eighteen months was unleashed. Hitler's last gamble had begun.

As the German infantry moved forward to assault the suddenly besieged Americans, SS panzer units began forming into their columns, awaiting word of the breakthrough that would allow them to surge forward. Jochen Peiper assembled his kampfgruppe in the woods around Blankenheim, ten miles east of the American lines at Losheimergraben. He spent much of that Saturday at the headquarters of the 12th Volksgrenadier Division (12VGD), the unit assigned to open the gap in front of rollbahn D. Following the ninety-minute early-morning barrage, 12VGD's commanding general, *Generalmajor* Gerhard Engel, had thrown his 27th and 48th Volksgrenadier

Regiments at American positions around Losheim, defended by 3rd Battalion of the US 99th Infantry Division's 394th Infantry Regiment.

Twenty-five miles to the west, at his group headquarters in Trois-Ponts, Wallis Anderson had started the day with routine assignments and activities. He had designated the 291st ECB as his security battalion, adding to their routine sawmill and road-maintenance tasks. With the 291st headquarters at Haute-Bodeux, about three miles west of Trois-Ponts along the N23 road, they were close at hand should the need for any protective measures arise.

Anderson's main concern that morning, however, was to support First Army's push toward the Roer Dams, which had started several days prior. First Army engineer Colonel William Carter had tasked Anderson with providing a company of engineers to support a combat command from the 9th Armored Division. Tanks in the attack against prepared positions often need engineer support to clear mines and other defensive obstructions, a practice Anderson first took part in during the Meuse-Argonne Offensive in 1918.

Anderson passed the assignment to Lieutenant Colonel Pergrin and his 291st ECB. Pergrin selected his Company A, under the command of twenty-three-year-old Captain James H. Gamble, for the assignment.[222] Gamble's company headquarters had been located at La Gleize, a couple miles north of Trois-Ponts, for several weeks.

As with all of the 1111th's assigned troops, Company A platoons were spread across a wide swath of the Belgian Ardennes. Pergrin ordered Gamble to begin to move into the area around Born on Saturday, December 16, and to start consolidating his scattered company. Gamble's company command element was on the road by Saturday daylight, passing through Malmedy en route to Born, eleven miles southeast from Malmedy. He chose to establish his company headquarters in Amblève (also known as Amel), a couple miles northeast of Born, as the latter was already crowded with US troops, specifically a battalion of the US 106th Infantry Division, newly arrived to the area.

Another 291st unit, Company B, under Captain John Conlin, had been posted in Malmedy, conducting road and sawmill operations. At 0715 on Saturday, Conlin phoned battalion commander Pergrin and reported Malmedy had been hit early that morning by four heavy-caliber artillery shells,[223] a very unusual event. In the six weeks the engineers had been in the region, nothing like that had happened. Military and civilian casualties had been inflicted by the brief, unexpected barrage, though none were Conlin's men. Pergrin drove to Malmedy from his headquarters to inspect the area and talk to his engineers.

The Belgian telephones were so reliable, and the situation had been so calm, that this network was used for command and control by the engineers in the region, a practice modified only when enemy interception and disruption began. The radio network was maintained but used only as a backup and for emergencies.

Anderson and his subordinate commanders also used couriers to deliver orders and information; sometimes duplicate messages were sent to ensure delivery. Throughout the period in France and Belgium, Anderson had placed staff officers as liaisons to various higher Army headquarters in the area; in December, this primarily consisted of First Army and V Corps.

Throughout Saturday, December 16, as the German attack along the front unfolded, Anderson and his 1111th Group, twenty-five miles to the rear, received no definitive information that something was amiss. Scattered, isolated events were reported, but were too vague and not linked in any recognizable way to suggest a major German offensive was underway: the isolated, four-shell barrage in Malmedy; a report of general uneasiness in the area by the easternmost engineers of Company A, 291st ECB; and some minor movement by reserve infantry units toward the front lines.

Lieutenant Albert A. "Bucky" Walters, 1st Platoon leader of Gamble's Company A, reported some secondhand information acquired while supervising timber-cutting activities in the vicinity of Grand-Halleux, five miles south of Trois-Ponts. During a visit to his battalion headquarters on Saturday, he reported that some locals had seen a small plane circling and dropping parachutes. The report was shrugged off, and Walters was ordered to join the rest of his Company A in the Born area the next day, Sunday.

In all, the information was too fragmentary and sparse for any commander to reach any conclusions, let alone take definitive action. As with the prior evidence of the German buildup in the region during the preceding weeks, even these indicators were shrugged off as likely German responses intended to counter the US attacks toward the Roer dams, if they even meant anything at all.

For Jochen Peiper, the first day of the offensive was marked by frustration and exasperation. The Germans were paying the price for their desperate efforts to raise an army in the fall. Although they had managed to create and organize a sizable force in a remarkably short time, the overall quality of this cohort was low—especially in the infantry units. With little time and severely limited resources to train and prepare, the volksgrenadier units were inferior, generally, and not well led. US Army frontline defenders reported that they faced massed infantry assaults over open ground, with little or no combined arms use or coordination between supporting heavy arms—hardly the seasoned, professional Wehrmacht of earlier in the war.

The initial clash affecting Peiper involved fusiliers from the 12VGD attacking Buchholz Station, a railroad stop one mile from the Belgian-German frontier. Parading up the railroad track two abreast, as if on a routine training march, the Germans suddenly appeared out of the fog to find the outnumbered American GIs lined up for breakfast. The encounter in the low visibility surprised everyone involved,[224] but the Americans recovered more effectively and drove off the Germans, inflicting heavy losses on the attackers.

Peiper monitored the progress (or lack thereof), and by midafternoon, it was clear that the conditions at the front were not yet ready for his planned thrust. "The Americans were holding firm at Losheimergraben,"[225] which blocked Peiper's path and prevented the launch of his kampfgruppe on rollbahn D. Congestion on all the roads near the front slowed all progress to a crawl; the *spitze* (vanguard) of Peiper's column made its way to Losheim by 1700, well behind the meticulously planned (though unrealistic) timetable.[226] Even then Losheimergraben was still being held by the Americans, the 99th Infantry Division's 394th Infantry Regiment, whose stubborn defense had held off 12VGD throughout the day.

At this point, with daylight dwindling on this first day of the offensive,[227] Peiper was ordered to deviate from his original route. Instead of driving northwest along the national highway from Losheim to Losheimergraben, he was directed to proceed more westerly, using lesser roads from Losheim through Hüllscheid to Lanzerath. This move diverted KG Peiper away from the 12VGD's assigned area and into the zone under attack by the 3rd *Fallschirmjäger* (Parachute) Division (3FSD).

The 9th Fallschirmjäger Regiment had been assigned to capture Lanzerath and the surrounding area. Late on Saturday afternoon the German regiment had finally taken the town after being held off for most of the day by less than two dozen soldiers from the Intelligence and Reconnaissance (I&R) Platoon of the 394th Infantry, at the extreme right of the 99th Infantry Division's front.

As Peiper directed his column west from Losheim, he encountered a destroyed road bridge over a rail line. The panzers were forced to depart the road, descend the embankment, cross the railroad tracks, and then rejoin the roadway. In doing so, the lead panzer (a Mk V Panther) was damaged by an antitank mine. As darkness fell, another minefield was encountered 500 meters farther from Losheim. A third minefield was struck by the column even before reaching Merlscheid. In each of these incidents, a panzer was damaged and lost to the column. Each time, pioneers (engineers) were called to clear the minefield, causing further delays. Peiper finally reached Lanzerath just before midnight.

Less than a day into the offensive, Peiper was about twelve hours behind schedule. He had already been diverted, yet that apparently did not improve the situation: in detouring, he had lost three panzers[228] to mines, an ignominious affront to an SS panzer commander. And he had yet to be shot at—or even seen—by an American defender.

In Lanzerath, Peiper encountered the commander of the 9th FSJ Regiment, who informed the more junior SS officer that the 9th FSJ was blocked and awaiting additional support as the road and woods leading northwest from Lanzerath were heavily defended. To Peiper, the frontline assaults had been carried out with an apparent lack of skill and enthusiasm, and had not succeeded, resulting in the entire timetable being thrown off.

At this point, angrily confronting the higher-ranking Luftwaffe *oberst* (colonel), the famed SS arrogance and aggression emerged.[229] Peiper demanded to know details about the supposed heavily defended American positions that were holding up the advance. In turn, he demanded specifics from the fallschirmjäger regimental commander, then his battalion commander, and finally a low-level staff officer. None had personally seen any of the reported American defenders, or their prepared positions.

In a rage, Peiper demanded a battalion of fallschirmjägers to support an attack of his own to break through the alleged American defenses northwest of Lanzerath. No doubt intimidated by the renowned SS leader, the oberst complied, and assigned a battalion to support Peiper. The attack was organized to begin around 0400 the next morning.

Thus, by the end of the first day of the "Eifel offensive" (as the Germans referred to it), Peiper was still a bare mile across the border, his ostensible starting point. The most powerful column in the German Army, assigned to use its lethal combination of speed and firepower to drive through the American lines, splitting the Allies and causing a strategic crisis, had barely left the starting gate.

ENDNOTES

221   Germany had imposed "German time" on occupied countries in Europe. Meanwhile, the United Kingdom had instituted "British Double Summer Time." As a result, during the Battle of the Bulge, both sides were using the same time standard.

222   Janice Giles, *The Damned Engineers* (Washington, DC: Houghton Mifflin Company, 1970), 26. Gamble went by "Harry," his middle name.

223   Ibid, 49. Possibly, 310 mm shells from massive German "railroad guns."

224   Marvin D. Kays, *Weather Effects During the Battle of the Bulge and the Normandy Invasion* (Atmospheric Sciences Laboratory, US Army Electronics Research and Development Command, 1982), 19. The weather summary for US air forces that morning states, "Very low clouds and fog patches. Visibilities poor. Light rain."

225   Michael Reynolds, *Men of Steel*, 54.

226   Wilhelm Weiss, editor, *Standartenführer Joachim Peiper, The Interview*, 122. In the postwar interview, Peiper claims that the 12VGD commander expected to open the way for Kampfgruppe Peiper by 0700.

227   For the period 16 to 21 December, 1944, daylight in the Ardennes came just before 0800. Sunrise occurred at around 0830. The sun set around 1635.

228   In postwar interviews, Peiper claimed five tanks and five other armored combat vehicles lost during the initial push from Losheim to Lanzerath. He tended to exaggerate after the fact, in order to amplify the various difficulties he had faced. This behavior was not unique nor isolated to Peiper, nor to the Germans. In fact, about the only postwar correspondent related herein who *didn't* exaggerate was H. W. Anderson, who consistently and significantly downplayed his actions, difficulties, and dangers.

229   Twenty-year-old Lieutenant Lyle Bouck, I&R Platoon leader who had led the defense of Lanzerath against heavy odds, witnessed this confrontation. Bouck and his handful of soldiers had finally

been captured in the evening, having held off the German assault throughout Saturday. Every member of his platoon, plus the attached artillery observers, received commendations for valor (Bouck received the Distinguished Service Cross), although this recognition took place belatedly, in 1981. Bouck turned twenty-one on Sunday, December 17, while in captivity.

CHAPTER TWELVE

CRISIS

December 17, 1944
Sunday

As the cold night passed into Sunday, December 17, the curious and scattered events from Saturday that had only generated uneasiness in the American engineers behind the front now took on more sinister significance. At around 0100, a routine telephone connectivity check between 291st ECB headquarters in Haute-Bodeux and 1111th Group (less than three miles away in Trois-Ponts) indicated the landline was out, although contacts with the battalion's elements were working properly. Group was notified by radio, which took steps to find and repair the line break. The situation "was so unusual that the feeling was general that it was sabotage."[230] Anderson's group[231] thereupon notified its subordinate units to maintain continuous watch on the radio network.

Shortly thereafter, as the 291st headquarters alerted its companies' headquarters of the unusual event and the group's new continuous radio-watch requirement, Company A, now in Amblève, received a message that could not be decoded; a similar garbled message was received a second time, a half hour later.

Both the radio and landline disruption were likely caused by enemy activity deep behind American lines. As their offensive unfolded, the Germans actively sought to disrupt US Army command, control, and communications. One aspect included the insertion of German soldiers specially handpicked for their English-speaking ability. These troops were issued captured American uniforms, weapons, and equipment (*NB* the capture of Anderson's S-4 logistics officer, Captain Thomas Williams, in October).

SS-Obersturmbannführer Otto Skorzeny, another SS officer handpicked by Hitler, organized this effort. Given command of the independent "SS Panzer Brigade 150" with a special assignment to disrupt the Americans in advance of the armored assault, Skorzeny sent these saboteurs and covert operators to sow as much confusion as possible.

Infiltrating by small groups and as individuals deep into the American rear echelon, they conducted a wide variety of disruptive activities. They cut phone lines, changed signs and road posts, spread false rumors, acted as military police to misdirect US Army troop movements, and generally caused turmoil throughout the battle zone. Although originally envisioned as coordinating and cooperating with the conventional SS panzer columns, Skorzeny's troops never managed that kind of close support.[232]

At around 0130, the First Army Security Command issued an alert—the first widespread notification of the German offensive— notifying all commands of the possibility of a large-scale German attack, accompanied by paratroops, and for precautions to be taken immediately.

In Trois-Ponts, Anderson—awake, alert, and in command— issued immediate security measures. By now wary of the vulnerability of electronic communications, he sent special orders via messenger to his battalion commanders. He ordered immediate security patrols and the posting of guards at strategic locations throughout his area of responsibility—bridges and road crossings were to receive extra protection. Tension built even more when, around this time, his communications personnel reported that they had discovered the telephone line between Trois-Ponts and Haute-Bodeux had indeed been cut, likely by saboteurs, as suspected.

For Jochen Peiper, the early hours of Sunday were exceedingly active. Between midnight and 0300, his column closed on Lanzerath, negotiating the blown bridge, minefields, and traffic congestion caused by all the other vehicular traffic supporting 6. *Panzerarmee* units around Losheim. Peiper, having essentially taken charge despite the more senior commander of the 9th FSJ Regiment, organized an assault on American positions reported to be in the woods and road northwest from Lanzerath. Peiper intended to create his own breakthrough, then to finally launch his armored thrust along rollbahn D, as originally intended, albeit almost a day behind schedule.

Peiper placed two Mk V Panther tanks in the lead, carrying paratroopers, to be followed by SPW half-tracks, then more of his Mk IV and Mk V panzers. The rest of the battalion of paratroopers accompanied on foot, anticipating enemy action.

The assault force rolled out of Lanzerath in darkness at around 0400, "broke through the area without firing a shot[,] and found it completely unoccupied."[233] The kampfgruppe carried on 1.5 miles through the forest road to Buchholz Station.

Buchholz Station had been vigorously and successfully defended the day before by elements of the US 394th Infantry. The 12VGD attacks against the 394th at Buchholz Station and Losheimergraben had come from the east. Before first light on Sunday, however, Peiper's forces came slowly toward the Americans along the road from an unanticipated direction, the woods to the southeast, catching the Americans unprepared.

The head (spitze) of Peiper's mobile column bypassed the railroad station and continued northwest toward Honsfeld. The fallschirmjäger and panzergrenadier troops following on foot quickly took the surprised (and sleepy) Americans in Buchholz Station without a serious fight. Honsfeld was ostensibly defended by elements of the 14th Cavalry Group in addition to 99th Infantry Division troops; the regiment-sized cavalry unit had only been assigned to the area in the previous several days, and was intended to fill the gap and corps boundary between the 99th (V Corps) and 106th Infantry Division (VIII Corps). Attacking a corps boundary is an especially effective way to keep the defender off balance, as a coordinated response is more difficult.

The cavalry group's mobile armored forces were widely scattered and caught unaware. Peiper's spitze, encountering the American armor and finding the defenders sleeping, pressed on toward Büllingen without delay, leaving the main body of the kampfgruppe to take the village and capture the defenders. Peiper's fallschirmjägers and panzergrenadiers quickly subdued the surprised Americans in what author Michael Reynolds describes as "a disaster for the Americans. They lost seventeen TDs [tank destroyers], some fifty reconnaissance vehicles and over 300 men as prisoners."[234]

Büllingen was a further two miles northwest from Honsfeld. Along the way, the spitze ran into an American column of about eight supply trucks, which were captured without firing a shot. As the kampfgruppe approached the southern end of the town at around 0700, it received automatic weapons fire from positions south and west of the town, from an airfield along the spitze's route.

Peiper directed the spitze to continue into the town, rather than stopping to engage the American defenders, thereby "leaving the clearing of American defensive positions to his main body."[235] A further prize awaited Peiper in Büllingen: fuel for his panzers. The town was a major supply depot for two American divisions, 2nd and 99th Infantry. Knowing his own fuel and supplies were unlikely to reach him in a timely fashion, Peiper intended to capture everything he could from the enemy along the way.

For the first time in the advance, Peiper's SS spearhead encountered organized defenders. On the southern outskirts of Büllingen, US Army engineers of the 254th Engineer Combat Battalion had been sent to establish a roadblock on the roads leading southeast from the town.[236] Expecting to be supported by in-place armored forces, the engineers instead found themselves the sole defenders that Sunday morning.

After a stubborn fight, the outgunned Americans gave way and withdrew back through Büllingen, fighting as they retreated. Peiper took the town, whose organized defense collapsed after the engineers pulled back. Scattered fighting took place in the confusion that followed. Peiper was able to capture a large amount of fuel (he claimed 50,000 gallons), allowing him to refuel all his tanks.

Although Büllingen had not been on his rollbahn originally, Peiper had been adapting to the circumstances and modifying his route from the start, either under orders or on his own initiative. The city of Büllingen, with its complex road network, caused some confusion as some elements of Kampfgruppe Peiper wandered off in the wrong direction upon continuing their advance.

By 0900, Peiper's column had resumed its breakthrough westward, with various elements branching off from the main road, seeking the best available tracks for the panzers. An American artillery barrage struck Peiper's extended column while in Büllingen, as did an attack by American P-47 fighter-bomber aircraft.[237] Both efforts caused some delay and losses; the SS column pressed ahead.

Having received the alert from First Army in the early hours of Sunday, Anderson at the 1111th Group headquarters had been directing the establishment of more active defensive measures in his area, but had not issued orders to cease the routine road-maintenance, quarrying, and sawmill work. The FUSA alert "advising of the possibility of a large-scale enemy attack accompanied by paratroopers"[238] had stopped short of declaring that an actual attack was underway.

Accordingly, most of the engineers began the day in their scattered work parties, as they had the previous several weeks. The engineers engaged in road and lumber jobs east and southeast of Malmedy soon noted the heavy concentration of west- and northwest-bound traffic, including combat vehicles and troop transports, not just the routine Army support vehicles. A withdrawal from the front line was underway.

One platoon leader, Lieutenant Frank Rhea, 3rd Platoon, Company A, 291st ECB, asked an MP west of Bütgenbach what was going on, and was told the Germans had broken through and were heading in their direction. Rhea noted American fighter-bombers were bombing and strafing the enemy to the east; these were likely the same P-47 Thunderbolts attacking Peiper's column in Büllingen. Rhea collected men from the work parties and returned to his Company B headquarters in Malmedy.

Gamble's Company A had a similar experience. The company first sergeant, William Smith, noticed the same air attack happening, this time from the vantage of Amblève, seven miles southwest of Büllingen. Smith drove closer to investigate, then hastily reported back to Gamble upon seeing Peiper's column of panzers approaching (probably in the vicinity of Möderscheid).

Shortly thereafter, company personnel reported panzers not just to the northeast (Peiper) but to the east and southeast as well— Kampfgruppe Hansen, whose rollbahn E ran through Amblève. Company A quickly found itself amid a massive confusion of vehicles. Frontline troops from the 99th Infantry Division, 106th Infantry Division, and 14th Cavalry Group, after a valiant defense on Saturday, had been overwhelmed on Sunday, and were in full—and often disorderly—retreat. They poured westward, clogging the road network that was never designed to handle such traffic.

Adding to the confusion and congestion, US 7th Armored Division had been activated late Saturday night,[239] and sent into the area from the north to help stem the German attack, on the chance that it was more than a local action. Not knowing of the breakthrough, these units filled the roads leading south toward St. Vith, but not in combat formations; 7th Armored was moving into the area, not attacking.

Into the midst of this disarray, the SS columns suddenly appeared. Both Peiper's and Hansen's kampfgruppes, spread over multiples roads, were trying their best to race along their respective rollbahns. SS wolves amid herds of panicked American sheep, they shot and machine-gunned disorganized Americans as they continued along their routes. According to Reynolds in *Men of Steel*, "By midday Hansen's leading elements were 5km to the south of Peiper's and only a short distance behind them. The Leibstandarte had accomplished its breakthrough."[240]

Gamble collected his partial company (Walter's 1st Platoon was in Grand-Halleux, out of direct contact and as yet unaware of the developing crisis), as well as various stragglers escaping the front, and made his way back to battalion headquarters in Haute-Bodeux. Such was the chaos encountered by Gamble and his company—who had been directly fired upon by the Germans—that the twenty-mile drive from Amblève to Trois-Ponts took more than eight hours.

Midmorning Sunday, Anderson received additional, unsettling news. At 1005, his liaison officer assigned to V Corps headquarters in Elsenborn, Captain Richard Carville (the 1111th's S-2, or intelligence section head), called on the telephone net. Carville reported that "enemy tanks had penetrated [their] lines and were in the vicinity of the CP [command post] of 629th Engr Lt Equip Co north of Bütgenbach."[241] Bütgenbach was also where the valiant 99th Infantry Division's headquarters was located.

The news would have been daunting as Anderson surveyed the situation; this new development placed him squarely in the middle of an extremely exposed and perilous position. Although the extent of the breakthrough was not yet known, the fact that the Germans had punched through the 99th Infantry Division represented a major danger. With a large part of First Army's front gone, and with German forces now rampaging toward him, no organized infantry, armor, or artillery defenders stood in their path. No reserves were maintained, as the Roer Dam offensive had shifted all available units to the northeast.[242]

Only Anderson's handful of engineers, scattered across sixty miles of forested terrain, barred movement to the northwest. He knew he had no support and no heavy weapons; with only a few bazookas and machine guns, he would soon be facing the German forces that had apparently rolled over two entire divisions in front of him.

Anderson did not hesitate. With a lifetime of experience, six weeks of area knowledge, and skilled, confident troops under him, he knew he held an advantage that no armored force could overcome: he held the bridges; the panzers would need those bridges to cross the Ardennes.

Two of his four engineer battalions were effectively out of position to the northeast. His light equipment company was already withdrawing in front of the German advance. Only the 291st ECB, under Dave Pergrin, and farther back, the 51st, under new commander Harvey Fraser, were positioned to block any advance.

He called Pergrin as soon as the warning arrived from Carville.[243] Anderson directed Pergrin to "proceed to Malmedy, ascertain the situation, establish road blocks, and take charge of the defense of Malmedy, Belgium, as no other combat units [were] known to be in the immediate vicinity at that time."[244] Pergrin wrote that Anderson had called and advised, "The *boches* are loose east of Malmedy. Take the necessary action to defend."[245] By referring to the Germans using a dismissive, disparaging WWI term, Anderson may have been trying to convey and instill confidence, as if to say, "We have faced German threats before, and we beat them. We will do the same today."

While a good part of First Army was pulling back, Anderson directed his forces *forward* on his own initiative to establish defensive positions in that gap, while he himself remained directly in the Germans' path, at Trois-Ponts, with his eighty-man staff of clerks and administrative personnel. At this point, Pergrin had only scattered troops himself, with elements of just one company at Malmedy. Anderson's orders were of his own authority; First Army had issued no such guidance.

Anderson told Pergrin of the danger to the 629th Engineer Light Equipment Company, which had been directed to fall back on Malmedy. Pergrin was to take charge of all these scattered 1111th units, which included the 962nd Engineer Maintenance Company, already in the town.

Pergrin immediately headed for Malmedy and began repositioning his Company B to defend the town. He reported back to Anderson on his progress in establishing roadblocks and defensive points throughout the Malmedy area. By now the 291st's Company A (Gamble) had returned and been ordered by Pergrin to head farther back to Werbomont. While major elements of First Army retreated westward through Malmedy, Pergrin was establishing a defense with less than 130 men and no heavy weapons. They had not wired any bridges for demolition, as they had an insufficient quantity of explosives as yet.

The assault on December 17 east of Bütgenbach that had been reported to Anderson had been conducted by the forces supporting Hitlerjugend Division (12th SS Panzer), not Leibstandarte. Although forced back, the American front was still intact, largely due to the veteran US 2nd Infantry Division, which had been positioned to launch their own offensive, unknown to the Germans. After the initial surprise, the Americans were able to mount a furious defense in the area, with combined infantry, armor, and artillery forces repelling the Germans with heavy losses. While Hitlerjugend was thus blunted attempting to take Elsenborn Ridge, Leibstandarte continued to slice westward, just to the south.

Paralleling Peiper to the south, Kampfgruppe Hansen, with Schnellgruppe Knittel trailing, continued on their rollbahn until confronted by an armored force of 14th Cavalry at Recht. After a fierce fight in the afternoon, Hansen paused for the night.

That left Kampfgruppe Peiper still unchecked and virtually unopposed. Departing Büllingen southwestward, Peiper's column continued to Möderscheid, then northwest to Schoppen. The kampfgruppe was determined and confident. They felt "there were no American combat units deployed anywhere on Peiper's planned route to prevent him reaching the Meuse river."[246] The column swept west from Schoppen to Odenval along the more direct yet smaller tracks. Skirting south of the major towns (Faymonville and Waimes) to avoid being bogged down, Peiper continued west to Thirimont, reaching the village at around noon.

THIRIMONT

At Thirimont Peiper's SS troops had their first direct contact with Anderson's engineers. The SS panzers shot up a 291st ECB, Company A, 3rd Platoon truck as it tried to make its way north to Malmedy for refueling; the soldiers escaped and returned south to Captain Gamble to report. Around the same time, a reconnaissance patrol from the 291st's Company B out of Malmedy spotted Peiper's column to the south and reported back to Pergrin in Malmedy; they had counted sixty-eight tanks and combat vehicles. Pergrin duly reported this information back to Colonel Anderson; Anderson, in turn, advised Pergrin of new security procedures—no use of radios to contact the group headquarters, only telephone and messenger.

With this news, Anderson now knew he faced yet another threat, this time from southeast of Malmedy. And in this instance, the German panzers appeared to be "running free" without any opposition. The German attack looked more extensive with every passing hour.

Peiper sent some of his column directly west from Thirimont toward Ligneuville, on forest tracks unsuited for panzers. Peiper had learned from a captured American officer that Ligneuville was an American headquarters of some type, and he was eager to take the town and capture anything of intelligence or logistic value. He sent his spitze north to Baugnez via Bagatelle, in a roundabout effort to make for Ligneuville from the north on the N23 highway, a road more useable by armored vehicles. The road conditions eventually forced his entire column along this routing—to the north, then south along the N23, through Ligneuville, to continue its advance westward.

Back in Malmedy, the withdrawal of American forces continued, eventually leaving Pergrin and his handful of engineers in sole possession of the town. His efforts to add to his paltry command from the scattered groups passing through the town were fruitless; he and his small band of engineers were the only troops with orders or inclination to stay and defend. Nevertheless, Pergrin continued to bolster his position in Malmedy, as he sought to defend the town and the area surrounding.

In early afternoon, he radioed back to his battalion headquarters for his Company C under Captain Lawrence Moyer to be sent forward to reinforce his meager defenders. Significantly, he also ordered Moyer to establish a roadblock south of Stavelot, on the bridge approach. Stavelot was five miles southwest of Malmedy, midway on the N23 toward Trois-Ponts. In midafternoon, he radioed again to Haute-Bodeux for his battalion to "send him all the ammunition and explosives, mines and wiring, they could spare."[247] Anderson had ordered him to defend Malmedy, and Pergrin intended to stay and fight with everything he could lay his hands on.

The scattered advance of US 7th Armored Division into the area continued as well. Around noon, one of these units passed through Malmedy, southbound. Battery B, 285th Field Artillery Observation Battalion, under the command of Lieutenant Virgil Lary and accompanied by a routing officer, Captain Mills, were ordered to move through Malmedy south to St. Vith. Although Pergrin warned them of the German panzers in the area, the officers chose to continue their assigned route. The small column of lightly armed artillery observers in about thirty unarmored vehicles reached Baugnez (known to the engineers as "Five Points"), turning south on the N23 highway around 1300 hours.

The American column passed the Baugnez crossroads and continued southbound just as Peiper's spearhead, led by SS-Obersturmführer (Lieutenant) Werner Sternebeck, commander of the spitze, was heading north along the parallel smaller road less than a half mile to the east. The SS element of two Mk IV panzers and two SPW halftracks were rigged for combat; the Americans were not. As the American jeeps and trucks came into view, moving in the opposite direction, the Germans opened fire across the field separating the two formations.

After a short one-sided firefight, the Americans surrendered and were herded into a field near the crossroads. Peiper, further back in the column, contacted Sternebeck and ordered him to continue to Ligneuville, pressing ahead as he had done previously and leaving the American captives to be handled by trailing Germans.

As Kampfgruppe Peiper circled north to Baugnez, then south to Ligneuville, there occurred what became known as the Malmedy Massacre:[248] more than 100 unarmed American prisoners were suddenly shot down by their guards and bypassing panzers of the kampfgruppe. Dozens escaped, but around seventy were killed, either outright or execution-style by the SS. Although this was the most extreme example, the incident was by no means an isolated case. Peiper likely wasn't on the scene for the killing, and probably did not directly order it, but the "ground rules" his men followed were well established and commonly understood: for the SS, killing prisoners was an acceptable act.

About two miles up the N23 highway and on higher ground, Pergrin in Malmedy heard the sudden eruption of firing, and drove to investigate. Escapees from the massacre began to filter up the road toward Malmedy and were recovered by Pergrin and his men; more continued to trickle in throughout the next day. Pergrin reported directly to First Army the details of the atrocity he was able to collect from the survivors.

Peiper pressed on. His column fought its way into Ligneuville, entering the town from the north, from Baugnez. The American defenders there (elements of the 49th Anti-Aircraft Artillery [AAA] Brigade and others) were surprised yet offered a brief, fierce fight before their unsupported efforts collapsed and they retreated.[249]

In Ligneuville, Peiper stopped to consolidate and reorganize his column, which was in some disarray due to the combat and diffused advance over the previous few hours. Throughout the day, he had launched scattered probes along various paths, tracks, and roads as he sought the best way forward. In Ligneuville, Peiper now organized his spitze to be led by a company of Mk V Panthers.

In the late afternoon, Peiper again sent his column forward, resuming its movement westward, albeit at a slow pace as the light faded, along "narrow, icy, tree-lined, and twisting roads."[250] The kampfgruppe track took it through Pont, Beaumont, and Lodomez, approaching Stavelot from the high ground to the southeast. Peiper himself lingered behind to organize, interrogate captured Americans, and to meet with his commander, 1st-SS Panzer Leibstandarte Adolph Hitler Division leader Wilhelm Mohnke, who had moved into the breakthrough zone with an advance headquarters element.

⚒

Midafternoon Sunday, some aspects of the situation became clearer to Anderson in Trois-Ponts. The expected breakthrough east of Malmedy at Bütgenbach, which galvanized Anderson to commit Pergrin to Malmedy's defense, never materialized. The northern sector of First Army appeared to be holding the shoulder along Elsenborn Ridge. (The capture of this terrain feature was a battlefield objective of the 12th SS Panzer Division, Hitlerjugend.)

However, the situation southeast of Trois-Ponts and Malmedy was a different story. The First Army units there, in the ten-mile gap between Bütgenbach and St. Vith, appeared to have collapsed and were retreating in great haste. SS panzers were loose, driving deeper while committing atrocities against defending Americans.

First Army was in a crisis that extended all the way up to the commander, Lieutenant General Courtney Hodges: "Midday on Sunday he closed his office door in the Britannique [hotel, in Spa, location of First Army headquarters, north of Stavelot], sat at his desk, and laid his head on his arms. He took no calls, and for the better part of two days showed symptoms of incapacitation."[251] Hodges, the only senior US officer in theater to have been an enlisted soldier and to have seen close infantry combat in WWI, seemed to suffer a temporary failure of leadership.

With frontline combat units streaming westward through Trois-Ponts, to retreat with them was a natural point of discussion for the engineers in the town. Anderson was asked by a staff member if the 1111th was going to withdraw with all the other Army units presently escaping to the rear areas. His reply was that of a patient and determined leader, reminding his nervous juniors of a simple fact: "We have come several thousand miles to fight these Nazis—not to withdraw from them."[252]

The response reveals layers of leadership principles that are simple in concept yet difficult to achieve under stress in a crisis.

Leaders often are called upon to remind their charges of the job at hand; this is especially true when difficulties or dangers arise and the temptation to take an expedient or convenient lesser path emerges. Anderson's statement reminded them of the training and preparation the engineers had undergone, specifically to meet the challenges they now faced. And that with this capability comes an expectation and obligation—their country sent them to fight.

Finally, Anderson knew that although his young troops had months of combat support and related experience, they had not yet faced direct attacks as were now looming. A good leader projects that which he expects of those around him: Anderson's reply was one of quiet determination and resolve. There was no indication of surprise or anything other than calm matter-of-factness.

Anderson in Trois-Ponts tracked the developments in Malmedy, as relayed by Pergrin. With that battalion commander personally directing the action forward, Captain Edward Lampp managed the remaining 291st elements in and around Haute-Bodeux. Lampp reported to Anderson in midafternoon and discussed the situation. Anderson approved the move to Malmedy by the 291st's Company C, which was to also establish a roadblock south of the Stavelot bridge.

Anderson modified Moyer's orders: He was to leave a squad in Trois-Ponts to guard the Amblève bridges there immediately, until a more substantial force could be brought up. This move reflects Anderson's judgment that the approaching SS column presented a serious threat; with only headquarters and staff personnel, the group's position in Trois-Ponts was extremely vulnerable. The official group report states, "The situation became more serious and it was apparent that the breakthrough had not been blocked, but instead was extending towards the MALMEDY—STAVELOT—TROIS-PONTS area."[253]

Having sent Pergrin to establish a defensive posture along the Malmedy-Stavelot line, and upon hearing reports that the German armor could be expected anywhere south and southwest of Malmedy, Anderson sought to extend the defensive barriers and focus his forces on the bridge crossings. He knew that although there were no American positions other than his, the Germans would have to come to him, eventually, if they wanted to continue to the northwest, behind First Army. Moreover, Anderson knew that help was coming, and it would come from the north.

Anderson had of course no knowledge of the German plan, but he was well aware of First Army and Allied troop dispositions, and of the danger a German drive toward Antwerp west of Liège represented. He planned his defensive strategy accordingly. If he could prevent the Germans from crossing the Amblève and thrusting northwest, they would be forced to head in a more northerly direction. This would take them directly into the face of expected American reinforcements.

With an enormous area to screen, Anderson picked two river crossings at which to concentrate his scant forces. Pergrin was established in Malmedy, although he was able to muster less than half his battalion. The force was inadequate, to be sure, but give the fragmented starting situation, it was a remarkable effort. Pergrin energetically fortified the town and its bridge and road network. Next along the line was Trois-Ponts. Anderson had placed his headquarters there to sit astride the natural confluence of road, river, and rail lines of communications. Anderson determined to make his stand in Trois-Ponts.

Sunday, in the darkness after dusk, Peiper's spitze made its way along the high ground approaching Stavelot from the southeast. Author David Cooke writes, "Moving slowly along the narrow Rue du Vieux Château, with a steep hill to its left, and a precipitous drop into the river valley to its right, the lead tank was crawling around a sharp corner, when a shout of 'Halt!' challenged them."[254]

The 291st's Company C, under Captain Lawrence Moyer, had begun to move by late afternoon, with enough elements of his scattered command having been gathered to La Gleize, the company headquarters. Directed by Pergrin to help defend Malmedy, Moyer made his assignments for two of his three available platoons.[255] He directed Lieutenant Donald Davis to proceed to Malmedy with 1st Platoon, which Moyer himself would accompany. Lieutenant Warren Rombaugh, 2nd Platoon leader, would take about two squads to Trois-Ponts, providing Anderson with much-needed manpower to prepare an immediate defense there, working with the group staff, which had begun to establish machine-gun and bazooka defensive positions. The remaining 2nd Platoon squad would establish the roadblock above Stavelot bridge.

For the Stavelot roadblock, Rombaugh assigned Sergeant Charles Hensel and twelve men. They took a single truck loaded with a .30-caliber medium machine gun, some demolitions (although not enough to blow up a road bridge, there was sufficient quantity to knock over trees), some mines, a bazooka, and assorted ammunition and demolitions equipment. Departing just before 1700 hours, they navigated the westbound traffic still fleeing the front lines. Hensel's truck arrived in Stavelot around 1830 (ninety minutes to travel a little more than six miles), finding the town crammed with vehicles escaping the German onslaught.

With extensive knowledge from having maintained roads in the region for six weeks, the engineers knew the area intimately, and knew where a roadblock would be most effective on the road that approached the Stavelot bridge from the south. Rombaugh had given Hensel precise direction on where to place his position. Accompanying Hensel and his squad was (likely) Lieutenant Cliff Wilson, the battalion's assistant motor-transport officer. Wilson had been detailed by Captain Lampp to direct Hensel where to place his men and mines, then to return to Haute-Bodeux. Wilson and Hensel chose a spot where the road was cut from the rock cliff face, as the hill dropped steeply down to the Amblève River. An armored column would have to come straight down the road, with no room to maneuver or outflank a defender.

Hensel had his men place about a dozen antitank mines atop the road, around a curve and thus out of sight to any oncoming panzer until it rounded the curve and was on top of the (hopefully unavoidable) mines. He established his bazooka team behind the mines, and his machine gun behind them. Hensel sent Private Bernard Goldstein up the road in front, as sentry. Goldstein, a big, rangy man with wide shoulders, hailed from Brooklyn; Hensel likely deemed him a good choice to first face any oncoming Germans. It was a wise decision. Hensel turned the truck around so it faced back downtown toward Stavelot. He figured if he needed to clear out, he should be able to do so quickly.

Less than an hour after Hensel prepared his position, at around 1930 hours, Peiper's lead panzers inched forward in the darkness, down the hill toward the stone bridge that crossed the Amblève and into Stavelot. The panzers carried infantry on their decks, anticipating a fight for the bridge. As the panzer column approached the cliff along the road, Private Goldstein heard the engines and the voices of the riding soldiers, stepped out from a small hut along the road, and with his M1 rifle at the ready shouted a sentry's command to Kampfgruppe Peiper: "Halt!"

Astoundingly, the panzers complied. Then all hell broke loose. The lead panzer opened fire with machine guns and then its main gun, a 75 mm cannon. Goldstein somehow managed to avoid getting shot, and ran up the steep slope to the west, escaping unscathed from surely one of the most lopsided encounters imaginable.

Hensel had been approaching Goldstein from behind, bringing a second man to place as an additional sentry. These two heard Goldstein's "Halt!" and the panzer engines. They threw themselves to the ground, fired a couple rifle shots, then ran back around the curve. The bazooka team fired one round blindly in the commotion.

Hensel gathered his squad around and behind the curves, and waited for the panzers, and for the absent Goldstein. He sent men forward to try to locate Goldstein, but the Germans were still present along the cliffside road. After a twenty-minute wait, Hensel decided to head back down the hill to the bridge.

Peiper's column, stopped by a single rifleman's challenge, an errant bazooka round, and a few hurried rifle shots in the dark, now waited. They had been in recurring running combat for more than twelve hours, and now showed signs of fatigue and faltering aggression.

Ahead in the darkness lay Americans armed and apparently willing to fight; everything else was unknown. From their vantage point above the town, the Germans could see and hear a hive of activity, with hundreds of vehicles moving about the town below, although in the dark the SS men could not know that all of this involved units retreating in near panic.

Peiper came up the column and, reaching the lead panzers, decided to bring up more forces to take Stavelot, and to pause to rest. A further push down the hill to take the bridge would require a coordinated assault by infantry, armor, and supported by artillery; the spitze spearhead racing forward would no longer suffice. Peiper delayed above Stavelot, choosing to rest and organize—not unreasonably, given the state of his troops and column. The delay sealed the fate of his kampfgruppe.

Private Bernard Goldstein of Brooklyn—still unaccounted for—had done his part to save the American army.

In the early evening of Sunday, Anderson activated another element of his command. The 202nd ECB had been attached to the 1111th on December 11 and was in place around Spa to support the push against the Roer dams by December 13. One part of that command, Company C, under the acting command of Lieutenant Joe Chinlund, was in Stavelot when the Germans launched their offensive.

The 202nd was a somewhat unknown quantity, having only recently been attached. Anderson does not mention them at all in his reminisces, nor does the 1111th make any detailed mention of the 202nd in official reporting. Others offer confused and contradictory accounts; not surprising, given the coming events.

As best as can be pieced together, Anderson sent orders for 202nd ECB Company C to rig the Stavelot bridge for demolition. It is possible this happened because the company, isolated from its higher battalion headquarters, prudently decided to pull back with all the other First Army units that were retreating westward through Stavelot. Upon reaching Trois-Ponts, however, and coming to the attention of Colonel Anderson, they were stopped and ordered to return to Stavelot, to mine the bridge there for destruction.

Lieutenant Chinlund took his company back to Stavelot to prepare the bridge Sunday night, around the time Hensel and his men were returning from their confrontation with Peiper's column. Hensel and his small group arrived back at the Stavelot bridge at around 2100 hours, whereupon he encountered the 202nd engineers working at the bridge. Hensel was debriefed by Captain Lloyd Sheetz, the 291st battalion staff officer assigned as liaison officer to group headquarters; Pergrin had sent him from Malmedy back to Trois-Ponts Sunday night to brief Anderson on the improving situation in Malmedy.

In Stavelot, having briefed Sheetz, and with 202nd engineers on the scene as well as Lieutenant Wilson (the 291st officer who had previously directed the establishment of their now-abandoned roadblock), Hensel then returned to Trois-Ponts to rejoin his Company C, 2nd Platoon officer, Lieutenant Rombaugh.

Thus, by midnight, the engineers knew that Peiper was close by, above Stavelot. However, in the confusion that reigned in Stavelot that night, specific information about Peiper's close proximity above Stavelot was not passed up to higher authorities, including Anderson.

As First Army in Spa became aware of the general threat posed by the nearby SS panzers, combat units in reserve were rousted and sent south. However, the thinking was that Malmedy was more severely threatened, not Stavelot. Despite Hensel having directly confronted Peiper's SS panzers less than 2,500 yards from the Stavelot bridge, the bulk of First Army's reinforcements were sent to Malmedy. Stavelot remained only lightly defended, with Peiper's column poised above.

Throughout Sunday Anderson "received numerous reports of enemy activity in all directions."[256] With such a vital and extensive network to cover, Anderson realized on Sunday afternoon that the mere squad he had called for from the 291st (Rombaugh's platoon elements) would be insufficient to hold Trois-Ponts. He was determined to stop the panzers from crossing at his headquarters. He would stand fast, but he would need more defenders. And with a powerful, mobile force of murderous SS approaching, he would need them quickly.

Twenty miles southwest of Trois-Ponts, the next major bridge town was Hotton, on the Ourthe River, another tributary that fed north, joining the Meuse at Liège. With his 51st ECB located nearby at Marche-en-Famenne, Anderson could quickly position this battalion to cover the important crossings along the Ourthe. As with the Amblève, the Ourthe had minor bridge points along its length, stretching southeast from Hotton.

At around 1600, Anderson transmitted orders to Lieutenant Colonel Harvey Fraser, the commanding officer of the 51st ECB, who Anderson had placed into the job only about seventy-two hours prior, to do two things: "Colonel Anderson orders you to send one company to Trois-Ponts to defend and prepare the bridges there for destruction and to set up a barrier line along the Ourthe River from Hotton to Bastogne—only about 20 miles."[257] Anderson ordered the 51st company to bring "a maximum supply of demolitions, mines, bazookas, and machine guns" to Trois-Ponts.[258]

Fraser reacted quickly, justifying the confidence Anderson had recently placed in him. As with the other engineering units under Anderson's command that Sunday morning, the 51st was scattered throughout a wide area, engaged in sawmill and road-maintenance operations. Collecting these troops and redirecting them to a combat posture began immediately. Fraser was in charge, but most of the troops and officers had served with and been trained by Anderson, going back to the summer of 1942 for some, including the intense winter in Plattsburgh. These were men Anderson personally knew and could count on.

Fraser gave the Trois-Ponts assignment to Company C and Captain Sam Scheuber. Scheuber had joined the 51st ECB in July 1943; although he had just missed the training in Plattsburgh that contributed so greatly to the unit's personality, he had been with the battalion for a considerable time, and had commanded his company since before the Normandy invasion. Scheuber began recalling his scattered troop elements from over three dozen sites running sawmill and lumber operations.

A Company C advance party departed Melreux (northeast of Marche) around 2100 Sunday and arrived in Trois-Ponts ninety minutes later. The main body of the company trailed by about an hour, with the final elements reaching Trois-Ponts in the early-morning hours of Monday. During their road movement to Trois-Ponts, the company passed by a large volume of First Army elements moving the opposite direction, away from the Germans. Lieutenant Joseph Milgram, leader of Company C's 3rd Platoon, observed, "Although it was pitch black, our eyes had grown somewhat used to seeing and it seemed to us that every conceivable kind of vehicle including tanks, tank destroyers, artillery pieces in tow, command cars, jeeps, and trucks was coming the other way, bumper to bumper, sliding off the road and having all sorts of trouble moving. And here we were idiots, heading east."[259]

When the 51st's Company C arrived, Anderson released Lieutenant Rombaugh and his 291st Company C, 2nd Platoon element back to La Gleize, to act as a standby force. Rombaugh's small force had screened Trois-Ponts for a few critical hours. Anderson was no doubt acutely aware of how thin his forces were; he might yet need to send troops to critical junctions, with little warning.

Anderson immediately set Scheuber's company to the task of preparing Trois-Ponts for the expected panzer assault. He directed Scheuber to set up roadblock positions east of the town on the N23 road. With approximately 140 men, six .50-cal machine guns, eight bazookas, and four .30-cal machine guns, the company commander began to establish positions along the west bank of the Salm, and to further bolster the positions begun earlier by Anderson's staff elements and Rombaugh's men.

Anderson further directed Scheuber to prepare the Trois-Ponts bridges for demolition. Two main bridges controlled east-west travel. As the Amblève curved in from the east along the town's north end, it had two parallel bridges over it, a road bridge and, atop a twenty-foot-high embankment, a dual-track railroad bridge. Just west of these two bridges, the Salm joined the Amblève as it curved north. The N23 road from Stavelot paralleled the Amblève's north bank. With the road bridge blown, vehicular travel would be forced to bear to the north on the N33 along with shifts in direction of the river.

The second critical bridge was over the Salm, in town center, at the T-junction of the N33 and N23 roads. While the Amblève was somewhat wider, the Salm was narrow, only thirty feet across. However, with its steep ten-foot banks cut into the stony ground, the Salm was an effective barrier to tanks. Vehicles transiting westward through Trois-Ponts must cross the Salm bridge.

Anderson had his engineers prepare three additional bridges. South of town, on the road from Vielsalm (N28, an offshoot from the north-south N33), a road bridge crossed the Salm. This was not considered to be as important, as no Germans had yet been reported in the vicinity of Vielsalm, ten miles south of Trois-Ponts. Another bridge, southeast of town, was an N33 road bridge over a train track as it emerged from a tunnel and entered Trois-Ponts rail station from the south. Again, this bridge posed no immediate threat to an east-west crossing, but dropping the bridge would inhibit any potential German vehicular movement east of the Salm. Finally, a footbridge crossed the Salm on the southern end of town. Although this bridge could not support panzers, Anderson wanted to stop all easy access to the town by the SS, even for foot soldiers.

Finally, during the night of December 17, Anderson discussed the situation directly via radio with the First Army engineer, Colonel Bill Carter. Concerned about Anderson's exposed position, given the SS sightings, Carter directed Anderson to shift 1111th Engineer Combat Group farther back, to Modave, fully thirty-four miles to the rear. Although the details from this conversation—and orders—are not known, the actions Anderson took are revealing; he would only depart his post after dealing with the "*boches*." Expecting a panzer column to bear down on him in the morning, Wallis Anderson was not going anywhere.

Meanwhile, Lieutenant Colonel David Pergrin's isolated, daylong stand in Malmedy at last received some assistance. According to Pergrin, "Unknown to me, my messages through 1111th Group to 1st Army headquarters throughout December 17 were having a chilling effect upon the top Allied military leaders in Europe."[260] Although First Army commander General Hodges was having a personal crisis, by Sunday evening his staff were responding to the German attack and began to send scattered reinforcements into the area.

At around 2200 hours, First Army sent an independent unit from Army headquarters in Spa to Malmedy: the 99th Infantry Battalion (separate), a force of 900 comprised of Norwegian-speaking soldiers (Norwegians who had fled Germany's occupation of Norway earlier in the war, and Norwegian-Americans). This welcome formation began to immediately bolster the defenses in and around the town. Although Pergrin had not been attacked, his solitary post had been subjected throughout the day to reconnaissance probes, which had been repelled, indicating to the Germans that Malmedy was defended, and therefore to be bypassed; Pergrin's 150 men with light weapons had successfully screened the vulnerability of First Army.

Had Anderson—on his own—not sent Pergrin to establish

defensive positions before noon, the German taking of an undefended Malmedy would have severely threatened First Army's defense of the high ridge behind Bütgenbach, as well as directly endangering Army headquarters in Spa, a scant nine miles northwest of Malmedy. Loss of Malmedy would have undermined First Army's entire defensive position.

As midnight Sunday passed, Anderson's busy day had produced some startling results, although the full significance was yet to be revealed. The day began with his four battalions engaged in three separate activities: the 296th, 202nd, and elements of the 291st were at or moving into position to support ongoing offensive actions against the Roer dams to the northeast; the remainder of the 291st and the 51st were carrying out wood-mill, logging, and road-maintenance work; finally, due to the alerts, active security measures were established throughout the area for key road and bridge points under the threat of German parachutists and saboteurs or limited spoiling attacks. His arc of responsibility was massive; most of his engineers had been greatly dispersed into squad-sized elements and work parties.

When news of the German breakthrough reached him, Anderson reacted decisively. Throughout the day, multiple reports indicated that his post, twenty-five miles behind the front lines only one day before, stood squarely in the apparent path of the panzers. He provided clear and resolute guidance: Hold the key bridge towns and blow the bridges as necessary to stop the Germans. He placed his best battalion commander at one flank and a new yet promising commander at the other, while he remained in the most critical center.

The stage was set. The ruthless SS panzer commander had marshaled his powerful column above Stavelot, ready to break through the thin, makeshift defensive line there, and to continue his advance. He was behind schedule, but he had not yet been confronted by a sizable, organized defense. The Americans were still reeling. Punching through at Stavelot would lead his kampfgruppe to Trois-Ponts. According to Peiper, "If we had captured the bridge at

Trois-Ponts intact and had enough fuel, it would have been a simple matter to drive through to the Meuse River early that day."[261]

In Malmedy and at Stavelot, the defenses consisted primarily of infantry units, under infantry officers, with engineers in support. In Trois-Ponts, however, only the 1111th's engineers were present, with Colonel Anderson commanding.

ENDNOTES

230   Janice Giles, *The Damned Engineers*, 57.

231   Likely from or through 1111th communications officer Second Lieutenant G. R. Donelson.

232   Wilhelm Weiss, editor, *Standartenführer Joachim Peiper, The Interview*, 81. On the other side of the planned collaboration with Skorzeny's operators, Peiper was dismissive and disdainful of this special effort, stating in a postwar interview, "They might just as well have stayed at home, because they were never near the head of the column where they had planned to be."

233   Ibid, 178.

234   Michael Reynolds, *Men of Steel*, 61. Peiper's troops were later charged with killing some fifteen American prisoners of war at Honsfeld.

235   David Cooke and Wayne Evans, *Kampfgruppe Peiper at the Battle of the Bulge*, Mechanicsburg, PA: Stackpole Books, 2008, 42.

236   The 254th was operating under the 1171st ECG, a corps-level engineer group assigned to support V Corps of FUSA.

237   These aircraft were from the 366th Fighter Group, Ninth US Air Force. The tactical air force weather summary for December 17 reads, "Overcast clouds, bases 1000 to 2000 feet, with intermittent rain. Visibility 3 to 5 miles." Marvin D. Kays, *Weather Effects During the Battle of the Bulge and the Normandy Invasion*, 19. While not particularly well suited for flying, this weather would allow for tactical sorties.

238   Unit History, 1111th Engineer Combat Group, 17 December 1944.

239   Outside Paris at Supreme Headquarters Allied Expeditionary Force (SHAEF), Eisenhower had read the scattered reports coming in from the Ardennes and viewed them in a more serious light than did his visiting guest, Twelfth Army Group commander Omar Bradley; Eisenhower directed Bradley to send 7th Armored Division to St. Vith.

240   Michael Reynolds, *Men of Steel*, 63.

241   Unit History, 1111th Engineer Combat Group, 17 December 1944.

242   The HQ Twelfth Army Group (Bradley) situation map for 16 December 1944 lists only one German infantry division (incorrectly identified) opposite the US 99th and 106th Infantry Divisions. Behind the 99th ID are listed zero US forces, all the way to Antwerp.

243   Anderson would have likely used his call sign, "Missouri," while Pergrin at the 291st would have used "Missouri-Baker." Similarly, the 51st ECB was designated "Missouri-Dog." First US Army Telephone Code Name Directory, Amendment No.1, 27 July 1944.

244   Unit History, 1111th Engineer Combat Group, 17 December 1944.

245   Janice Giles, *The G.I. Journal of Sergeant Giles* (Boston: Houghton Mifflin Company, 1965), 206. Anderson's use of the WWI slang, a disparaging term for Germans—*boches*, or "blockheads" —was not uncommon; his contempt for the Germans, who had now involved him in two world wars, was certain.

246   Michael Reynolds, *Men of Steel*, 67.

247   Janice Giles, *The Damned Engineers*, 182.

248   The Malmedy Massacre is an extremely well-documented event. Every major account of the Battle of the Bulge records the incident, and there are numerous books and articles dedicated to describing the episode. Peiper's name is forever tied to this brutal war crime.

249   David Cooke, *Kampfgruppe Peiper at the Battle of the Bulge*, 55. Peiper personally took part in the fighting, and tended to the wounds of one of his lieutenants suffered in forcing the entry into Ligneuville.

250   Michael Reynolds, *Men of Steel*, 69.

251   Rick Atkinson, *The Guns at Last Light*, 440.

252   Ken Hechler, *Holding the Line* (Fort Belvoir: United States Corps of Engineers, 1988), 16. The quote was relayed to Army historian Captain Hechler from Captain Sam Scheuber during an interview on February 23, 1945. Scheuber and his 51st ECB Company C did not arrive in Trois-Ponts until very late on December 17, as part of Anderson's effort to defend Trois-Ponts and to deny the Germans from using the westbound roads. Anderson's quote would indicate his intent earlier on Sunday, *before* definitive steps to defend Trois-Ponts had been taken, when the question as to whether the town was to be defended or abandoned was still in doubt. For this reason, the author believes the question and Anderson's reply were likely to have taken place midafternoon Sunday, before Scheuber and his company arrived. In fact, the exchange probably took place among Anderson and his staff, and likely happened before Lieutenant Rombaugh arrived to provide some semblance of defensive coverage at around 1400. The exchange probably was then relayed to Scheuber later.

253   Unit History, 1111th Engineer Combat Group, 17 December 1944.

254   David Cooke, *Kampfgruppe Peiper at the Battle of the Bulge*, 56.

255   Most of Moyer's Company C 3rd Platoon, under Lieutenant John Perkins, had been working in the Sourbrodt area northeast of Malmedy when the German offensive struck. As a result, the larger part of this platoon was isolated from the rest of the company and battalion, cut off from communications and involvement.

256   HWAMil, 38.

257   Barry Fowle, *The 51st Again!*, vi.

258   Janice Giles, *The Damned Engineers*, 225.

259   Albert Radford, *Unbroken Line*, 197.

260   David E. Pergrin, *First Across the Rhine*, 105.

261   Wilhelm Weiss, editor, *Standartenführer Joachim Peiper, The Interview*, 250.

CHAPTER THIRTEEN

COLLISION

December 18, 1944
Monday

T hroughout Sunday night and into the Monday predawn, the opposing sides prepared for what would be a decisive day. Senior levels of the US Army had begun to shift reinforcements into the area; it would take some time for these units to arrive, prepare, and engage the enemy. The window of opportunity for Hitler to tear the Allies apart was closing.

First Army units were alerted on Sunday; notably, the 30th Infantry Division began to pull off its eastward-facing positions north of Aachen and redirect its efforts south. Similarly, the 1st Infantry Division was ordered southeast to bolster the 2nd Infantry Division as it continued to hold off 12th SS Panzer (Hitlerjugend) Division.

Also on Sunday, Eisenhower took more measures to deal with the crisis, tasking XVIII Airborne Corps to move into the area to block the Germans. This corps was comprised of two veteran American airborne divisions, 82nd and 101st. Both were "recuperating and re-equipping in training camps near Rheims, France, from their recent heavy fighting in the Arnhem drop."[262] The paratroopers were not a designated reserve force, per se, but they were available. Both airborne divisions and their superior corps were in various stages of readiness, with much of their senior leadership absent for various assignments and leave.

The 82nd was more prepared; its commander, Major General James Gavin, was "dual-hatted" as acting head of XVIII Airborne Corps. The 82nd was notified, and the process of collecting the troops, equipping the division for combat, and finding transportation began and continued throughout Sunday. This organizing took time. The airborne units did not begin to move until Monday.

On the heights overlooking Stavelot, Jochen Peiper organized his kampfgruppe to force the bridge crossing and continue his drive to the Meuse. He still carried almost all his offensive capability, having only lost a handful or two of his panzers in the drive thus far, which had taken him twenty miles behind the American lines.

In Stavelot itself, disjointed efforts trickled into the town as various American army reinforcements tried to piece together a hasty defense to prevent a further German breakthrough, apparently unaware of the specific threat posed by Peiper.

Anderson too had spent an active night, preparing for the expected panzer assault. Weighing his limited manpower, time available, and areas to defend against likely outcomes, Anderson had to decide how best to use his resources. Aware that only 202nd ECB Company C was in the Stavelot, barely enough to offer even a perfunctory defense, and with Hensel's new information regarding panzers threatening the bridge there, Anderson committed additional men, such as he could spare. Around 0200, he ordered a platoon of the recently returned Company A of the 291st, under Captain Gamble, to Stavelot to assist with the defense. This move placed a more senior man, and one known and trusted by Anderson, to bolster the efforts of the much less familiar 202nd Company C.

Presumably, from his viewpoint a breakthrough at Stavelot would result in only one of two outcomes: the Germans would either proceed north, into the Army's reinforcements, in which case the strength of the US Army would prevail, or the Germans would continue west to Trois-Ponts, where he was much better prepared.

Meanwhile, scattered reserve units from First Army began to arrive along Malmedy-Stavelot. One of the first to move was the 526th Armored Infantry Battalion, from positions west of FUSA headquarters in Spa. The 526th AIB was a somewhat unusual unit. It was formed and organized as an independent battalion, not as a component of any higher regiment or division, and assigned various special tasks during the push across France, as directed by higher headquarters.

Under the command of Lieutenant Colonel Carlisle Irwin, the 526th traveled from the Remouchamps area to Malmedy, accompanied by a company of the 825th Tank Destroyer Battalion.[263] In Stavelot, a company from the former and a platoon from the latter peeled off to establish defensive positions. The executive officer of the 526th, Major Paul Solis, was placed in command, responsible for the defense of the town.

Gamble and his 3rd Platoon, under Lieutenant Archibald Taylor, arrived in Stavelot at around 0400 to reinforce the 202nd ECB, Company C roadblock, as ordered by Anderson. Company C had prepared the bridge, although they had merely dragged a daisy chain of linked antitank mines across it.

Gamble also encountered troops from the 526th and 825th, which Anderson knew nothing about, as First Army had not sent word of this move to Trois-Ponts. Further, Gamble became aware of a missing reconnaissance team sent by Lieutenant Wilson at around 0100 hours across the bridge, back up the hill toward the last known German positions. Wilson had sent his driver, Private Lorenzo Liparulo, and Private Goldstein, who had escaped his earlier encounter with Peiper's column and eventually made his way back down to the bridge.

During the night, this patrol had run into some of Peiper's SS troops, who were conducting a similar reconnaissance toward the bridge. Both Liparulo and Goldstein were seriously wounded, Liparulo mortally so. Goldstein, with three gunshot wounds, managed to crawl back down the hill.

Gamble and Taylor crossed the bridge and found the two wounded 291st soldiers. They evacuated the wounded, and decided to return to Trois-Ponts to brief Colonel Anderson, as the situation in Stavelot, now with a full company of infantry supported by tank destroyers defending, was significantly different from what they had expected.

Meanwhile, the reinforcements under Major Solis began to arrive piecemeal in Stavelot between 0300 and 0400 Monday. Solis set about to defend the town and bridge over the Amblève, although he appeared either to be unaware or to not fully appreciate the danger of Peiper's panzers. He planned to establish a roadblock on the high-ground approach south of the bridge and river, approximately where the 291st's Sergeant Hensel (and Private Goldstein) had stopped Peiper the night before.

The rest of his command Solis placed in the town to interdict the Germans should they break through his roadblock above the stone bridge; 291st ECB's Captain Sheetz was also in Stavelot, assisting the 526th with their defensive placement. Solis sent two infantry squads, a 57 mm antitank gun from the 526th, and two (of four) of the 825th's towed three-inch tank-destroyer guns to establish the roadblock. All these elements began to deploy between 0600 and 0630 hours, crossing the bridge to climb the hill.

✗

Across the river to the south, on the high ground overlooking Stavelot, Peiper spent the early hours of Monday preparing his assault. He anticipated a fight against a prepared enemy who, for the first time, would likely have some appreciable antitank capability. With his column collected now, Peiper reordered his forces for a strong push down the hill, as he fully expected to have to fight for the town and route west. He placed two companies of Mk V Panther panzers in the lead, supported by panzergrenadiers and pioneers.

Significantly, Peiper now had his artillery available, unlike his prior encounters, which were "running fights." For Stavelot, Peiper intended to bring more of the weight of his powerful SS column to bear; after that, he could again resort to a mobile armored race to reach the Meuse. As he had the day before, Peiper sent another column on a westerly alternate route, probing for any gaps in the Allied road network that he could exploit. He sent two companies of Mk IV panzers (with accompanying pioneers) along a looping, roundabout course through the hills toward Trois-Ponts via Wanne and Aisomont.

Major Solis's motor column ran directly into SS forces who were beginning to infiltrate down the hill in advance of Peiper's assault to take and cross the bridge. Losing the two 3-inch towed tank-destroyer guns and their half-tracks and crews, Solis pulled back and maintained defensive positions in town, across the bridge on the north bank of the Amblève. There he waited for the Germans. Peiper unleashed a mortar and artillery barrage, preparing his assault. The battle for Stavelot had begun before dawn on Monday.

In all, the six hours in Stavelot between midnight and 0600 Monday morning had been a swirl of confusion for the engineers under Anderson. During this period, he had sent elements of three companies from two battalions to the town. As dawn approached, only one remained, Lieutenant Chinlund's Company C, under the command of the 526th and Major Solis. The bridge was inadequately mined with only a thin chain of aboveground antitank mines.

In Trois-Ponts, less than four miles farther west, Colonel Wallis Anderson prepared a much more vigorous defense. Deep behind the front line only forty-eight hours previous, Anderson now commanded the last remaining barrier to the German thrust; behind his thin line of engineers holding the bridges stood no organized American defenders, all the way to Antwerp.

By dawn, Anderson's engineers (primarily Company C of the 51st ECB) in Trois-Ponts had prepared the two key road bridges over Amblève and Salm for destruction. Interestingly, Anderson mined none of the five rail bridges or viaducts north and south of town, as he had determined none could be used by the panzers. He left untouched a road overpass leading down from the heights east of the town, on an unpaved track that led to Wanne. Anderson judged this road span over the train tracks would not support an armored threat and did not cross a river in any case. He did not have the resources to destroy every pathway to Trois-Ponts, so he selected for destruction only those he judged capable of supporting tanks.[264]

As more of Company C's men arrived in town (having been recalled Sunday from their scattered previous locations around Marche), Anderson further directed their company commander, Captain Sam Scheuber, to prepare defensive positions around Trois-Ponts with machine guns, bazookas, and mines. Still concerned about the German paratrooper threat, Anderson sent out security details, patrolling the area for airborne commandos and saboteurs. Using whatever manpower he had available (now a mix of his own group staff plus 51st and 291st personnel), Anderson was preparing for anything the enemy might throw his way.

American convoys and scattered random vehicles were still transiting Trois-Ponts, heading both toward and away from the front. One such detachment was another of the 526th AIB elements, en route from Comblain-la-Tour to Malmedy. This small group consisted of a half-track towing a 57 mm antitank gun, with the gun's crew. In Trois-Ponts, the half-track slipped a track on the icy roads, temporarily stranding men of the 3rd Squad, 526th Company B Antitank Platoon. Well aware he had no substantial antitank weapons, Anderson countermanded their orders on the spot and commandeered the gun and crew. As the battle for Stavelot began up the river, Anderson now had at least some means to delay a charging panzer column.

Another random event added to the confusion that predawn in Trois-Ponts. A southbound 7th Armored Division vehicle, probably an open-topped armored vehicle on its way to the St. Vith area, had tried to negotiate the sharp right-hand turn onto the bridge over the Salm in city center. In doing so, it lost control and tipped over, off the bridge and into the river, about a ten-foot drop. The crew abandoned the vehicle and scuttled it with a thermite grenade. The heat of this incendiary caused the tank's ammunition to "cook off" periodically throughout the day and night from below the bridge.[265]

Early in the morning, another 1111th element joined Anderson's improvised force in Trois-Ponts. Just at daylight, Lieutenant Albert "Bucky" Walters, 1st Platoon leader, Company A, 291st ECB, appeared at his battalion headquarters in Haute-Bodeux after a grueling night working his way back from wood-cutting around Grand-Halleux, to the south. Anderson called upon the 291st to provide another detachment, to prepare the road bridge south of town for destruction, on the N28 leading to Vielsalm. Walters's platoon drew the assignment, and Anderson had him prepare this road bridge with demolitions. The group commander intended to seal Trois-Ponts off completely from road traffic along any axis the enemy panzers might use.

Walters's men loaded the demolition charges on the bridge and erected a roadblock. When it was completed, Walters left Sergeant Jean Miller in charge with specific orders to blow the bridge upon seeing any enemy. Walters then returned to Trois-Ponts to report back to Colonel Anderson.

After the 526th half-track was repaired, Anderson sent the gun, crew, and other 1111th and 51st men on the road to Stavelot, under the leadership of his S-4, Captain Robert Jewett.[266] He directed Jewett to place the 57 mm antitank gun just east of the two elevated railroad viaducts over the N23, in order to fire at tanks approaching from Stavelot. He had Jewett place a string of daisy-chained antitank mines along the road further along, as well as the half-track with its machine gun, to provide covering fire for the troops.

Anderson's use of the antitank gun, mines, and handful of troops beyond the bridges set to be destroyed is intriguing. One could look at the situation and conclude that one need only to man positions *behind* the mined bridge, with nothing forward. After all, any friendly forces placed beyond were, by design, positioned to be cut off once the bridges were blown. With such a small band forward in such an exposed position, the purpose of this outpost should be examined closely. The meager force could not be expected to stop an entire column of rampaging panzers. They could, however, impose a short delay. With the bridges wired and with line of sight on the enemy's expected approach road, Anderson would have ample time to blow the bridges before the Germans reached the spans, if all went well. However, this small element of uncertainty reveals Anderson's judgment. With the weight of responsibility that came from knowing a breakthrough at Trois-Ponts could split First Army wide open, Anderson could not afford to take chances, however small.

Bridge demolition operations under fire are fraught with risk, especially in the appalling weather and environmental conditions his young engineers faced. Electric firing devices, wiring, freezing temperatures, and hurried loading by tired troops in the middle of the night can all combine to undermine the certainty the task demanded. Should an initial attempt to demolish the bridges fail, his engineers would need time to find and resolve any problem. Anderson gave them time and sacrificed good soldiers on a fatal yet vital mission: engage and delay a column of panzers with a completely inadequate force. Making such decisions is the burden of command.

Peiper's charge into Stavelot was a one-sided affair. After the initial German barrage and infantry clash around the bridge, which destroyed the American attempt to establish a roadblock up the hill across the bridge, Solis pulled his men back to await the panzer assault. The Mk V Panthers forced their way across the bridge, having engaged in a one-sided duel with the remaining antitank guns.[267] The US infantry and tank destroyers (with 202nd ECB Company C assisting, with machine guns and riflemen) destroyed a couple German tanks but could not stop the numerically superior and more heavily armed SS troops. With half his antitank capability destroyed in the opening round without having fired a shot, no artillery, and less than 400 troops, Solis had to give way, pulling his forces back to the north and east, defending the path to First Army headquarters ten miles to the north. Solis's withdrawal also screened an important resource Peiper had no knowledge of—a series of gasoline dumps along the road leading to Spa at Francorchamps.[268]

The attempt to destroy the bridge and stop the panzers had failed, and Peiper threw his assault forces across it. By 1000 hours, Peiper controlled the part of Stavelot that included the bridge and road leading west. He sent his column down the N23 to Trois-Ponts, with a company of Mk V Panthers in the lead. The relentless push into First Army's rear echelon continued; Hitler's Ardennes gamble was still alive.

X

As the sounds of battle echoed down the Amblève valley from Stavelot, Wallis Anderson continued to position and prepare his engineers to defend Trois-Ponts. Other stragglers (including a random British officer) drifted into town throughout the morning and were promptly incorporated into Anderson's small command. He placed a rearguard to cover the approach on the N23 from Werbomont. He had Captain Scheuber send 51st Company C, 2nd Platoon under Lieutenant Fred Nabors across the river and railroad to the high-ground approach east of the town, to establish an outpost there with bazookas.

Sent by Anderson to detect and delay the panzers, Captain Jewett placed the 57 mm antitank gun on the south roadside, just east of the dual railroad viaducts, so that it could aim down the N23. The gun, manned by four 526th gun crew, had virtually no cover, and was expected to engage the onrushing panzers from only a couple hundred yards—point-blank range. Jewett sent two more 526th men, Bruce Frazier and Ralph Bieker, another 250 yards up the road toward Stavelot, with instructions to verify that any oncoming traffic was German (as there were still random Americans fleeing the front). Once so determined, Frazier and Bieker were to yank a daisy chain of ten linked antitank mines across the road, then return to rejoin their colleagues back at the antitank gun.

Lieutenant Richard Green, 51st ECB, Company C, 1st Platoon leader, under Jewett's direction, positioned himself behind the 57 mm antitank gun, and scattered some of his men in a roadside ditch behind it as well. Green placed another three of his men with a jeep forward, to watch over Frazier and Bieker, and to provide additional warning of the German approach.

Jewett himself commanded from the 526th half-track, across the road from the gun. Just in front of the railroad embankment, two 51st Company C men in a truck ran a field telephone wire back to the company command post, where Captain Scheuber monitored the action from behind the Amblève, at the train station. All the men thus placed in forward positions along the Stavelot road were fully cognizant of their isolated positions, with the bridge behind them wired for destruction.

Anderson established an overwatch, up on the hillside resort hotel that he had been using as his command post. This hotel (present-day Le Beau-Site) provided an excellent panorama from slightly northwest of the T-junction of N33 and N23, on the north end of Trois-Ponts. From this vantage he could observe part of the Stavelot road, the northern road bridge, and downtown Trois-Ponts. His engineers' headquarters in town were located adjacent to the Salm bridge on the N23 at town center, at the Hotel Crismer.[269] Although he could not directly observe the site where Jewett placed the antitank gun, Anderson could see the demolition-rigged road bridge 300 yards downhill, and the N33/N23 T-junction about 200 yards north of it.

Peiper's Mk V Panthers barreled down the Stavelot road, approaching the northern Trois-Ponts railroad viaducts at around 1030 hours. Frazier and Bieker bravely yanked their daisy chain of mines across the road and pitched themselves into the river beyond, determining it was safer than running back down the road. The panzers halted briefly and began firing machine guns at the American scouts; the three-man jeep raced back to the antitank gun position, warning Lieutenant Green of the approaching tanks. Meanwhile, a cluster of panzers had negotiated the curve (and presumably the daisy chain) and now came into view of the gun crew. A gun duel ensued between the 57 mm and at least three of Peiper's Panther tanks. Starting the firefight with only seven rounds at hand, the 526th crew quickly required additional ammunition, so "the little crew of defenders started an ammunition bucket brigade, with Captain Jewett tossing the shells across the road to Lieutenant Green, who forwarded them to Private Salazar, who handed them to the gun crew."[270]

The 57 mm crew hit and knocked out or immobilized the lead Panther, leaving it smoking. Sadly, the other panzers continued to fire and knocked out the gun, killing all four members—Donald Hollenbeck, Lillard McCollum, James Higgins, and Dallas Buchannan—of the valiant crew. Anderson wasted no time, and "the bridge over the AMBLEVE River was blown on order of Colonel

ANDERSON when enemy tanks approached it about 1045A hours."[271] Two explosions boomed, and the road span over the Amblève was now a shattered gap.[272] After the war, Anderson wrote, "I personally directed the explosion of charges which destroyed the two bridges at Trois Ponts."[273]

Although he had plenty of personnel present capable of rendering this action, he likely reserved it for himself due to the responsibility such a decisive act entailed. For the moment, he had just stopped the panzer thrust westward.

The engineers beyond the demolished bridge span were now stranded. Rapidly withdrawing in the truck and half-track, they headed north on the N33 toward Stoumont, escaping the oncoming panzers. Eventually Lieutenant Green and his truckload of survivors made their way back to Trois-Ponts, using backwoods paths. Captain Jewett in the 526th half-track took a longer route, ending up back at the new group rear headquarters at Modave.

Rolling past the destroyed antitank gun, Peiper's column pressed forward, up to the T-junction just north of the demolished bridge. With their route west no longer possible, they stalled on the east bank of the Amblève, deliberating. An ad hoc pile of mines was stacked on the N33 road leading north, Peiper's only remaining avenue. This had possibly been placed by the engineers as a cratering charge intended to damage the roadway. In any case, it had not been detonated; a panzer set off this large pile of mines with a cannon shot. No appreciable damage to the road was noted by the Germans.

Immediately after destroying the bridge, Anderson issued a flurry of orders. He sent his S-3, Major Henderson Webb, to First Army headquarters to notify them of the action and resulting situation. Earlier that morning, Anderson had dismantled his communications station in preparation for the move back. With the Amblève bridge gone, but the panzers still present, First Army needed to know. Anderson wanted to warn FUSA that Trois-Ponts could no longer be used as a north-south transit point. Reinforcements coming into the area would have to adjust their travel farther westward.

Anderson sent his 1111th Engineer Group staff back down the N23 to Haute-Bodeux, near the 291st CP, as a preliminary move. He remained in Trois-Ponts, however, to monitor the panzers, which were still coming up to the blown span. Major Webb alerted the CP of the 291st ECB when he passed through Basse-Bodeux. This command post duly notified the 291st element in La Gleize, part of Company C, which now lay on Peiper's route, should he decide to turn north.

Jochen Peiper, meanwhile, collected his column around the vicinity of the T-intersection of the N33 and N23, on the east bank of the Amblève. His accompanying SS panzergrenadiers patrolled into the houses in the area. Panzer crews and soldiers committed several atrocities during this period, including the murder of Belgian civilians, witnessed by Colonel Anderson from his observation post above at Le Beau Site. Anderson watched a tank crew machine-gun an elderly couple as they tried to escape the battle area. Seeing the horrific incident through binoculars from only 200 yards away, Anderson could hardly have mistaken the act. Other murders were revealed at various times over the next several days by others in Anderson's command. After the massacre at Baugnez twenty-four hours previous, the pattern of SS criminal brutality was by now well established.

As the SS panzers collected on the northern end of Trois-Ponts, streaming in from Stavelot, an additional element of Peiper's force emerged to threaten the town. A part of the two companies of Mk IV panzers sent from south of Stavelot toward Trois-Ponts earlier that morning, a probe of three Mk IVs, had rolled along the circuitous, looping route through Wanne and Aisomont, emerging from the woods on the track along the high ground east of Trois-Ponts.

Anderson had placed a platoon of the 51st Company C there, under Lieutenant Nabors. With two bazookas and a daisy chain of antitank mines, Nabors men tried to ambush the panzers near the hamlet of Noupré. A brief, sharp fight ensued, with the engineers withdrawing under heavy fire, although neither side took any losses. The panzers spotted and set off the daisy chain with machine-gun fire. One bazooka fired but missed; the other bazooka was shot out of the operator's hands and damaged.

Preventing any further action, however, Peiper radioed the tank element and withdrew them, ordering them back to Stavelot in order to join his column along the N23. From his map, Peiper would have seen that no direct entry from the Mk IV's positions led across the Salm and into Trois-Ponts (Anderson had reached the same conclusion the night before).

At around the same time, Colonel Anderson left his observation post at the hillside hotel and moved the half mile downhill to the town proper. His lower headquarters, at the Hotel Crismer, lay fifty yards west of the Salm River bridge, which was wired for destruction. Lieutenant Albert Walters, 291st Company A, 1st Platoon leader, reported back to Colonel Anderson on the completion of the demolition charges on the Salm River bridge along the N28 two miles south of town. Anderson and Walters stood in front of the hotel, conferring. Other 291st men, including Sergeant Paul Hinkel, stood nearby, guarding the hotel (Peiper's column was a mere 600 yards up the road, although around the road curve and across the blown bridge).

Author Janice Giles writes, "Suddenly a burst of machine gun fire from the heights across the river sprayed the wall of the hotel, just above their heads. Hinkel recalls that the two men looked up, observed the pattern of machine gun bullets, went on talking a moment or two longer, then separated."[274] Preparing to depart the town, Anderson attached Walters's platoon to the 51st and Captain Sam Scheuber's company.

Anderson thereupon encountered Scheuber, who had shifted his company command post from the train station on the high ground east of town back to town center. Years after the war, Scheuber described what happened next:

> [Anderson] said, "Captain, can you show me those German tanks?" I said, "Certainly, Colonel Anderson." We were close by the near side of the blown bridge over the Amblève and from there I climbed a steep hill east of us to a ridge of that hill which afforded a view of the Malmedy-Trois-Ponts highway. I had not anticipated a forward movement of the tank column since last viewing them and inadvertently we exposed ourselves while getting to the view point on the ridge. Colonel Anderson had an unknown staff officer along. There we all stood, exposed. Col. was counting "Fourteen, fifteen, sixteen" when an 88 mm tank shell went between us or slightly overhead to explode on the hillside beyond. Now anyone who has had the privilege of hearing an 88 pass close by will never forget the sound or how it will immediately get your attention! When we three finished tumbling off that ridge (there wasn't time to run) Col. Anderson and I ended up in about the same pile! Now remember back about him. Always neat, even prim; always of erect military posture, never perturbed and totally calm. I never ever heard him raise his voice or indulge in profanity ever! Yet when he was in that pile of bushes and people, I found him still on the ground looking at the ground from knee height and softly saying "God Damn! God Damn!" Then he got up, starting to brush himself off and his eyes met mine. "Captain, any

man who has been through this once and then asks to come back to it does not have a brain in his head!" (Really he didn't say those words exactly. He used a much more earthy, and pungent expression as to what might pass for brains.) You see, Col. Anderson had been in WWI![275]

Anderson's act might be viewed as mere bravado, or worse, foolhardy. But as usual with Anderson, there was probably an underlying intent that goes to the heart of good leadership in combat: shared risk. He could easily have remained in his lofty resort observation post, relatively safe and with an excellent panoramic view of much of the battlefield. And although his troops down in the town were safe from armored assault, numerically superior German forces were close in, to the north and east. His little band clung to the town, behind the narrow Salm.

Well aware of the effect his presence among the troops would have, he descended to interact and share the risks. Clambering up a steep twenty-foot embankment to nonchalantly count enemy tanks 250 yards away may not be considered normal behavior for a colonel and group commander, let alone a middle-aged grandfather, but for Anderson it was perfectly in character. If his young engineers were expected to face the enemy in such a manner, then he would demonstrate to them that he held himself to those same expectations.

The destruction of the Trois-Ponts Amblève bridge forced Peiper to delay at the N23/N33 junction and devise a new plan. Still intending to find a way to the northwest, to cross the Meuse at Huy, he was now forced to detour by following alongside the Amblève north, then west. If he could reach the bridge at Cheneux, he could cross the Amblève, proceed southwest and across a minor creek, then resume his westerly original route on the N23. It was feasible, but this detour would take additional time, and additional fuel; the SS kampfgruppe leader was rapidly running out of both. Peiper turned his column north.

Seeing Peiper on the move again and now heading north, Anderson needed to keep First Army apprised of this new development. He sent a second courier, Captain A. P. Lundberg, his motor officer, in a 51st ECB jeep driven by Private James Snow Jr. As Major Webb had done an hour or so earlier, Lundberg took a very roundabout journey to Spa, proceeding west to Werbomont, then north, then east, in order to avoid the Germans north of town.

With the Germans to the north and east (even though the panzers posed no direct threat to the town), and with his intention to move his headquarters to the rear as ordered, Anderson decided to take no chances. He ordered three other bridges destroyed.

First, Anderson had Nabor's 2nd Platoon destroy the road bridge over the railroad tracks just south of the train station, which had earlier been threatened by the three Mk IV panzers. He pulled the 51st engineers back across the Salm and destroyed a foot bridge over the Salm on the southern end of town. In doing so he simplified the defense of the town, making it more difficult for any infantry to attack across the Salm.

Next, he directed the destruction of the Salm River bridge on the N23 in town center. This span went up at 1300.[276] Now even if the Germans somehow managed to cross the railroad embankment that ran north-south along the eastern boundary of the town, they would not be able to proceed further.

A fifth overall bridge was destroyed, this time south of town on the N28, a southern road bridge over the Salm. Loading this bridge had been Lieutenant Walters's responsibility; having supervised the bridge preparation and roadblock construction during the late morning, Walters had left the location to report back to Colonel Anderson, leaving Sergeant Jean Miller in charge. Walters instructed Miller not to blow the bridge unless Germans directly threatened to cross it.

Miller and his half dozen men had watched the approach by the Mk IV panzers on the hill overlooking Trois-Ponts. Although the tanks had no road down the steep hill to threaten Miller's bridge south of town, they were accompanied by foot soldiers; in fact, the troops escorting the panzers were some of the remaining *fallschirmjagers* and SS pioneers[277]—combat engineers themselves. The SS officer commanding the panzer element[278] sent his troops down the hill to seize the road bridge. Miller and his men remained hidden as the SS soldiers descended the hill and approached. As the Germans swarmed onto the bridge, attempting to dismantle and remove the demolitions, Sergeant Miller detonated the charge. The bridge was destroyed, taking a number of SS men with it. Miller's men escaped to the south, all the way to Grand-Halleux, before working their way to Modave.

Trois-Ponts was now isolated. No road bridges still stood. Germans could only watch the small force of Americans from across the Salm and Amblève Rivers.

While Peiper pressed ahead, seeking to detour his way back onto a westward route (he anticipated American forces coming down from the north as well), behind him a renewed fight was building in Stavelot. Due to congestion and combat delays, Kampfgruppe Sandig, which was supposed to trail behind Peiper, had been held up and lagged far behind. Kampfgruppe Hansen, on rollbahn E south of Peiper, had been stopped at Poteau, between Vielsalm and Recht, confronted by 7th Armored Division forces; a stalemate there ensued, as neither side could shift the other. As a result, the trailing Schnellgruppe Knittel exercised the option to switch rollbahns rather than get jammed behind Hansen. Knittel detoured his route northward, to Stavelot. Arriving around midday, Knittel was able to send much of his column westward, behind Peiper, even as American forces were moving into the area to contest ownership of this vital town.

Under Major General Leland Hobbs, 30th Infantry Division had gotten the call to move south and confront the German breakthrough forces. His three regiments, 117th, 119th, and 120th Infantry, began to sweep south toward the Trois-Ponts-Malmedy line. By Monday afternoon, forward elements advanced into northern Stavelot. Peiper had blasted his way through, but the following elements of his column, and now Knittel's, were going to have to fight to keep open his lines of communication.

In early afternoon, before departing Trois-Ponts, Colonel Anderson made three more moves in his running chess match with the Germans. First and foremost, when he saw the SS column turn to the north, Anderson again anticipated what this development meant in terms of the overall strategic situation. If the German column continued north, past Stoumont and toward Spa, it would bring them into contact with First Army forces. Already 7th Armored Division was forming to the south and west; more reinforcements were sure to follow. A clash with Leibstandarte would be a fight, but that was preferable to allowing a breakthrough.

However, if the push north by the SS panzers was just a detour around Trois-Ponts, the northwestern route to the Meuse was still a possibility, and a threat. Two bridges had to be crossed along that route. The first of these Peiper would encounter was south of Stoumont, across the Amblève, at Cheneux; from Trois-Ponts, Peiper was less than seven miles from there. Moreover, of all the bridge sites in the region, the river at Cheneux bridge was the most likely to be potentially fordable (bypassing the bridge), as it was shallow with low banks. Anderson therefore ignored the Cheneux bridge as impractical; Peiper would likely get to it first, in any case.

After Cheneux, Peiper would have to continue looping to the south, then connect again to the N23, leading west to Werbomont, and Huy, on the Meuse, twenty-five miles further along. Before Werbomont, however, was a final bridge over a tiny creek at the hamlet of Habiémont.

La Lienne creek was barely noted on maps and fed into the Amblève a few miles to the north. Not particularly deep, its one significant feature was that La Lienne was cut into steep rock banks. It was essentially a fifty-foot-wide tank barrier, with no other tank-capable bridges for several miles in any direction.

Anderson recognized its strategic importance and called the 291st ECB command post at Haute-Bodeux, ordering Major Lampp (acting in command, with Pergrin still in Malmedy) to immediately send a detail to the Habiémont[279] bridge, and to prepare it for destruction. Habiémont was a direct eight miles west of Trois-Ponts, whereas Peiper's route there was longer and more circuitous. Even more fortunate, a last remaining element of the 291st was in Werbomont, only two miles west of Habiémont. Company A, 2nd Platoon was the last of Anderson's engineers in the area that had not yet been employed.

Lampp radioed to 2nd Platoon and passed the order to the platoon sergeant, Edwin Pigg; the platoon leader, Lieutenant Alvin Edelstein, was presently in Haute-Bodeux.

The race to Habiémont, the last defended bridge to the Meuse, was on.

Anderson's next two moves ensured that he left Trois-Ponts in a solidly defensible state. Although the blown bridges protected his band of engineers from armored assault, he was still acutely aware that his entire force consisted of less than 200 men, and was only lightly armed, at that. He had pulled them back into a tight perimeter, forming Company C "on a 500-yard front to keep the Germans from crossing the river."[280]

And finally, Anderson left the defense of Trois-Ponts under strong leadership. As group commander, Anderson was responsible for coordinating the actions of four engineer battalions, three of which were now deeply involved in direct combat with the enemy across a broad front. He had temporarily postponed that responsibility in order to deal with a crisis, the attempted panzer breakthrough at Trois-Ponts. Having stopped that emergency, he was anxious to reestablish his higher headquarters in order to more effectively manage his overall responsibilities. Within this complex scene yet another fortuitous event occurred.

As mentioned previously, Major Robert "Bull" Yates, executive officer of the 51st ECB, had returned to his duties on Friday, December 15, after more than three months' absence while convalescing for a foot injury. As he was becoming reacquainted with the 51st mission area and activities, the Germans had struck. With a brand-new commanding officer as well, the leadership of the 51st scrambled to prepare their own lines for combat action, farther south and west, around Hotton.

On Monday, Yates drove to Trois-Ponts to be briefed on the situation.[281] Yates was a well-known "Plattsburgh-trained" member of Anderson's command; Anderson considered Yates a strong and capable leader. Arriving shortly after Anderson's orders to destroy the bridges into Trois-Ponts, Yates's presence was a welcome development. Although the immediate crisis had passed, Trois-Ponts was anything but safe. If the Germans had bridging material somewhere in their column, they had ample forces to yet push their way over the Amblève and Salm. The town still needed to be defended, and Anderson was confident in Yates's ability to do so. Anderson placed Yates in command of Trois-Ponts: "Mission assigned by Group C.O. [Anderson] was to hold TROIS PONTS and prevent enemy establishing bridgehead west of SALM River."[282]

HABIÉMONT

Throughout Monday morning, senior US commanders in the area were gathering in Spa, First Army headquarters location, to discuss how to respond to the German offensive. Lieutenant General Courtney Hodges, emerging from his stress condition of the previous day, held a series of meetings to assign actions to counter the German breakthroughs. Major General James Gavin, division commander for the 82nd Airborne and acting commander of the XVIII Airborne Corps, met with FUSA commander Hodges. By then, "the situation had changed and the greatest threat to First Army was now Peiper's column."[283]

Hodges ordered Gavin to take his 82nd Airborne Division, still en route from France, and to shift its destination to Werbomont instead of Bastogne where it had originally been directed. Gavin departed to make a personal reconnaissance of that area, in advance of his division.

Shortly thereafter, Major General Leland Hobbs, commander of the 30th Infantry Division, arrived in Spa to discuss with Hodges how to employ his division, which was moving into the area from the north.

Both of Anderson's couriers sent from Trois-Ponts arrived to report while Hodges and Hobbs conferred. From Webb, FUSA learned of Peiper's arrival at Trois-Ponts and the blown bridge over the Amblève; Lundberg relayed the additional information that Peiper had turned north and was on the move. Information came in from Army Air Corps reconnaissance aircraft,[284] identifying Peiper's column now winding its way along the Amblève valley in the vicinity of La Gleize. The weather had broken, allowing the air force to fly.

Hodges ordered Hobbs to spread his initial infantry regiment, the 119th Infantry, in a wide swath, from Stavelot to Werbomont, in order to cover any Peiper push to the north and northwest. This blocking movement would help screen the arrival of the 82nd Airborne west of Werbomont. Both infantry units, still scattered and piecemeal, needed a little more time to form up and establish effective positions to block the German advance.

Peiper wound his way through the Amblève river valley, heading north, then west to La Gleize. Midafternoon, the skies cleared somewhat, allowing the sun to shine through the broken clouds. The German column extended twenty miles along the entire route Peiper had taken, all the way back to the vicinity of Ligneuville. Allied tactical aircraft, mostly from American IX Tactical Air Command under Major General Elwood "Pete" Quesada, spotted Peiper's exposed column and pounced.

Around three dozen fighter-bombers from the 365th Fighter Group and others attacked all along the extended length of panzers, from Stavelot to La Gleize. At the head of the column, around sixteen P-47 Thunderbolts[285] bombed and strafed the SS armor, forcing crews to halt and take cover as best they could. Peiper's mobile antiaircraft *flakpanzers*[286] fought back, shooting down at least one Thunderbolt. During the aerial assault, Peiper lost around eight armored units, three Panthers, and five SPW half-tracks. More significantly, his column was delayed two full hours.

After clearing the damaged vehicles off the road and reorganizing his column after the air attack, Peiper resumed his advance at around 1530 hours. An hour of daylight remained. He guided his panzers across the Cheneux bridge, crossing south over the Amblève, less than six miles to the final bridge at Habiémont.

Meanwhile, Sergeant Edwin Pigg, platoon sergeant for 291st ECB, Company A, 2nd Platoon, had received Major Lampp's radioed order from Anderson to prepare the Habiémont bridge for demolition. His platoon was billeted in a Werbomont schoolhouse, the last and rearmost of the 291st elements. Pigg rushed to gather what men he could find (some were still out on paratroop-hunting patrols), mostly from the platoon's 3rd Squad.

The only vehicle large enough to carry the dozen or so men and explosives was the platoon truck, which had burned-out valves as it awaited repair. However, it was the best available transportation; Pigg loaded men, TNT, mines, Primacord,[287] wires, and detonators, and set off for Habiémont, two miles east . . . at the speed of ten miles an hour. Arriving at Habiémont on the N23 at around 1500, Pigg hurriedly set his men rigging the bridge with explosives. He had his truck driver point the truck back west and keep the questionable engine running. They might need to make a quick getaway.

Working rapidly, the 3rd Squad men loaded the bridge with TNT and Primacord, and ran blasting-cap wires back to the electric firing device located in a roadside sentry box only 100 feet back from the west bank of the span. While Pigg supervised, Sergeant R. C. Billington and Corporal Fred Chapin—the demolitions expert— did most of the rigging. Two independent charges totaling more than 2,000 pounds of TNT, one on each bridge end, were placed. At around 1600, Colonel Anderson's convoy of 1111th Group personnel passed through, westbound on the N23, bound for Modave. They had stopped temporarily in Haute-Bodeux, picked up 291st Battalion headquarters staff, and continued west. At Habiémont bridge, Anderson dropped off the 2nd Platoon leader, Lieutenant Edelstein, placing him in command with orders to blow the bridge at the first sighting of the expected German column. Anderson then continued on to reestablish his group command in Modave, another twenty-four miles to the rear, just shy of Huy.

Shortly after Anderson's column departed west, the Habiémont bridge crew, now under Lieutenant Edelstein, received another visit by a senior officer. Major General James Gavin, commanding the 82nd Airborne Division, was scouting the area ahead of his paratroops as they began to arrive and assemble west of Werbomont.

Stopping to discuss the situation with the young lieutenant, Gavin departed a few minutes later. At around 1630, the bridge demolition rigging was completed. Edelstein ordered other details to lay mines on intersecting roads as well, on the west bank.

On the move again, with *1. Kompanie* Panzer Regiment 1's Panthers once more in the lead, as they had been since Ligneuville, Peiper pushed on down the road from Cheneux, determined to continue his breakthrough, now forty hours old. His spitze snaked southwest through Rahier and then Froidville, before the road merged with the east-west N23.

Shortly after Gavin departed the Habiémont bridge, a two-jeep convoy of Anderson's couriers, Major Webb and Captain Lundberg, returning from having briefed Hodges in Spa, entered the area. They carried messages directing Anderson to relocate the 1111th to the west, not realizing Anderson had already departed Trois-Ponts. (Tragically, they didn't stop to talk to the bridge-rigging crew, who would have informed them Anderson had already passed by, westbound.)

In the lead jeep, Lundberg, with 51st ECB's Private James Snow driving, wound their way using secondary roads on their roundabout journey from Spa. Lundberg and Snow crossed the Habiémont bridge eastbound on the N23 at around 1645, heading toward Trois-Ponts. They drove directly into the entire panzer column. Suddenly encountering German soldiers along the road, the engineers tried to shoot their way past, until a Panther tank fired, killing both. Webb, farther back, had only just crossed the bridge. Seeing the fate of Lundberg and Snow, Webb and his driver abandoned their jeep amid gunfire and escaped westward.

In the fading light, Peiper's panzers made the sweeping right-hand curve on the N23 that brought them fully into view of the tiny Habiémont bridge, 100 yards ahead. The panzers began firing at the soldiers they saw around the bridge. Corporal Chapin, holding the blasting machine, ducked and looked to Lieutenant Edelstein, who frantically signaled for Chapin to fire the circuit.[288]

Chapin cranked the handle, and more than 1,000 pounds of TNT erupted, even as the panzers approached. With the debris still falling from the detonation, Chapin quickly rewired the blasting machine to blow the second charge (on the bridge's far side), but the first shot had destroyed the wiring to the second charge. No matter—the first charge had demolished the entire bridge. Peiper's SS panzers could only watch helplessly as once again they were prevented from crossing a major barrier by a matter of yards. For the third time in less than twenty-four hours, combat engineers of the 1111th Engineer Combat Group had faced the Leibstandarte panzers, eyeball-to-eyeball. The first encounter had been an unexpected, bold bluff; the next two were more emphatic TNT showdowns.

The panzers closing on the creek could only rake the scattering Americans from across the demolished span with machine-gun and cannon fire. Edelstein and his men made good their escape without casualty, in a 10 mph truck.

Peiper sent a reconnaissance force of panzergrenadiers in half-tracks across a light bridge farther up the valley, hoping to find a way across for his panzers. Anderson had ignored this bridge—in the vicinity of Froidville—and others he knew could not support panzers and therefore posed no serious threat. His path west now impassable, Peiper's only option was to reverse course and backtrack to the north, back to Stoumont and, he knew, into the arriving American reinforcements. The race to the Meuse was over.

The destruction of the Habiémont bridge was not the end of Peiper's saga. Hard days of fighting lay ahead for his embattled and increasingly outnumbered force. However, Peiper's failure to cross the fifty-foot-wide La Lienne creek reverberated up the German command structure, affecting the entire offensive. His kampfgruppe column was still strung out for twenty kilometers, extending back to Stavelot and across to the south bank of the Amblève. Renewed fighting at the Stavelot bridge chokepoint backed up his column traffic even more.

That Monday evening, the SS forces earmarked to follow up and exploit Leibstandarte's success were diverted to the south. The 9th SS Panzer Division Hohenstaufen, one of the two remaining SS panzer divisions and part of II SS-Panzerkorps, was ordered onto a more southerly line of advance. Peiper's breakthrough had been sealed by the engineers, and "it was recognized already on the 18th or 19th of December that [they] should not succeed in gaining the Maas [Meuse] or crossing it by surprise."[289] The latter-day "Siegfried of the Waffen-SS" had been stopped.

AFTER HABIÉMONT

Colonel Anderson arrived in Modave at around 1800 Monday night. He reestablished his group headquarters in "the beautiful and historic Château de Modave."[290] Lampp similarly set up his 291st headquarters nearby, later in the night. The 291st was highly fragmented, with elements scattered from Malmedy back to Modave, across more than forty miles of forested Belgium, with German-held territory interposed throughout. The 51st ECB was somewhat more intact, with only their Company C apart, still holding isolated Trois-Ponts. The remainder of the battalion held a series of bridge and road positions in a line southeast from Hotton.

In Modave, Anderson's 1111th carried out new First Army orders: "continuation of delaying actions, construction of road blocks and establishment of barrier lines in the zone of enemy advance."[291] A period of reorganization ensued, as elements of the group finally caught their breath after a very hectic two days. The 202nd and 296th

ECBs, with the 767th Engineer Dump Truck Company (last seen in the Bütgenbach area, in what must have seemed a lifetime previous, though only forty-eight hours before), had now been out of contact with the 1111th since Sunday. Both were reassigned, out from under Anderson's responsibility, to the 1105th Engineer Combat Group. The elements of Pergrin's 291st ECB were assigned to 30th Infantry Division, which had moved into the Malmedy area in force.

By Tuesday, December 19, the Americans had taken control of the entire northern bank of the Amblève at Stavelot. The veteran 30th Infantry Division, shifted off the line north of Aachen on Sunday, had moved south on a broad front by midday Monday. Division commander Major General Leland Hobbs had been given the assignment to push against the northern flank of Peiper's column, from Malmedy to Werbomont. His 117th Infantry Regiment entered Stavelot in early afternoon on Monday. Encountering elements of Peiper's kampfgruppe as well as the other trailing SS armored units, fighting over the city continued for the next two days.

The 12th SS Panzer (Hitlerjugend) was supposed to block this anticipated American response, but had failed utterly; as a result, units trying to catch up to Peiper were forced to run a gauntlet through Stavelot. Tuesday evening, the engineer battalion assigned to 30th Infantry Division, 105th ECB, demolished the Stavelot bridge under fire. Using the cover of an artillery barrage that fired high explosives and smoke against the Germans south of the bridge, the engineers carried twenty 50-pound boxes of TNT, and in five minutes placed them in a pile on the roadbed where the near span was thinnest. Using multiple time-fuse blasting caps, the engineers pulled three redundant fuse igniters and ran to safety. At around 1930 Tuesday night, the Stavelot bridge, which had been at the center of fighting and provided the key access to Peiper's breakthrough, went up in a thunderous blast of a thousand pounds of TNT. Now Peiper was trapped; his escape route was blocked, and increasingly stronger forces were coming into position from the north.

Germans attacked for two more days to try to force their way back into Stavelot. Peiper sent units back as well to aid the effort, and to reestablish his line of communications. By the nineteenth, two infantry divisions, the 30th and 82nd Airborne, with ample armor support, were in position to hem in Peiper's regiment-sized column. His forces grew increasingly desperate and were eventually overwhelmed in the vicinity of Stoumont.

Commanding officer David Pergrin of the 291st ECB in Malmedy, meanwhile, helped to guide the defensive preparations of the growing American forces. Early-morning Tuesday, additional reinforcements arrived as 30th Infantry Division infantry, artillery, and armored units took positions throughout Malmedy. The city was now well defended, no longer the isolated outpost held by a thin line of engineers. Before dawn on Thursday, December 21, the SS finally struck, in a last-gasp effort to break the American hold on the Elsenborn ridge line.

From the start of the offensive, SS commando Otto Skorzeny sent his American-garbed and equipped infiltration troops to sow confusion and chaos throughout the 6. *Panzerarmee* zone. Some of those had managed to filter through the lines and been somewhat effective. However, Skorzeny had three kampfgruppes of American-equipped (or disguised to resemble US) units as well, independently organized as the 150th SS Panzer Brigade. These had been intended to precede the panzer columns and seize key points, such as crossroads and bridges. In this, Skorzeny had failed completely. None of his columns had been able to even cross through the front lines; Skorzeny cited poor roads, traffic congestion, and the failure of a frontline breakthrough.

With Peiper cut off and increasingly desperate, Skorzeny was ordered instead to use his three kampfgruppes in a more conventional role: to launch a frontal assault to take Malmedy. Accordingly, before dawn on December 21, he threw his forces against the thoroughly prepared defenses, which included Pergrin's engineers. By that date, Malmedy was defended by five infantry battalions, with engineer, artillery, tank destroyer, and antitank support. Skorzeny had only ten tanks, a mix of Mk IV and Mk V Panthers, all disguised to pass for US M4 Sherman medium tanks. Skorzeny was outnumbered and had little artillery to support his effort. The fight was sharp, lasting all day, but never in doubt for the stronger American defenders. Skorzeny was thrown back with heavy losses.

This was not the end of Pergrin's engineers' ordeal in Malmedy, or even the worst of it. The two instances of fortuitous air interdiction against Peiper's column on December 17 and 18 might suggest that close coordination between ground and supporting air forces was a routine and polished affair in 1944. Not so. Cooperation between air and ground forces was still fraught with disconnects and mistakes. This peril was tragically demonstrated for three straight days, from December 23 through Christmas Day. Malmedy had never been occupied by the Germans throughout the Ardennes period. On Saturday, December 23, having withstood the SS armored attack, the engineers in Malmedy were now hit by the US Army Air Force. Twenty-eight 9th Air Force B-26 medium bombers skimmed beneath the low-lying clouds and initially mistook Malmedy for Zülpich, Germany. Zülpich, which lay a full thirty-three miles northeast of Malmedy, sat on the broad plain between the mountainous, forested Ardennes and the Rhineland; Malmedy was nestled amid the rugged Ardennes. Twenty-two of the bomber crews realized their mistake and veered away before dropping bombs. However, six of the B-26s unloaded their ordnance payloads over Malmedy. Each B-26 typically carried eight 500-pound bombs each; they struck town center, where Pergrin and his engineers had established their headquarters. Soldiers and civilians were killed and wounded as the bombers destroyed numerous buildings.

The next day, eighteen B-24 heavy bombers, bombing through the cloud cover, dropped more bombloads onto the city. The much larger bombers caused even more casualties, including some of Pergrin's engineers. Finally, on Christmas Day, Malmedy was once again struck mistakenly, again by four B-26s thinking they had targeted German-held St. Vith. Malmedy continued to suffer occasional German artillery barrages until the lines were pushed back, but the air force caused far more damage and casualties.

On December 26, Pergrin finally left the town his engineers had held since the start of the Ardennes offensive. He took the battered elements of his 291st to rejoin the 1111th Group in Modave. Anderson's posting of Pergrin in Malmedy in the opening hours of the crisis was strategically significant; the 291st's commander had provided strong, determined leadership. Pergrin made it possible for First Army to transform Malmedy from an isolated, undefended outpost into a strongpoint along the line that stopped the German offensive. For its efforts, the 291st was recognized with a Presidential Unit Citation.

Anderson wrote, "Pergrin finally got back to me today—and apparently had quite an experience—and has done [an] excellent job. He was tired naturally—but quite happy as he had collected a Silver Star and Purple Heart as souvenirs of his weeks work—plus a letter of commendation from a division commander. I am very glad as he is a good conscientious boy—and I sent him to his Hq to get some rest."[292]

In Trois-Ponts, Major Robert "Bull" Yates took over the defense of the town, his small band of engineers precariously holding the west bank of the Salm. Yates and Trois-Ponts were cut off and isolated; however, without any bridges standing to allow vehicular assault, he and his engineers were largely protected from any direct threat. They were subjected to mortar, artillery, and machine-gun fire, however, and endured two days under fire.

Across the stream, the Germans held a similar position, screening any American effort to threaten the Trois-Ponts-Stavelot road and Kampfgruppe Peiper. Neither side was capable of crossing in force. On December 19, Yates's position was strengthened by a platoon of three M8 Howitzer Motor Carriages, which could provide supporting fire should the Germans try to push across the Salm and into the town.

Throughout his stand in Trois-Pont, Yates engaged in various active measures to deceive the German forces overlooking Trois-Ponts. At night he had trucks roll into and out of the town, departing in blackout and returning with headlights on and tire chains, to give the impression of reinforcements of heavy vehicles arriving. He had men shift locations while shooting across the river, to suggest his forces were more numerous than they actually were. Yates had his troops shoot bazookas, hoping the Germans would think he had artillery in support. The scuttled tank at the bottom of the Salm cooked off throughout the first night as well; Yates suggested this might have added to the deception, with Germans potentially mistaking this activity for outgoing artillery fire.[293]

Finally, on Wednesday, December 20, elements of the 505th Parachute Infantry Regiment of James Gavin's 82nd Airborne Division pushed into the town. On the fifth day of the offensive, the paratroopers had arrived. With the airborne division coming into the line, Anderson withdrew Yates and the engineers, which included troops from the 1111th Headquarters Company, 291st ECB, and 51st ECB. Yates actively supported the 82nd into December 21, providing covering fire when a probe across the Salm was beaten back by the still-dangerous German forces.

The 51st ECB, under Harvey Fraser, had carried out Anderson's orders of December 17 to defend the Ourthe River from Durbuy to La Roche-en-Ardenne, a twenty-mile line. Anderson sent instructions with a map overlay indicating which key bridges and roads to defend. As other American units came into the line, Fraser spread his two remaining companies (Company C was in Trois-Ponts with Anderson, then Yates) along the key points, mining and defending crossroads while preparing bridges for destruction. The 51st and other engineering units established a strong line of defense along the Ourthe, holding positions at Hotton, La Roche, Champion crossroads, Rochefort, and on minor road and river points.

Several minor skirmishes with German patrols ensued, with a somewhat larger clash taking place on Thursday, December 21, in Hotton. On that day, a platoon of four panzers from the 116th Panzer Division, supported by infantry, probed toward the bridge over the Ourthe at Hotton. With the help of American armor and infantry, the engineers repulsed the German probe, driving off the Germans with a loss of all four panzers.

Fraser had assigned Captain Preston Hodges to organize the defense of the town and bridge. Hodges was one of the early 51st men, having been assigned to the unit since June 1942, predating even Anderson's arrival to the regiment. He was part of the Texas and Plattsburgh training, and in the Ardennes commanded Company B. At Hotton, Hodges coordinated the mixed collection of antiaircraft, armor, infantry, and engineers to fend off the Germans on December 21. Hodges personally directed the bridge defenses, which included a 37 mm antitank gun.

When the regular crew hesitated to put the undersized gun into action against the German panzers, Fraser's driver, Private Lee Ishmael, operated the gun, along with other 51st engineers.[294]

Eventually five Army divisions moved into the line where the 51st was positioned. The 51st was awarded a Presidential Unit Citation for its actions in Trois-Ponts and along the Ourthe during the first week of the Ardennes offensive.

Anderson wrote to his wife, "As a matter of fact most of my gang gave an excellent account of themselves during the trying days they went through and I am very proud of two outfits in particular and the rep they made for themselves and the outfit in general."[295]

Thus, by the end of the "Bulge," both of Anderson's active engineer battalions (subtracting the 202nd and 296th, both of which were cut off from his command and assigned elsewhere) had been recognized with Presidential Unit Citations for "outstanding performance of duty in action against the enemy." In both instances, he had positioned their forces and given clear and direct guidance. In the confusion and stress that ensued, both battalion commanders had risen to the challenge, as had their junior officers and men.

THE DAMNED ENGINEERS

Legend has it that Jochen Peiper, in his command SPW a few vehicles from the front of his column when the Lienne creek bridge erupted into dust and debris, slammed his fist into his knees, exclaiming, "The damned engineers!"[296]

No battles are won by individuals or units operating in a vacuum. Every event is connected to another, and every outcome is reliant upon surrounding and preceding factors. The Battle of the Bulge continued for another four weeks after Corporal Chapin twisted the handle of his blasting machine, blowing Habiémont bridge into La Lienne creek. The hard fighting that followed smashed the German units, with US and British forces suffering heavy casualties. Nazi fanaticism died hard.

There are numerous perspectives of who stopped Peiper, and who won the Bulge. Successful outcomes inevitably attract credit claims; human nature compels feelings of significance. The more so if the actions are desperate, important, and uncertain. And to be fair, many such claims have elements of reasonable justification.

The Ardennes was the largest land battle for the US Army in the war. It is the most and best documented, allowing us to evaluate the many, many instances of significant actions that played a part in stopping Hitler's last offensive. Some have been alluded to here. Others are noteworthy: The desperate resistance of 99th Infantry Division—outnumbered, surprised, and unsupported—in the tiny twin villages of Krinkelt and Rocherath in the opening hours completely disrupted the German's timetable and initial objectives, from which they never recovered. Like a boulder in a river, 7th Armored's tenacious defense of St. Vith prevented *5.* and *6. Panzerarmees* from blasting through the American lines, linked side by side. And of course, the 101st Airborne's epic stand in Bastogne vaulted that storied unit into legend, as they held out against repeated assaults by the furious, vengeful Germans.

While recognizing the contributions above, one inescapable conclusion stands out: In the initial assault, when the Nazis enjoyed their fullest advantage, only one group of Americans prevailed against the SS unit specifically selected to lead the Germans to victory. In the early hours of the Ardennes offensive, while much of the American First Army reeled and fell back in shock, small bands of engineers, well placed and exceptionally well led, caused the delays that doomed Hitler's last offensive.

The 1111th Engineer Combat Group and its subordinate elements caused delays, detours, and, in the end, a complete halt of the Waffen-SS force designated by Hitler himself to save the Reich. The 1111th did so while isolated and with virtually no direct support for a pivotal twenty-four-hour period. One brilliant stroke by the Army Air Corps—and luck—played significant roles as well and are fully acknowledged. The steadfastness and fatal sacrifices of the engineers and supporting troops under Anderson's steady hand proved critical.

Hitler had designed *Wacht Am Rhein* from the start to achieve strategic objectives before the weight of Allied reinforcements could be brought to bear. The initial guidelines stated that "all planning would aim at securing tactical surprise, and speed."[297] Wallis Anderson and the combat engineers he commanded blew the bridges of Trois-Ponts and Habiémont, and the SS kampfgruppes could race no more.

ENDNOTES

262   Robert E. Merriam, *Dark December* (New York: Ziff-Davis Publishing, 1947), 104.

263   Tank-destroyer units were equipped with either self-propelled or towed guns. The 825th's platoon in Stavelot had towed antitank guns, the 3-inch (76.2 mm) M5. Although they had the same basic mission—to kill tanks—in WWII Army doctrine, "antitank" elements were part of offensive infantry and armored units, while "tank destroyers" were used in a defensive role. The primary distinction between the two lay in doctrinal employment, not in hardware.

264   He also ignored a span over the Amblève one mile east of Trois-Ponts, known as Petit Spai. Anderson's judgment was validated several days later when a German *Jagdpanzer* IV tank destroyer tried to cross it after the Stavelot bridge was blown; the bridge collapsed under the weight of the armored vehicle, dumping the panzer into the river.

265   Some confusion surrounds exactly what type of armored vehicle this actually was. The M7 Priest Howitzer Motor Carriage has been mentioned, as has the M5 Stuart light tank. However, the available data suggests it was likely an M8 Howitzer Motor Carriage (HMC), a self-propelled 75 mm gun used for artillery support. The vehicle was specifically described as open-topped, which eliminates the M5 Stuart. The Priest's ammunition load was carried in the open gun-crew compartment, with storage for about seventy rounds; the explosive charge was just under five pounds of TNT for each high-explosive shell. A Priest's 105 mm shell cooking off would very likely either detonate the other shells or blast them away from the storage rack, making them less likely to catch fire and cook off regularly. For the open-top M8, with much smaller blasting charges in each round (under 1.5 lb. explosive per round, typically), repeated cooking off over a period of hours would be a reasonable outcome if a thermite grenade were set off in the crew compartment. The M8 is built on an M5 chassis, a fast, narrow platform (only 7.5 ft. wide, capable of 36 mph). On icy roads, negotiating an unfamiliar 90-degree turn in bad weather by a driver in a hurry might have contributed to the accident.

266 Captain Robert Jewett replaced Captain T. J. C. Williams, who had been captured in October, as Anderson's S-4.

267 The daisy chain of mines laid by the 202nd ECB would have been removed to allow the column sent by Major Solis to cross the bridge, and their subsequent retreat. Apparently, the mines were not replaced, or had been removed. Giles suggests that the mines were removed by enemy subterfuge, a definite possibility.

268 Accounts vary as to the quantity of gasoline First Army had placed along roadside dumps; between one and three million gallons seem to be the common understanding. Several dumps were thus situated, with the gas in five-gallon cans for easy use by First Army units. The Germans were unaware of these dumps. Despite numerous fanciful accounts of Peiper's panzers being turned back by sheets of flames as the Americans destroyed gas to prevent capture while thwarting the panzers, Peiper crossed the Stavelot bridge, turned left, and continued west to Trois-Ponts. The road leaving Stavelot to Spa and Francorchamps led northeast—exactly the opposite direction Peiper wanted and was directed to pursue. His postwar interview in the fall of 1945 may indicate when Peiper first heard of the Francorchamps gas dumps.

269 Present location of a tourist information's office, Trois-Ponts, although artillery fire destroyed much of the original building on December 20, 1944.

270 Ken Hechler, *Holding the Line*, 20.

271 Unit History, 1111th Engineer Combat Group, 18 December 1944.

272 The two explosions may indicate the bridge had been wired with two independent firing circuits and charge loads at either end of the bridge, for redundancy.

273 H. Wallis Anderson, letter to Captain Robert Merriam, dated January 23, 1950.

274 Janice Giles, *The Damned Engineers*, 245.

275 Albert Radford, *Unbroken Line*, 191. The other 1111th staff officer was probably Captain A. P. Lundberg, who had been assigned to the 1111th on October 28; Anderson made him assistant S-4/motor officer for the group. The hill/ridge to which Scheuber refers was likely the railroad

embankment that ran north-south along the eastern edge of the town. Finally, much as US soldiers invariably and too often erroneously described every German panzer they encountered as a "Tiger tank," they often called cannon shells "88s"; as described earlier, Peiper kept his Tigers well to the rear in his column. Although it is possible a Mk VI *Ausf.* B Tiger had advanced up the column, the tank shot that Scheuber described was more likely a 75 mm, main armament of the Panther. As ever, Anderson makes no mention of the incident in his notes.

276   Janice Giles, *The Damned Engineers*, 247. The Salm bridge in town was not completely destroyed. The bridge piers and girders remained twisted but intact; it was unusable for vehicles, but could still be used by infantry.

277   From *3. Kompanie* Panzer Pionier Abteilung I, commanded by SS-Obersturmführer Franz Sievers.

278   *7. Kompanie* II Abteilung Panzer Regiment I, commanded by SS-Hauptsturmführer Oskar Klingelhofer

279   Sometimes referred to as the Neufmoulin bridge.

280   Barry Fowle, *The 51st Again!*, 79.

281   Accounts vary as to the purpose of Yates's driving to Trois-Ponts that Monday afternoon. Yates was neither "just passing through" (Anderson's postwar recollection), nor was he sent to take over in Trois-Ponts (Giles). Almost certainly he had been sent to be briefed on the specific situation of the ongoing crisis. Which makes Heckler's account closest—"unaware of the situation and merely bound for the daily liaison meeting"—although this version implies the meeting was routine and that Yates wasn't aware of the danger of the German assault; the author disagrees.

282   Unit History, 1111th Engineer Combat Group, 18 December 1944.

283   Janice Giles, *The Damned Engineers*, 251.

284   Marvin Kays, *Weather Effects During the Battle of the Bulge and the Normandy Invasion*, 20. The weather forecast for tactical air force bases on Monday read, "Overcast clouds, bases 1000 to 2000 feet, with intermittent rain, becoming 500 to 1000 feet broken during late afternoon. Visibility 2 to 6 miles. Also, fog patches in the southern sector."

285   Called *"Jabos"* by the Germans, from *Jägerbomber*, or "hunter-bomber."

286   Notably *Wirbelwind* ("Whirlwind") vehicles, mounting quad 20 mm automatic cannon.

287   *Primacord* is a brand of detonating cord, a flexible plastic tube filled with explosives. It is used in demolitions to connect components of the charge together, so that all elements are set off at once. An electric firing device would send an electrical current to detonate an electric blasting cap, which, connected to one or more main charges by Primacord, would ensure the entire demolition charge goes off at once.

288   Chapin used a handheld US Army Ten Cap Blasting Machine, a standard piece of demolition equipment in WWII for small jobs such as Habiémont. Turning the handle sends an electrical current to attached electric blasting caps.

289   Danny S. Parker, editor, *Hitler's Ardennes Offensive—The German View of the Battle of the Bulge*, 238–239.

290   Janice Giles, *The Damned Engineers*, 269.

291   Unit History, 1111th Engineer Combat Group, 18 December 1944.

292   H. Wallis Anderson, letter to Marietta Anderson, December 29, 1944. Anderson typically closed letters to his wife with "The Ancient," Marietta being eight and a half years younger. The division commander referred to was Major General Leland Hobbs, commanding the 30th Infantry Division.

293   The author is highly skeptical that German troops across the river would have mistaken bazooka fire for artillery, let alone that exploding tank rounds at the bottom of a riverbed inside Trois-Ponts would be mistaken across the river by German soldiers as outbound artillery fire. Nevertheless, all Yates's efforts would have had a positive effect on his isolated troops by showing engagement and effort, which would have greatly increased morale and a fighting spirit. And for that Yates should be respected and commended.

294   Private Ishmael and the others had received instruction on the 37 mm gun—which was not part of the engineers' equipment—during

Anderson's comprehensive training program in Plattsburgh. During the action at Hotton on December 21, battalion commander Harvey Fraser was present but became isolated on the enemy side of the river for much of the morning and the fight. Hodges, who was wounded during the action, received a Silver Star for his leadership and valor during the battle; Ishmael received a Bronze Star.

295   H. Wallis Anderson, letter to Marietta Anderson, December 29, 1944.

296   This episode and quote may be one of the more widely known anecdotes in modern military history. The author is unable to find the original source reference.

297   Winston Ramsey, editor, *After the Battle, Number 4*, 1.

CHAPTER FOURTEEN

INTO GERMANY

December 1944–March 1945

The combined Allied armies hammered the German forces of the Ardennes offensive, which had been exposed as they lunged into Belgium. Having failed in their bid to split the Allied lines, the 6. and 5. *Panzerarmees* instead created a bulge with the initial momentum of the German surprise attacks; by late December this only served to extend the lines they were now required to defend. The vastly more powerful combined Allied armies now took advantage of the Wehrmacht being out in the open, away from their prepared positions along the western German border. As both sides knew, German war-matériel production was rapidly collapsing. The German armed forces were dying, the end hastened by the lavish expenditures of men and arms for the ill-fated Eifel offensive.

Colonel Wallis Anderson established his new headquarters in Modave, a dozen miles behind the new defensive line established along the Ourthe River. A period of reorganization followed as reinforcements and reserves poured into the area. Having stopped the Germans, now the Allies began operations to cut off, push back, and destroy the Wehrmacht and Waffen-SS units. The new XVIII Corps (Airborne) took over responsibility for operations encompassing Modave.

Accordingly, on December 19, First Army assigned Anderson's 1111th Engineer Combat Group the mission of supporting this corps. Further command shuffling followed, on December 24, with the group being assigned to support VII Corps; thus, for the first time since entering combat, the 1111th ECG was operating directly under a corps, not First Army. Jockeying all along the Allied line reflected the massive reinforcements that were joining the Allied effort.

Various unit assignments followed. The 300th ECB was attached to the 1111th. The 207th and 61st ECBs were attached on December 23; these units were shortly reassigned, however. Operational activities to strengthen the barrier line along the Ourthe occupied most of the group's activities. The engineers established and fortified a second barrier line along the Lesse River, ten miles behind the Ourthe. This time, Army commanders were taking no chances.

The prominent 1111th units, the 51st and 291st ECBs, having been scattered and fragmented during the first week of the German attack as Anderson conducted his chess match against Leibstandarte, were eventually consolidated again, and back under the direction of the 1111th. As the momentous month ended, the 1111th Group took the time to sum up its recent contribution. The unit diary comments,

During the period 17-31 December 1944, the 1111th Engr C Grp assumed a rather prominent role in stemming the advance of the Germans in the ARDENNES breakthrough. Approximately 1709 mines were laid and five (5) enemy tanks disabled or destroyed. One (1) officer and nine (9) enlisted men were killed in action; two officers (2) and fifteen (15) enlisted men wounded; and one (1) officer and six (6) enlisted men were listed as missing in action.

During the German break-through, the Group had demonstrated its ability to come through with the goods when the heat was on.[298]

Addressing what was to come with the new year, the unit history continues,

Because of their effective and efficient completion of their assignments in the face of enemy opposition and the hazards of severe weather the Group was called upon more and more for tasks of prime importance. The VII Corps was to launch an attack with two Infantry Divisions abreast, closely followed by two Armored Divisions. The 1111th Engr Combat Group was to support the attack by removal of mines and maintaining routes for the advance.[299]

As January 1945 began, Anderson's command now consisted of the following:

- 51st Engineer Combat Battalion
- 291st Engineer Combat Battalion
- 300th Engineer Combat Battalion
- 505th Light Ponton Company

Supporting VII Corps' push to retake Houffalize, Anderson assigned the 291st ECB to the 84th Infantry Division, and the 300th ECB to support 2nd Armored. Additional high-level reorganizing continued as the American army continued to adjust during the final phases of "the Bulge." Anderson's group was reassigned, again to XVIII Corps (Airborne). More Army-unit hopscotch followed, weekly, throughout the month. At one point, on January 4, ironically the 1111th had assigned to it (briefly) the 238th ECB, marking the first time both the 51st and 238th were attached to the 1111th since the training period in Plattsburgh.

A small but satisfying coincidence took place on January 8, at Trois-Ponts, where Anderson and 51st Company C had destroyed bridges while under fire and in the face of Peiper's charging panzers. Supporting the 82nd Airborne Division in early January, the job to rebuild the Amblève bridge was assigned to the 238th ECB. Past met present as the 238th, once again directed by Wallis Anderson, spanned the Amblève with a Bailey bridge built under fire from the beaten but not yet defeated Germans, who fought fiercely to delay and disrupt the engineers. It was common practice during this period for the engineers to construct bridges under enemy fire; the Germans destroyed bridges wholesale as they retreated. Engineers throughout the group units took casualties. The 238th constructed a double-single Bailey (that is, two 10-foot panels wide by one panel high) class 40, eighty-foot bridge, over a two-day period, and according to the unit history, "The intensity of the enemy artillery can be appreciated when one reads the casualty report[;] 18 men and 3 officers are listed."[300]

Group units continued to conduct other standard army engineering projects in addition to bridge construction, including removal of mines, and snow clearance, to assist the forward movement of infantry units. The particularly severe winter of 1944 to 1945 added "further difficulties and hazards to the orders of winter fighting."[301]

Anderson shifted his group headquarters on January 15, taking up residence in the Château de Froidcourt, near Stoumont.[302] This was very near where Kampfgruppe Peiper, in its death throes, had met its end as combined American infantry, armor, and artillery pounded the SS men trapped in the hills between Stoumont and Le Gleize. Cut off and low on all supplies, Peiper's men abandoned their remaining tanks and armored vehicles and made their way back to German lines on foot; 770 returned to Germany on Christmas Day, out of his original force of 4,800.

In this period, Anderson wrote up one of his junior officers for a Silver Star for gallantry in action, demonstrating another embodiment of principles of sound leadership: recognizing worthy individuals. Approved by XVIII Corps on January 16, 1945, Captain Sam Scheuber was awarded the medal for his "outstanding work in holding the Germans at Trois Ponts."[303] Scheuber, of course, commanded the 51st ECB Company C, ordered by Anderson to take positions in Trois-Ponts, where it blew the bridges while holding its position throughout December 17 to 21.[304]

Ice, snow, and cold weather continued to be the major concern as offensive actions continued. Enemy resistance faded and was now more sporadic as the Germans pulled back behind their border defensive positions. Occasional thaws turned roads into quagmires, adding road-maintenance operations for the engineers.

Meanwhile, Anderson himself had been recognized for his actions during the Ardennes action. He was presented the Silver Star "per General Order No.17, Hq First U.S. Army dated 27 January 1945, for the part he played in stopping the German breakthrough during December."[305] The citation reads,

For gallantry in action against the enemy from 17 to 18 December 1944 in ***. Colonel Anderson, displaying great personal courage, remained constantly exposed to intense artillery, machine gun and small arms fire to personally direct the defense of a vital village against a strong German armored column. As the enemy exerted pressure upon his small group, Colonel Anderson, with coolness and determination, supervised the demolition of two bridges, thus forcing the enemy column to change its course and permitting his troops to hold the strategic defensive positions in the town. By his marked valor and devotion to duty, Colonel Anderson reflected great credit on himself and the military service.[306]

Reorganizations and unit shuffling continued. On January 28, Anderson again shifted his 1111th Group headquarters, this time to Malmedy; another forward move took place three days later as Anderson placed his group headquarters in Born. More traditional, routine engineering jobs started up again as well—quarrying and the establishment of water points. One unusual result of the continuous organizational shuffling was the 1,700 officers and men from 7th Armored Division who were assigned—with their armored vehicles—to the 1111th in order to provide additional manpower to assist with road maintenance.

Into February now, the 1111th was attached to the XVIII Corps (Airborne), again. On February 5, Anderson departed on detached service, and spent a week in the United Kingdom. During his absence, the first since landing in France the previous June, Lieutenant Colonel James Kirkland assumed temporary command of the 1111th. The group was shifted once again, this time into Germany itself. Kirkland established the new group headquarters in Walheim, Germany, having made the twenty-mile tactical road march to the northeast under blackout conditions. This move was followed by another organizational shift, as the 1111th was transferred once again, this time to III Corps,[307] which took over XVIII Corps' area of responsibility. Anderson returned on February 13 and resumed command of the group.

Crossing into Germany proper meant a new and heightened level of excitement. Anderson wrote, "Enemy resistance dwindled and town after town hung out their bed sheets in token of surrender as our leading elements approached."[308] Bridging operations continued, and on February 27, the Roer River was crossed at Zerkall by Army units, with engineers supporting. The Roer was a major barrier, the last defensive terrain feature until the Rhine River fifteen miles further east. To assist the Army units, notably the 9th Infantry Division, the 51st ECB provided treadway, foot, and Bailey bridges. Commenting on the variety of equipment the group now had assigned, the unit history states, "The Group at this time looked like a miniature army with all its equipment including tanks and DUKWs."[309]

Anderson continued his standard leadership practices, unchanged throughout the war. He ranged around his area of responsibility, personally inspecting his units' work projects, and sending his staff officers to do the same. At Bruck-Hetzingen, on the Roer, the 51st Company C built a Bailey bridge under enemy fire. Anderson, noting a flaw in its construction, chewed out Captain Scheuber—Silver Star notwithstanding—as well as his battalion commander, Lieutenant Colonel Harvey Fraser.[310] The flaw was corrected without mishap.

The group entered March still assigned to III Corps. This corps, led by Major General John Millikin, had been part of Lieutenant General George Patton's Third Army, and was the first to break the siege of Bastogne to relieve the 101st Airborne Division during the Ardennes campaign. The 1111th Group consisted of the following:

- 51st ECB
- 291st ECB
- 300th ECB
- 467th Engineer Maintenance Company (one platoon)
- 629th Engineer Light Equipment Company (less one platoon)
- 738th Tank Battalion (ME; mechanized engineer), Company B
- 994th Engineer Treadway Bridge Company (less one platoon)
- 501st Engineer Light Ponton Company

Supporting the 78th and 9th Infantry Divisions, the 1111th Group constructed several bridges over the Roer. The 291st alone built three class 40 Bailey bridges over the Roer at Heimbach, Blens, and on the Schwammenauel dam over the river at Hasenfeld. Although the German Army was in a state of near collapse, it still fought back.

The first two of the bridges were built under fire as the Germans sought to impede the US Army. Anderson again visited his field units engaged in operations. On March 3, he visited Pergrin's Company C as it erected a Bailey bridge over the dam's spillway the Germans had demolished. They watched bridge construction proceed smoothly, and Pergrin mentioned, "I knew things were going well as soon as I saw the twinkle in the Old Man's eyes."[311]

As the engineers spanned the gap, Anderson chatted with Pergrin on the campaign, which had begun in October and November with the 28th Infantry Division attacking through the Hürtgen Forest, twelve miles behind them now. As both were Pennsylvanians, Anderson reminisced with Pergrin about his time in the 28th Division; Anderson, whose history with the division went back to 1912 and the National Guard of Pennsylvania, had of course commanded engineers in combat in WWI with this unit. In this war, the division had been badly mauled, first in the Hürtgen, then during the Ardennes, and "the colonel waxed nostalgic about the many scores of Pennsylvania infantrymen and engineers who had died on their way to this dam."[312]

That night, Anderson wrote his wife, "I didn't sleep well last night. Pergrin was involved in building three bridges across a river where the danger was extremely in evidence from all the hazards of war. When I didn't hear from him this morning, I went to the sites and saw three masterpieces of engineering skill and courageous leadership. I will sleep well tonight."[313]

Other attached units conducted the standard road-maintenance operations, mine-clearing, and other support. On March 5, the 51st ECB was detached, along with the 994th Engineer Treadway Bridge Company. The 299th ECB and 998th Engineer Treadway Bridge Company were assigned to the 1111th. The group advanced with III Corps as it closed in on the Rhine River, in the vicinity of Remagen.

Although the war was entering its final phase, one more critical episode lay ahead for the engineers to demonstrate their worth.

Anderson and his engineers would once more find themselves in the center of a momentous action, with far-reaching consequences.

Ironically, having been a key component in "denial of enemy mobility" operations during the Ardennes, now the mission would be flipped: in March, the engineers would be called upon to provide vital access for the US Army to close with and finish off the Wehrmacht, ending the war. Failure would mean delays, which would extend the fighting, with additional lives lost.

ENDNOTES

298 Unit History, 1111th Engineer Combat Group, 1 December 1944–31 December 1944.

299 Ibid, 1 January 1945–31 January 1945.

300 Ibid.

301 Ibid.

302 Anderson's château headquarters was about a mile from the present-day December 44 Museum—Battle of the Bulge in La Gleize, Belgium.

303 Ibid.

304 Another engineer was awarded a Silver Star medal the next day, from the 51st. Technical Specialist/5 Oliver Connelly Jr. was recognized for his gallantry for action on December 29, while supporting Ourthe River barrier operations. While operating a bulldozer in a mined area, his vehicle struck a mine, which blew Connelly to the ground while the vehicle continued toward enemy lines. Connelly chased after the runaway, caught it, and returned it safely to complete the job. Only then did Connelly submit to medical attention, whereupon he had twenty-seven shrapnel fragments removed.

305 Ibid.

306   H. Wallis Anderson service record. Note the reluctance to list any/ all locations, as the war was still ongoing, and such details were classified.

307   On February 15, III Corps was reorganized under First Army, from Third Army.

308   HWAMil, 39.

309   US Army six-wheel amphibious trucks. Colloquially called "ducks," the letter designations stood for D—design year (in this case, 1942); U— mission (in this case, Utility); K—drive configuration (all-wheel drive); and W—axle configuration (dual tandem rear axles).

310   For his leadership during the Ardennes action along the Ourthe River, Fraser received the Legion of Merit. Although sometimes displayed as higher in the order of precedence for military awards, the Legion of Merit is two placers lower than the Silver Star.

311   David Pergrin, *First Across the Rhine*, 214.

312   Ibid, 215.

313   Ibid.

CHAPTER FIFTEEN

REMAGEN

T he shattered remnants of the German Wehrmacht pulled back from their ill-fated Eifel offensive desperately low on manpower, firepower, and horsepower, as conscription efforts, war-matériel production, and petroleum-product levels hit rock bottom. Many German divisions, brigades, and batteries were bare skeletons lacking any real strength or capability. Nevertheless, the Wehrmacht was still capable of resisting as it conducted a mostly orderly retreat, delaying everywhere.

The Allies pressed ahead relentlessly. As ever, the senior army commanders had differing opinions on how to finish Germany off, and who would get the major share of credit. Field Marshal Bernard Montgomery, directing the 21st Army Group on the left, northern portion of the Allied line, favored of course the main thrust to his front. This would take the Allies into and through northern Germany. Such a thrust had the advantage of traversing more gentle terrain, as well as heading directly for Berlin, the German capital.

Bradley, commanding 12th Army Group, instead argued for a heavier push in his sector, in the middle. A main effort here would rip through the center of Germany, destroying the war industries and coal centers, and splitting the country in half. One of the main drawbacks to this approach was terrain; Bradley's armies faced much more rugged topography, which would assist the German defenders.

Eisenhower had decided to go with Montgomery's strategy as far back as August. The supply delays, the Hürtgen forest, Market Garden, and the Ardennes Counteroffensive had all disrupted this strategy; in early 1945, it was back on track.

The Allies rolled across the German border while planners worked to put the original idea back into place. Montgomery would cross the Rhine first, north of the industrial Ruhr. Once his 21st Army Group poured into northern Germany, Bradley would follow up and cross the Rhine somewhere between Cologne and Koblenz.

The Rhine was on everyone's mind, as it was the last and most serious barrier into the heart of Germany. Flowing south to north, approximately forty miles east of Germany's western border, the Rhine was broad and deep, one of Europe's most significant waterways.

As the Allies approached, the Germans carried out the strategy of destroying all the bridges across the Rhine. At each main bridge point, they faced the difficult decision of timing. If they blew the bridge too soon, they risked leaving desperately needed armed forces stranded on the west bank, almost certainly to be quickly crushed or taken by advancing Allied units.

Conversely, if the withdrawing defenders waited too long to destroy a bridge, they ran the risk of a bridge being captured—a cardinal sin at this point in the war, and one that would likely cause a catastrophe and lead to utter collapse. Renowned military author and Army historian S. L. A. Marshall wrote, "No decision in combat is more difficult to make, and to time correctly, than the blowing of a bridge. There is an awful finality about it."[314]

Indeed, Wallis Anderson had dealt with this very issue at Trois-Ponts and had made the extraordinarily difficult decision to sacrifice good men to delay the enemy, precisely so that his blowing of the bridge over the Amblève would not be mistimed.

In early March, the First US Army launched Operation Lumberjack, the purpose of which was to drive all the way to the banks of the Rhine River, on a fifty-mile-wide front, from Koblenz to Cologne. Anderson's 1111th ECG supported III Corps, which contained the 9th Armored Division and three US infantry divisions: 1st, 9th, and 78th.

As it rolled eastward over crumbling German resistance, 9th Armored sent one element on a more southerly thrust, south of Bonn, in the direction of a bridge city, Remagen. Anderson recorded, "By March 7th we were within a few miles of the Rhine and it was the tactical plan for that date to clean out all resistance west of the river and the next day to turn our axis about 90° and attack south along the west bank of the river—to eventually meet Patton's Third Army which was coming north to join us."[315]

No one in the US Army had much hope of capturing any of the Rhine bridges. After the war, Anderson wrote to combat historian Ken Hechler, "The hope of securing a bridge intact was merely a glint in the eye of a few people."[316] Several attempts had been made to no avail as the Germans destroyed the spans. First Army continued to task the Army Air Force with destruction of the Rhine bridges, hoping to further disrupt the German Army. The US 9th Armored Division, which pressed into the Remagen sector on March 6, was directed to destroy the Ludendorff Bridge by fire "if necessary, to prevent enemy from using it."[317] The plan was to secure the west bank, then wait for Montgomery's forces to breach the Rhine; afterwards, the Americans would follow with their own river crossings.

The component of 9th Armored that drove toward Remagen on March 7 was a task group (not unlike the equivalent German kampfgruppes) of mixed forces, Combat Command B (CCB). CCB was led by Brigadier General William Hoge, a Corps of Engineers officer who had commanded engineers at Omaha Beach on D-Day. Hoge aggressively pushed his forces to the Rhine's west bank north and south of Remagen. As the CCB troops reached the town, they were surprised to find the bridge still standing.

Built during WWI, the Ludendorff Bridge at Remagen was a dual-track railroad bridge with an overall length of 1,069 feet. On the eastern shore the heights of Erpeler Ley rose; a train tunnel ran into this mountain immediately upon exiting the bridge eastbound. These heights provided a commanding view of the entire area.

Warned by a German prisoner of war that the plan was to destroy the bridge at 1600 hours, Hoge's troops instead quickly fought their way across, capturing it intact. The Germans attempted to impede the Americans, blowing a large crater at the bridge's western approach. This failed to stop the American infantry, who rushed onto the bridge with covering fire provided by armor and artillery.

When the Germans tried to blow the bridge, some of the demolition wiring and explosive-charge connections had been cut; the subsequent partial detonation only damaged the bridge, leaving it standing. Hoge wrote, "I issued my orders. First, we sent the infantry across. Right with them I sent a squad of Engineers to remove any demolitions that were on the bridge, and we found maybe 1,000 pounds or something like that underneath. They cut those loose and dropped them into the river."[318]

The heavily damaged bridge did not support tanks or heavy vehicle movement across, but infantry moved to establish a foothold on the east bank. The Rhine barrier had suddenly and unexpectedly been breached.

The seizing of the Ludendorff Bridge caught everyone by surprise. In preparation for providing engineer support for the upcoming drives south along the west bank, Anderson was at III Corps headquarters at Zülpich when word of the Remagen capture reached the corps commander. As Anderson described it, "That happy event completely changed the whole picture. The anticipated attack south was cancelled and all troops available—of any arm or organization—were pushed toward the Remagen crossing. Naturally one of the results was a massive traffic jam from the bridge head west."[319]

Coincidentally, the III Corps engineer, Colonel F. H. "Rusty" Lyons, had been part of the occupation forces after WWI, and had inspected that very bridge; he was familiar with its construction and vulnerability.

Lyons sent Anderson to First Army headquarters with the recommendation to immediately construct floating bridges as "insurance" for the Ludendorff Bridge. Once again, Anderson's group happened to be "in the wrong place at the right time—or vice versa," and so after "driving through the traffic tangle to Army Hdqrs.—and back," Anderson returned "with the bridge 'contract' in [his] pocket as it were."[320]

As III Corps prepared to throw as many troops as it could across the Ludendorff Bridge, opening a second avenue to push forces over the river was a top priority. Speed was critical, as the Germans were expected to react quickly and forcefully once they realized the severe danger now posed by the Americans on the east bank of the Rhine.

The Americans were acutely aware of how badly the Ludendorff was damaged; it was not expected to last long. Of the four trusses supporting the main arch that held the three spans, one was destroyed. That left only the downstream truss on the east bank supporting the entire east-bank bridge load. Although Army engineers swarmed over the bridge trying to fashion repairs, this effort was patchwork and not expected to provide a long-term solution. Until floating bridges could be constructed, there was a very real danger of the bridge collapsing, stranding American forces on the east bank and trapping them, the only Allied troops east of the Rhine.

Anderson's task: build a bridge across the thousand-foot-wide Rhine, with the far bank being contested and the construction crews isolated and exposed to enemy fire. As always, before he sent men into harm's way, he had to see for himself. On Thursday morning, March 8, Anderson headed to the bridge site. When his jeep arrived, he drove along the west bank north of the river, encountering officers from Pergrin's 291st ECB, who were scouting on their own.

The presence of Anderson's jeep seemed to attract attention from the Germans across the river because "as soon as the colonel's [Anderson] jeep appeared, mortar and machine-gun fire from the east bank hills overlooking the river had driven it and our recon team to cover behind buildings fronting the waterway."[321]

Anderson, along with senior engineers Hoge, Lyons, and Colonel Carter, "all examined the Ludendorff in the face of extreme personal risk, and all agreed that its life was very short."[322] Constructing the floating bridge would be a difficult and dangerous affair.

With the stakes so high, Anderson turned to his foremost battalion for the critical assignment. On Thursday March 8, Dave Pergrin and his 291st ECB were dispersed throughout the area around Euskirchen, providing support to the 78th Infantry Division, another III Corps unit. As usual, the engineers were conducting a variety of jobs to assist the line divisions—mine clearance, bridge-building, and road clearing and maintenance.

When word spread of the bridge at Remagen, all engineers were of course eager for any news that might affect them. Anderson summoned Pergrin in the early evening to report to group headquarters. Arriving at Anderson's headquarters, Pergrin wrote, "I could feel the tension before I even entered the group operations center. Colonel Anderson was deep in thought alongside a map that evidently had just been tacked to the wall. When he became aware of my entrance, he took off his helmet and said, 'Hi Dave. We've got a little job for you.'"[323]

Anderson's operations officer (S-3), Major Henderson Webb, briefed Pergrin on his assignment. The 291st was to construct a floating treadway bridge over the Rhine, just 400 yards downstream (north) of the Ludendorff Bridge, as quickly as possible. Anderson concluded his meeting with Pergrin, walked the twenty-seven-year-old lieutenant colonel to the door, and closed with, "Good luck, Dave. You and your men have the most important and dangerous bridge assignment in the history of the Corps of Engineers. We know you can do the job because the 291st has proven itself many times over."[324]

Even before assigning Pergrin this weighty task, Anderson had begun to tap other units for critical support roles. Establishing a forward headquarters at Ringen, seven miles west of Remagen, Anderson started to organize and coordinate all his available resources. Recognizing that the task at hand was not a typical construction job, he knew material would be stretched. He anticipated that the Germans would do their best to interdict American efforts, which meant damage and casualties; more men, equipment, and supplies would be needed than for a typical bridge-construction effort. Accordingly, he distributed tasks throughout his units, while calling for additional support.

Anderson assigned his 299th ECB with preparation of the bridge approach, on the shore. He further tasked the 299th with replacing damaged floats; this was especially important once German efforts to destroy the bridge began. He ordered the 86th Engineer Heavy Ponton Battalion to build ferries to transport men and material between the banks. The 998th and 988th Engineer Treadway Bridge Companies were assigned the primary task of assisting the 291st with treadway materials.

In conjunction with the 291st and its Remagen assignment, Anderson's former battalion, the 51st ECB, received a similar tasking: construct a heavy ponton bridge across the Rhine, upstream (south) from Remagen, between Linz and Kripp. As this sector was not yet securely in American hands, this second effort would lag the 291st's bridge by a day or two.

Work began on the treadway bridge site at around 0400 on Friday, March 9. Pergrin had men working on both banks, preparing the bridge approaches and foundations.

Having set into motion the construction enterprise, assigned tasks, and coordinated all the group activities in support of the all-important effort, Anderson turned to his next most important task as senior in charge: supervision and morale. These two are in a delicate balance; too-heavy effort in the former would negatively affect the latter. But with his engineers under fire (the 291st took its first casualties from German artillery shelling at around 0830, not long after dawn visibility allowed artillery spotting), Anderson felt compelled to quietly show his presence. It was again vitally important for morale that the group commander demonstrate the principle of shared risk.

Pergrin wrote,

> Colonel Anderson had arrived in Remagen at around 1000 hours but had remained out of our hair, silently watching our progress from a remote vantage point. Even after I learned of the colonel's proximity and went up to greet him, he never took an active part in doing my job for me. He never had before, but even I was ready to admit that this bridge was the most important job we had ever tackled, and technically the most taxing. However, knowing the Old Man was there, silently approving my actions, was an indescribable tonic.[325]

The implied approval would have extended down to the last man as well, as would the confidence of seeing their senior colonel exposing himself to the same risks they all faced. The troops noticed. Sergeant Henry Giles, 291st ECB, Company A, 2nd Platoon weapons sergeant, who manned a .50-caliber antiaircraft machine gun along the west bank of the Rhine, wrote,

> We heard that Col. Anderson was here himself to help Col. Pergrin lay out the bridge. I wouldn't know myself, but some of the boys said there *was* a full Col. here, standing around with Col. Pergrin watching most of the time. Both of them as cool as cucumbers. Paying no more attention to the shells & bombs than as if they'd been in their own back yards. No ducking or flinching.[326]

Pergrin assigned his Company A under Captain Harry Gamble to the actual bridge-building, with his other companies providing support. The basic construction of the M2 treadway bridge consisted of three major subcomponents: float, saddle, and treadway. The floats were made of rubberized canvas, each thirty-three feet long, eight feet, three inches wide, weighing 975 pounds, and capable of supporting eighteen tons. Once the float was inflated, a saddle was installed atop the float. The saddles were steel frames weighing 2,200 pounds. The saddle provided the means to lay the treadway over the float; the saddle secured and distributed the weight over the float.

The treadways provided the roadway for the bridge. Each treadway section weighed 2,350 pounds and provided two parallel tracks with a grid flooring. Once the float-saddle unit was assembled, it was launched into the water, and a treadway section was lowered onto it and attached. This assembly was then pushed by utility boat into line at the leading edge. Float assemblies, one after the other, were connected to the leading edge extending across the river. The connection of each float assembly required treadway connecting pins to be hammered into place. Support against the running river (the Rhine at this site moved at seven miles per hour) was provided by anchors and steel support cables running the length of the bridge.

In all, the bridge-building effort was heavy work requiring a massive effort of coordinated activities, including boats, cranes, pneumatic air-compressors, bulldozers, and dump trucks, as well as back-breaking, old-fashioned sledgehammer work.

At the extreme leading edge of the bridge (referred to as the "nose" in bridge-building) was Company A, 2nd Platoon, under Lieutenant Alvin Edelstein, the same stalwart platoon that had blown the Habiémont bridge in the face of Peiper's panzers, stopping Leibstandarte in its tracks.

Although Pergrin had intended to rotate troops through this position, the most arduous and dangerous of all the bridge-construction tasks, once they began the platoon refused to be relieved. High morale of troops in combat is difficult to quantify, and is reflected in a variety of ways. Refusing to leave danger is one example.[327] Grim humor is another; the leading edge was quickly labeled "Suicide Point" by the troops.

As expected, as the work progressed, the Germans responded furiously. Artillery shelling rained on the engineers throughout the day, and "an indication of their opposition is the record that 32 of the 86 floats required by the treadway at Remagen were so badly damaged by enemy action as to require replacement even before the bridge was completed."[328]

Working from a temporary headquarters established by Colonel Lyons, III Corps engineer, just behind the west-bank work site on high ground, Anderson stayed at or near the bridge construction throughout the day. He had his executive officer, Lieutenant Colonel James Kirkland, spend time on-site as well; clearly the intent was to show the troops that the seniors were always close by.

Casualties occurred from German artillery throughout the day. All along the banks were burning trucks and damaged equipment; the bridge had taken several direct hits as well. A near miss of a large-caliber shell knocked Kirkland to the ground and concussed him, requiring his evacuation.

The artillery firing continued into the night. Across to the east side, a German counterattack sought to throw the American forces back to the bridge. Work halted when barrages reached a certain point; the engineers sought refuge until the firing relented. At around 0300 on March 10, the firing finally ceased. The German attack had failed to dislodge the Americans east of the river.

Work on the bridge resumed, although more damage had been done. At this time, the bridge progress had reached midway across, about 500 feet. More German artillery commenced during the predawn hours of Saturday, March 10, causing further damage to the floating bridge and the Ludendorff.

Daylight brought a new threat to the bridge work, this time from the sky. Although scattered air attacks had been conducted the two previous days, on Saturday much more concentrated raids were thrown at the bridge site. Included in the new assaults were Messerschmitt ME-262 jet fighter-bombers, the world's first. The German Luftwaffe made numerous attacks, beginning shortly after dawn. German attack aircraft also included JU-87 Stukas, Arado AR-234 bombers (also jet powered), FW-190, BF-109, and ME-410 fighters.

Troops took cover, sometimes on the bridge itself, during the raids. German aircraft bombed and strafed the Ludendorff and the half-built treadway bridge. Once the air attacks subsided, bridge construction resumed. By midmorning, Anderson again visited the site, and "as always, the Old Man was well groomed, calm, and collected."[329]

Pergrin briefed him on bridge progress and the delays caused by the determined German air and artillery attacks. In response to the all-important question of the projected time of bridge completion, Pergrin provided Anderson with his estimation: early that evening. Even as they spoke, another flight of German jets attacked. By this point, the American army had concentrated a massive number of air-defense weaponry at and around Remagen. Pergrin describes,

Any weapon that could bear was firing as the string of jets swooped in. There was so much firing that the ground shuddered; it was awesome. The entire valley around Remagen became cloaked in smoke and dust before the Germans left— only three minutes after they first appeared. Throughout, Colonel Anderson never wavered, never flinched. Though I was by then extremely gun shy, I felt obliged to stand up beside this straight-backed veteran of Black Jack Pershing's raid into Mexico and the trenches of France during what we used to call The Great War. If nothing else, Colonel Anderson certainly impressed and inspired the troops. Word of his unfazed stance in the face of German jets passed through the battalion like wildfire.[330]

Perhaps without realizing it, Pergrin had absorbed the essence of leadership by example while under extreme stress. Although he felt severe anxiety—very understandably—while exposed to danger, he had stood his ground and presented an outward appearance of composure and confidence, purely so as not to disappoint the senior next to him, whom he so admired and respected. Projecting steadfastness outweighed his own instinct for survival. This is leadership in its rawest form. Undoubtedly, Anderson learned it the same way, in France twenty-seven years before, as he watched how his own senior officers behaved under fire.[331]

German artillery continued, causing delays from casualties and damage. Bridge work progressed, only halting during particularly heavy barrages. As the harrowing morning progressed, periodic shelling erupted, and the engineers sought cover. Anderson stayed to monitor the progress. He bore the burden of the extreme stress, shielding his engineers from the pressure of knowing an entire American army waited to use the bridge the moment it was complete. Not once did he urge Pergrin or his troops to hurry.

One barrage caught Anderson standing on the west bank, chatting with Pergrin. According to Pergrin, the rounds impacted a mere "twenty feet from where Colonel Anderson and [Pergrin] were standing." He continues,

> As I had minutes earlier, I continued to stand erect beside my superior. Lord knows, I wanted to run and hide, but I simply could not. Oh, how I wished he would break for cover! The troops who had gone to ground nearby were amazed. Finally, Sergeant Charlie Sweitzer, one of my leading demolitions men, crawled out and stood up beside us. A big, affable man who was as brave as anyone living, Sweitzer looked the colonel right in the eye and said, "Sir, you really ought not to take chances. We'd feel better if you and Colonel Pergrin would jump into a hole or something. We know when the Krauts are coming

in with something, so, when we yell, would you mind taking cover?" The old veteran looked back into Sweitzer's eyes and smiled. "Thanks Sergeant, we'll take that under advisement. You men are doing a good job and I wouldn't want to do anything to take your mind off the work."[332]

(Pergrin wrote that "good job" was "about the highest praise the taciturn group commander had ever been heard to utter, the ultimate superlative in his [Anderson's] limited lexicon of praise."[333] Giving effusive and therefore diluted praise was not a habit of Wallis Anderson's.)

Despite Sweitzer's plea, Anderson did *not* take cover. Pergrin says, "When the German shelling stopped, we were still standing in the open—the colonel, me, and Sergeant Sweitzer. Not then and not after would Anderson bow to the instincts of us mortals; no one ever saw him take cover in the face of German fire."[334]

By late Saturday morning, the bridge had reached two-thirds of the way across, despite all the delays and difficulties. Replacement floats were put into place by the 299th ECB along the bridge even as the nose extended farther across the Rhine. The bridle cable was prepared; this would provide much-needed stability and strength once the bridge sections were completed. As this bridge would be the longest-ever floating treadway, extraordinary measures were being put into place to ensure it stayed intact.

More German artillery barrages landed in midafternoon, the heaviest yet over the two days of construction. More floats were destroyed, more trucks hit, more equipment damaged; twenty more men were wounded as well. The artillery was followed by more jet aircraft attacks. American and British air forces provided fighter cover, aggressively defending the vital site.

Pergrin's men pressed on. With a determined effort at last light on Saturday, they reached the far shore. Officially at 1710 hours, the final connecting pin was driven in and the hook-end treadway wedge was secured. The Rhine River had been bridged; Hitler's last barrier was permanently breached.

Bridge support and strengthening continued, as well as repairs to damaged floats and treadways, in order to prepare the span to carry troops and vehicles; air attacks continued throughout, as more ME-262s tried to drop both bridges. Exhausted yet triumphant, Pergrin reported the completion to Anderson.

Later that night, Anderson wrote his wife (who he addressed as "My Dear Red Head"). After apologizing for not writing more frequently (and reassuring her that she would understand when he was able to give her the full account), he gave Marietta a version of events designed to pass the Army censors:

> I tell you that an old retread has just completed a job that every contemporary man or unit has been looking forward to for several years—and many have studied and trained particularly. The rest can now do what they please; ours was the first—and naturally that is quite gratifying. Now that I have actually been across a considerable river I really feel that I can say I have been in Germany—messing around on the west bank these several months has merely been a prelude.[335]

The next day he continued, in another letter to her,

> Yesterday we finished a job that every other similar group in service would have liked to have and many have specially trained for its prospect—as usual we just happened to be in the way and so stumbled into it—the first it has been done since the days of the little corporal some hundred and twenty five years back. Fraser and Big Bob got second honors being elsewhere at the moment.[336]

The 1111th unit history records the achievement:

On the 9th of March 1945 a class 40 steel treadway M-2 bridge was started across the RHINE River by the 291st Engr C Bn. The bridge was furnished by the 988th and 998th Engr Tdwy Br Companies, the bridge was started at 091300A March and completed 101710A March. The completed bridge was 1032 feet long. The longest tactical bridge ever built at that time. It was the first tactical bridge across the Rhine.

During the construction considerable damage was done by shell fire and necessary repairs precluded the opening of the bridge until 110700A [7 a.m., March 11]. Fifteen construction hours were lost due to enemy sniper, mortar and artillery fire. 17 casualties were suffered during construction of the bridge.[337]

Anderson and the group—privately and officially—reflected satisfaction that cascaded down through the ranks. The healthy sense of competition and unit pride—the much sought-after *esprit de corps*—established during training now paid off in lives saved during combat. Sergeant Giles wrote, "51st Engineers finished a pontoon upstream from the railroad bridge [Ludendorff] about three hours after we'd finished ours. Our boys worked like maniacs to get through first. We *weren't* going to let 51st beat us. Ours was a harder bridge, too. They built a heavy pontoon, but we built a floating treadway. And ours is longer."[338]

Starting on March 11, First Army could now throw many more resources across the Rhine, reinforcing the units trying to expand the bridgehead. The German effort to destroy the bridges continued, and included an effort by frogmen to mine the bridge foundations. The Germans even reportedly used their super-heavy self-propelled siege mortar, *Karl-Gerät*, which fired massive shells of either 540 or 600 mm. Air attacks and artillery continued as the desperate Germans tried to stop the American army from pouring across the Rhine into the German heartland.

The two floating bridges eventually were able to carry so much of the Army's movement that the Ludendorff was taken offline to conduct much-needed repairs. Additional floating bridges were constructed as the bridgehead expanded.

Even more desperate measures were attempted to stop the Allies at the Remagen. The German V-2 was the world's first operational long-range ballistic missile. It had been in service since the fall of 1944, used against city targets due to its imprecise accuracy. London, Antwerp, and Liège had been targeted, with more than 2,000 missiles launched. Hitler personally ordered V-2s to be used against the Remagen bridge site, despite the weapon's lack of suitability for such a point target; this was the only time these weapons were used against a target inside Germany.

On March 17, eleven V-2s were launched from sites in the Netherlands, aimed at Remagen, 150 miles to the south. Rocket launches began shortly before 1000 hours. The first V-2 impact came the closest to the Ludendorff Bridge, landing just under a half mile southeast of the bridge on the west bank, remarkably close for such an inaccurate weapon. Two other V-2s impacted at 1030 and 1220—the former five miles to the northwest and the latter a half mile west of the bridge. Due to the dense concentration of US Army troops in the area, the V-2s, with a 2,200-pound warhead, caused several military and civilian casualties.

V-2 barrage or not, Anderson visited Pergrin at the bridge site on that Saturday to discuss what new assignments were coming. As soldiers of the 1st Infantry Division crossed the treadway bridge that 291st men had built under shot and shell a week earlier, Anderson led Pergrin out along the bridge. While they chatted, Anderson inspected cable lashings and bridge components (of course), while enjoying the scenery and absorbing the deep sense of satisfaction they both must have felt.

Just after 1500 hours, with Anderson and Pergrin standing about midway along the treadway bridge, about a quarter mile upstream the Ludendorff Bridge suddenly trumpeted the loud and agonizing sounds of impending collapse, and, with much groaning, screeching, and cracking, fell into the Rhine. Ten days after explosive charges crippled it, and after countless high explosives hit on or near it, the bridge finally could stand no more.

Anderson, with an engineer's heart, wrote, "Then to our surprise and amazement before our eyes the immense structure just laid down in the River—as much to say 'I've done my part, but I'm tired—now you take over.'"[339] Anderson continued, "As to its final collapse, the mystery is not what caused it to fall but just why it kept up so long in its very damaged condition."[340] More than two dozen US soldiers—most of them engineers trying to save the bridge—were killed when Ludendorff collapsed.

Anderson and everyone else at the site rushed to help the survivors and to take measures to prevent damage to the floating bridge just downstream. Fortunately, the flotsam caused no permanent damage. After an hour's delay to rescue survivors and clear debris, troops continued to pour across the Rhine on the treadway, to be used to pound the German armed forces into final submission.

On March 26, the 1111th relinquished responsibility for the bridge at Remagen to the 1159th ECG. Germany was collapsing, accelerated by the exploitation of the Remagen bridgehead. German soldiers—and even entire military units—began surrendering in large numbers as the US Army pressed forward. The usual organizational shuffling occurred as the Army restructured to handle this new reality. The redoubtable 291st ECB was transferred to the 1159th Group, separating Dave Pergrin from Anderson's command.

The 51st ECB again returned to the 1111th, once more reuniting the Plattsburgh and Texas-trained engineers with Anderson. The group remained attached to III Corps, still under First Army, and built bridges to assist the advance deeper into Germany. During the month of March 1945, units of the 1111th built a total of thirteen bridges for III Corps, including the famous "First Across the Rhine"

1,032-foot floating treadway at Remagen. Units of the 1111th suffered thirty-nine casualties, most during or just after the construction efforts at Remagen.

In April, III Corps moved rapidly into the industrial Ruhr region of Germany, in the vicinity of Kassel, 125 miles east of the Rhine. The 1111th and its engineer units provided standard road and bridging support. In mid-April, German resistance in the Ruhr collapsed and III Corps was sent in its entirety—including the 1111th ECG—to Third Army under General Patton, who pinned on his fourth star, signifying the full rank of general, on April 14, 1945. III Corps moved south to Neustadt, taking up operations into southern Germany and Austria. There was fear that substantial German forces would try to establish a "redoubt" in mountainous southern Germany. Third Army and III Corps were sent to prevent this.

Danger for those engaged in close-combat support did not cease, even as the Third Reich went into its death throes. On April 26, the 51st ECB was assigned to build a bridge over the Donau River (the German name for the Danube) at Ingolstadt, which was still being contested by remaining German forces. The infantry present, US 86th Infantry Division, had presented an overly optimistic assessment, claiming the city was entirely in their hands. The 51st's Company A was assigned to build a floating treadway bridge over the Donau. In fact, fighting was still widespread in and around the city.

Late in the tense, dark night, battalion commander Lieutenant Colonel Harvey Fraser and Captain Floyd Wright scouted along the northern bank to find a suitable site to launch the bridge. Wright walked along the muddy bank, author Fowle describes,

> as quietly as he could when someone tapped him on the shoulder from behind and said in a low, but reassuring voice, "I think you can get started now." This scared the daylights out of Wright. He turned around and in spite of the darkness recognized Colonel Anderson, Commanding Officer of the 1111th ECG. With the group commander and the battalion

commander at the bridge site every soldier knew that somehow everything was going to be OK, even though the Germans still controlled the far bank.[341]

Once again, the presence and calm confidence of the senior officer ensured a sense of determined steadfastness that led to a successful mission.

As Anderson experienced on numerous occasions, such leadership practices entailed risk. The overnight Ingolstadt construction operation involved another such episode. When the 51st began its work, the far shore had not yet been cleared of German resistance:

[Before dawn] heavy small arms fire was received in the bridge site from the far shore. The fire was returned and with the help of an M-7 SP [self-propelled] gun and infantry the enemy finally surrendered. Approximately 300 prisoners were taken in all. No casualties were suffered and no damage sustained by the bridge. During this action the Group Commander, Colonel H. W. Anderson and the battalion commander Lt.Col. FRAZER had a close call. While on the bridge an enemy burp gun cut down on them. They had to hit the deck until the sniper had been eliminated.[342]

Inspiring the troops is a hazardous business.

On April 29, a happy event transpired for Anderson and members of his group. Forty miles southeast of Ingolstadt, the 14th Armored Division of Patton's Third Army overran a German prisoner of war (POW) camp, liberating the captives. Stalag VII-A was Germany's largest WWII POW camp, located in Moosburg, Germany, outside Munich. One of the POWs released was Captain Thomas Williams, Anderson's S-4 who had been captured in the Ardennes the previous October. Captain Albert Radford of the 51st ECB wrote to his wife,

Do you remember the captain I mentioned as captured?

Anderson got him out of a large prison camp day before yesterday [April 29]. He has lost a lot of weight and has marched hundreds of miles as a POW. He was once freed by the Russians and then recaptured by the Germans. He has seen most of Europe on foot and on 2 potatoes and a cup of soup a day.[343]

Shortly after, German resistance completely collapsed and the war in Europe ended. Victory in Europe (VE Day) was declared, May 8. At the time, 1111th ECG was in Altenerding, northeast of Munich. Happily, the 291st ECB was reattached to the group on that date, a fitting act to end the war. On May 11, the 1111th moved again, to the vicinity of Würzburg, where "the Group was billeted in an old 16th Century Castle named after its occupants: Castell-Castell."[344] The accommodations were "very comfortable," with ample space and time for relaxation, including sports and a chapel. Soon, "the entire combat Army rapidly completely fell apart. . . . The fact that [the Allies] were still involved in a very rough war in the Pacific seemed to be totally forgotten."[345]

Anderson performed one last service for his engineers. As the Army published its point scheme to determine who could go home and who should remain behind, it was left to unit commanders to single out those deemed "essential" and therefore to be held in service despite their accumulated point total. Anderson declared on May 24 that for the units in his group, no officer would be declared essential if they had the points to return home. Although no schedule for return had been published, Anderson's policy buoyed morale.

The Army had a final surprise for Wallis Anderson. Although he would have preferred to remain with his group, he received orders for transfer to a new and virtually unknown headquarters, to report on May 30. The Group Control Council (GCC) had been established to administer all governmental affairs in Germany, under the Four Power Council (United States, Great Britain, USSR, and France).

According to the unit history, "A farewell banquet was held in the Officers mess for Colonel H.W. Anderson, Group Commander who was reassigned."[346] The next day, as Anderson departed for his new staff assignment, he published one final formal order for his group, for May 30, 1945:

Order of the Day:

To: All officers and men of the 1111th Engineer
Combat Group.

Effective this date the undersigned is assigned to other duties. In relinquishing command of the 1111th Engineer Combat Group I desire to take this opportunity of expressing my appreciation of the fine work you have done in the campaign recently closed—both as units and as individuals.

During the training period in the United States, through the preparatory work in England and all during the operations on the continent, your performance has been outstanding. Severe weather, adverse conditions, new and unexpected situations and enemy action have in turn been met and overcome in stride. Through all phases your achievements have been noteworthy and meritorious—and second to none.

During the campaign in Normandy, on the advance through France and Belgium, in the Ardennes, across the Roer, over the Rhine, in the Ruhr pocket and in the final phase of the battle in and across Germany including the crossing of the Danube, you distinguished yourselves by always accomplishing every mission assigned, despite difficulties and with maximum despatch and minimum casualties, thereby bringing considerable credit to the engineers in general and yourselves in particular.

As a result of your excellent performance various decorations and awards have been made to you as individuals and as units. No doubt others were well earned and fully merited. However I wish to add my own congratulations and commendation for the excellent work you have done.

I feel that I have been particularly fortunate and honored in having commanded the group from its creation, during its training and throughout its active service in the European theater and wish to thank you all for the loyal support you have rendered.

This war started in the Pacific and [will] eventually end there. What the future holds for any of us is—as usual—most uncertain. However I will always recall with pleasure and gratification my service with the group and wish you the best of luck where ever you are assigned. May your future be as glorious as your past and early success to our arms in the Pacific result in your speedy return to your homes.

H. W. Anderson
Colonel, C. E
Commanding[347]

Wallis Anderson's journey with the 1111th Engineer Combat Group had begun three years before after an Army-wide reorganization removed him from the Pennsylvania National Guard with whom he had grown up, in a professional and military sense, and sent him to Texas. There, with almost no direct assistance, he had built a regiment-sized group—literally, as his new officers and men began training using facilities they had constructed themselves. Twice the age of his young draftees and volunteers, none of whom had experience in the military or even professional engineering, Anderson created a culture of excellence, discipline, and professionalism from a throng of untrained yet eager new combat engineers.

When the Army transferred his training effort to the frigid north, Anderson, eschewing the comfort of brick buildings with steam heat, instead compelled his trainees to learn their work while exposed to the most inhospitable of winter climes. Alone among his cohort in knowing the rigors of combat, he knew the value of hard, even harsh training. Throughout, he placed himself at the front of all unit activities, leading by example for his young officers and noncommissioned officers.

With the Allied invasion of France, Anderson's engineers contributed measurably to initial Army success on the continent. As they became seasoned veterans and gained confidence with combat experience under Anderson's steady hand, the engineers' reputation and abilities grew.

When crisis struck, the steadfastness built over two years extended from Anderson at the top down through the most junior ranks; other units broke under the stress, while Anderson's engineers stood their ground. Rebounding from that success, the engineers under his command were able to seize an opportunity to advance the war effort, at Remagen. The circumstances there were no less critical; failure would have allowed a still-dangerous enemy to regroup and extend the war for weeks.

Wallis Anderson's personal leadership style provided the foundation for dozens of young officers to study, learn, and emulate. Always composed, professionally turned out, and positive, Anderson was the epitome of leadership by example, bravery, discipline, and high standards of excellence so critical for combat-mission success.

In a Special Efficiency Report, his Army commander described Anderson as a "very quiet and unassuming man but extremely forceful and completely dependable in an emergency as well as in regular routine combat duties."[348] In that report, written just after the crisis of the Ardennes had peaked, the commander rated Anderson with the highest marks ("Superior") for leadership, initiative, and stability under pressure. Twice recognized with the nation's third-highest medal for valor in combat, to Wallis Anderson, the fact that the troops and units under his direction received recognition for their heroic contributions counted for more; his personal correspondence reflects this pride.

Transferred to an unsought-after staff job at war's end, Anderson bid farewell to his beloved engineers. The postwar Army needed administrative staff officers more than they needed fifty-four-year-olds with superior combat-leadership abilities. As he well understood, the Army needed to keep rolling along.

In his first deployed service, twenty-five-year-old Anderson had worn riding breeches and been issued saddle bags. Twenty-nine years later, during his final major action, he and his troops were subjected to attack by jet bombers and ballistic missiles that had traversed space. It was time to move on, and let others step up to the challenge of "let us try."

ENDNOTES

314   Ken Hechler, *The Bridge at Remagen* (New York: Ballantine Books, 1957), xiv.

315   HWAMil, 39.

316   H. Wallis Anderson letter to Ken Hechler, August 26, 1958.

317   Hechler, *The Bridge at Remagen*, 22.

318   William Hoge, *Engineer Memoirs* (Washington, DC: US Army Corps of Engineers, 1993), 144.

319   HWAMil, 40.

320   Ibid.

321   Pergrin, *First Across the Rhine*, 227.

322   Ibid, 231.

323   Ibid, 225.

324   Ibid, 224. Pergrin again mentioned Anderson's "twinkling eyes" in this exchange.

325   Ibid, 244.

326   Janice Giles, *The G.I. Journal of Sergeant Giles* (Boston: Houghton Mifflin, 1965), 295. Giles also helped to inflate the floats used for the bridge.

327   Occasional short-term replacements did provide the platoon with some respite.

328   HWAMil, 40.

329   Pergrin, *First Across the Rhine*, 262.

330   Ibid, 263.

331   David Pergrin was born July 26, 1917, one year before Anderson first faced combat in shallow trenches south of St. Agnan, France.

332   Ibid, 264.

333   Ibid.

334   Ibid, 265.

335   H. Wallis Anderson letter to Marietta Anderson, March 10, 1945. Anderson wrote in a tight, precise longhand. His wife, an office professional, *typed* her letters to him.

336   H. Wallis Anderson letter to Marietta Anderson, March 11, 1945. This letter and the previous reveal a more personal side of Anderson, reflecting pride and a competitive nature he was reluctant to display publicly. "The little corporal" is a reference to Napoleon, who was allegedly the last to cross the Rhine in a military action. In this way, Anderson could obliquely refer to the Rhine without mentioning it, and pass the censors. "Fraser and Big Bob [Robert Yates]" refer to the commanding officer and executive officer of his former 51st ECB, who constructed a ponton bridge upstream from Remagen; it was completed in the evening of March 11.

337   Unit History, 1111th Engineer Combat Group, 1 March 1945–31 March 1945.

338   Giles, *The G.I. Journal of Sergeant Giles*, 294.

339   HWAMil, 41.

340   Ibid.

341   Fowle, *The 51st Again!*, 164.

342   Unit History, 1111th Engineer Combat Group, 1 April 1945–30 April 1945.

343   Radford, *Unbroken Line*, 164.

344   Unit History, 1111th Engineer Combat Group, 1 April 1945–30 April 1945.

345   HWAMil, 43.

346   Unit History, 1111th Engineer Combat Group, 1 May 1945–31 May 1945.

347   1111th Engineer Combat Group Order of the Day, 30 May 1945

348   Anderson personnel file. Special Efficiency Report for the period 1 July 1944–25 December 1944, signed by Lieutenant General Courtney Hodges, commander, First US Army, 21 April 1945. The reader is left to decide what "regular routine combat" means.

EPILOGUE

Colonel Wallis Anderson reported for duty with the Group Control Council (GCC) in Paris on Saturday, May 5; two days later the command shifted to Frankfurt, Germany. He was assigned to the "Prisoner of War and Displaced Person Branch" of the G-1 (administration) section due to a personal connection.

As ever, Anderson's network and reputation were extensive and superlative. The former commanding general of the artillery brigade of the 28th Infantry Division—Anderson's former outfit—Brigadier General Eric Wood, had specifically requested Anderson, even before the war ended. Anderson took up his staff duties with the GCC, a policy headquarters charged with managing the administration of postwar Germany.

The Army's formal recognition of Anderson's exceptional performance after the Ardennes followed. On April 17, Anderson was awarded a second Silver Star; III Corps General Order 47 states,

> For gallantry in action. On 9 March 1945, in the vicinity of ***, ***, Colonel ANDERSON, as group commander, bravely and fearlessly under continuous heavy artillery and air bombardment, ably directed the construction of the first tactical bridge across the *** River and the operation of heavy

ponton ferries. With complete disregard for his safety, he remained at his post for eight days and, despite continued shelling and bombing, saw the bridge through to successful completion. Colonel ANDERSON's courage and gallant action under fire reflect the highest credit on him and the armed forces of the United States.[349]

In addition, Anderson was singled out for his overall senior leadership performance during the final push into Germany, without specific reference to a particular act, with the Legion of Merit, seventh in order of precedence of all US military awards (the Silver Star is third highest). Anderson's citation of 20 August 1945 reads, "For exceptionally meritorious conduct in the performance of outstanding services from 18 February to 8 May 1945."[350]

While attending meetings in London, Anderson learned of the end of the war with Japan. Repatriation followed quickly, as the Army quickly phased out service members who were not regular Army. Both Wood and Anderson soon found passage back to the United States, although the difference between a general officer and a mere colonel was on display: Brigadier General Wood flew back independently from Europe, while Colonel Anderson was assigned responsibility for a troop detachment and sent home on a returning Liberty ship, the *Arthur Moore*.

Coincidentally, Anderson made it home only a few weeks after his distinguished former battalions, the 51st and 291st, returned in much the same manner. For the 51st, their return voyage was marked by an unusual display of recognition and admiration. Aboard the SS *Eufala Victory*, the battalion members soon found that their reputation—so important among Army units—was held in high regard. According to one member, "The 51st was known. When we were coming home, when we got on the boat . . . it was a big troop ship. All different outfits on the ship. And when we went to mess hall one day, someone hollered '51st Combat Engineers! and you coulda heard, the whole place erupted. And we knew that we had been heard about. The infantry guys even knew us."[351]

The concept of "unit pride" was never more eloquently presented.

Back stateside, Anderson was undergoing out-processing from his home base for the National Guard of Pennsylvania, Indiantown Gap Military Reservation, when he received a phone call from a colleague at Army engineer headquarters in Washington, DC. For the first time in his long career, he was offered a job ("which in itself threw me off guard"),[352] a temporary assignment as VII Corps engineer, in Monterey, California. As Anderson describes,

> Then too it was snowing in Philadelphia at the time so California sounded much more attractive than railroading— and snow. Only a very brief consultant with my Chief of Staff was necessary for me to mumble acquiescence. That was December 1945—and the "temporary" job finally terminated in October 1950 when retirement was mandatory [on] account [of] reaching statutory age.[353]

Anderson established himself at the corps headquarters office in Fort Ord, while his quarters were in the Presidio in Monterey (present-day site of the Defense Language Institute). The accommodations were only partially furnished with Army Quartermaster furniture, as his was only a temporary assignment. Anderson goes on to say,

> Our own household effects—which were still in storage in Phila. would have been of course moved to San Francisco by the Government. However, our tenure out there was supposed to be only temporary—and we were superstitious enough to believe that a sure way to end a very agreeable assignment would be to have our furniture join us. We were quite comfortable as is.[354]

His assignment survived the usual reorganizations and structural shuffling, although his title and duties shifted several times. He was able to travel extensively throughout the Western United States, a region unfamiliar to him up to that point.

Upon reaching mandatory retirement age in October 1950, Colonel H. Wallis Anderson retired, having managed to extend a temporary assignment into a very fulfilling four and a half years. The next year, he was placed on the retired list of the Pennsylvania National Guard, which advanced him to the grade of brigadier general. He continued to serve with that organization's Veterans Association, including a term as president. Anderson continued his membership with the Society of American Military Engineers, of which he was a charter member.

Wallis Anderson returned briefly to Pennsylvania Railroad, his only other employer. After short stints in Altoona and Baltimore, he was able to meet retirement criteria, and retired from that company as well.

In retirement, Anderson kept in touch with many of his former colleagues and friends, in and out of the service, as he had done throughout his life. Anderson took part in several postwar return visits to his former battlegrounds. In 1969, to commemorate the twenty-fifth anniversary of D-Day, he visited many familiar sites. With various veterans' groups, he visited England and many of the places he saw in combat during two wars in France, Belgium, and Germany.

On one such visit, the tour director, behind schedule and having to hastily modify the itinerary, decided to forego the group visit to the Remagen bridge site on the Rhine. Anderson gripes, "His explanation that 'there was nothing to see anyhow—the bridge was demolished during the war' was little satisfaction to those of us who wished to revisit the site."[355] Fortunately, Wallis was able to make it to the Remagen site on a following trip.

The last entries in his commentaries are dated in the fall of 1972, six months before Anderson passed, on March 14, 1973, at the age of eighty-two. His remains are interred at the Arlington

Cemetery in Drexel Hill, Pennsylvania, four miles from the Sharon Hill neighborhood of his youth.

Tributes to Harry Wallis Anderson take several forms, direct and indirect. SS officer Jochen Peiper's alleged furious exclamation, having been stopped just shy of the Lienne creek at Habiémont, "Those damned engineers!" could well be directed at Anderson, the man responsible for sending the combat engineers to destroy that bridge.

Another form of tribute for a commander so committed to the development of his young officers is the gratification of seeing many of the officers he led in combat achieve lengthy and senior service positions. Several reached the rank of general officer and enjoyed long, successful careers.

Still others wrote of Anderson after his passing. Corporal Frank Lee, a Plattsburgh-trained member of the 51st ECB, provided his recollections for a book in 1998. Writing of his experiences with the 51st, Lee wrote,

> We became a very cohesive, close knit group. As much a family as is possible under military conditions. We cared about each other, individually and collectively. We were concerned with each other's welfare and safety. And we were and still are proud of our outfit.
>
> These are the many things I still thank God for amongst many others for looking after us as He did.
>
> For Colonel Anderson and for the hell he put us through.
>
> For changing our orders in North Africa and reassigning us to the E.T.O. [European Theater of Operations, which resulted in assignment to Anderson's group]
>
> For Major Yates for being the kind of officer he was and at the same time for being one of us.

For sending us Col. Harvey Fraser (Scrappy) when we needed a competent combat commander in the worst kind of way.[356]

In a 2017 interview, another member of the 51st who joined the battalion in Plattsburgh, Charles "Chuck" Kroen, commented on Anderson:

I joined them in New York, 30 below zero. During the Battle of the Bulge, nobody got frostbite. Everybody had learned how to take care of themselves. The training helped us.

He [Anderson] was out there, I mean, he slept out there, and the whole bit, you know, with us. Most of the officers, from West Point and all, were just a bunch of charlatans. As far as being an officer, he was good. I mean, he was one of the best. Him and Major Yates. They were two, you know, very good officers. The officers—the average soldier, he'd salute him, because he was an officer. But there were certain ones who would get a salute because they were who you are. And Yates and Anderson, they were two of those.[357]

Finally, a moving tribute was recorded, this time not by a service member but by a grateful wife, Laurie Radford, whose husband, Captain Albert Radford, commanded the Headquarters and Services Company of the 51st ECB. In 1988, Laurie Radford wrote to Mrs. H. Wallis Anderson (Marietta, the "Red Head" of Wallis's letters),

The more I read about the war and think about all that the men under him [Col. Anderson] accomplished, the more I admire him. He had so much common sense, foresight and anticipation of what sort of hard training they needed to be able to face and endure the drudgery, the misery, the horror of combat—they couldn't realize what was coming, but the colonel [a veteran of the Mexican War and WWI] knew and prepared them to face it.

I'm sure they grumbled and complained about all the hard training at Plattsburgh, but it paid off. So many of the men said later they never endured anything much worse in combat! So they got excellent training from your husband. And thanks to your husband, in large part, there were very few war widows (or grieving family members) among the 51st ranks, and others he trained.[358]

ENDNOTES

349 Anderson Service Record. The locations—Remagen and Rhine River—are withheld due to security in wartime.

350 Ibid.

351 Charles Kroen interview September 10, 2017, by author.

352 HWAMil, 45.

353 Ibid. Anderson's comment about consulting his "Chief of Staff" is a tongue-in-cheek reference to his wife, Marietta.

354 HWACiv, 29.

355 HWAMil, 48.

356 Radford, *Unbroken Line*, 219.

357 Charles Kroen interview September 10, 2017, by author.

358 Radford, *Unbroken Line*, 235.

SELECTED BIBLIOGRAPHY

"America's Wars Fact Sheet." Department of Veterans Affairs, Office of Public Affairs. May 2017. Accessed April 2020.

Anderson, H. Wallis. Letter to Captain Robert E. Merriam, author of Dark December, January 23, 1950.

———. H. Wallis Anderson to his wife, Marietta, December 29, 1944.

———. H. Wallis Anderson to his wife, Marietta, March 10, 1945.

———. H. Wallis Anderson to his wife, Marietta, March 11, 1945.

———. H. Wallis Anderson to Ken Hechler, author of *The Bridge At Remagen*, August 26th, 1958.

———. H. Wallis Anderson to wife, Marietta, late December, 1944

———. H. Wallis Anderson to wife, Marietta, March 3, 1945.

———. "Memoirs (Civilian)," 1971.

———. "Some Military Experiences," 1971.

Atkinson, Rick. *The Guns At Last Light: The War in Western Europe, 1944-1945.* New York: Henry Holt, 2013.

Beck, Alfred M., Abe Bortz, Charles W. Lynch, Lida Mayo, and Ralph F. Weld. *The Corps of Engineers: The War Against Germany.* Washington, DC: United States Army Center of Millitary History, 1985.

Bennet, Ralph. *Ultra in the West.* New York: Charles Scribner's Sons, 1980.

Bouwmeester, Han. *Beginning of the End: The Leadership of SS Obersturmbannfuhrer Jochen Peiper.* Fort Leavenworth, KS: US Army Command and General Staff College, 2004.

Buchan, John. *Days To Remember: The British Empire in the Great War.* n.p: Musaicum Books, 2017.

Cain, Francis M, III. *The 1111th Engineer Combat Group in the Bulge: The Role of Engineers as Infantry in AirLand Battle.* Auckland: Pickle Partners Publishing, 2014.

Carter, William A. Letter from William A. Carter to H. Wallis Anderson, September 4, 1969.

Centre de Recherches et d'Informations sur la Bataille des Ardennes. n.d. Accessed April 15, 2020. http://www.criba.be/.

Clendenen, Clarence C. *Blood on the Border: The United States Army and the Mexican Irregulars.* New York: Macmillan Company, 1969.

Cole, Hugh M. *United States Army in WWII—Europe—The Ardennes: Battle of the Bulge.* Auckland: Pickle Partners Publishing, 2013.

Coll, Blanche D., Jean E. Keith, and Herbert H. Rosenthal. *The Corps of Engineers: Troops and Equipment.* Washington, DC: United States Army Center of Military History, 1988.

"HQ Twelfth Army Group situation map." Library of Congress. Accessed various. https://www.loc.gov/collections/world-war-ii-maps-military-situation-maps-from-1944-to-1945/.

Cooke, David, and Wayne Evans. *Kampfgruppe Peiper at the Battle of the Bulge.* Mechanicsburg, PA: Stackpole Books, 2008.

———. *Kampfgruppe Peiper: The Race for the Meuse.* South Yorkshire: Pen & Sword Books, 2014.

Cora, Paul B., and Alexander A. Falbo-Wild. *The US Army Campaigns of World War I: Supporting Allied Offensives—8 August–11 November 1918.* Washington, DC: United States Army Center of Military History, 2018.

"The Zimmermann Telegram." *Cryptologic Quarterly.* National Security Agency, n.d.

Duncan, T. V2ROCKET.com. n.d. Accessed April 10, 2020. http://www.v2rocket.com/.

Elstob, Peter. *Hitler's Last Offensive.* S. Yorkshire: Pen & Sword Books, 2003.

Fowle, Barry W., Floyd D. Wright. *The 51st Again!* Shippensburg, PA: White Mane Publishing, 1992.

Gabel, Christopher R. *The US Army GHQ Maneuvers of 1941.* Washington, D.C: United States Army Center of Military History, 1992.

Gilbert, Eugene. *The 28th Division in France.* Nancy-Paris-Strasbourg: Berger-Levrault, 1919.

Giles, Janice Holt. *The Damned Engineers.* Washington, DC: Office of the Chief of Engineers, United States Army, 1987.

———. *The GI Journal of Sergeant Giles.* Boston: Houghton Mifflin, 1965.

Hechler, Ken. *Holding The Line.* Honolulu, HI: University Press of the Pacific, 2005.

———. *The Bridge At Remagen.* New York: Ballantine Books, 1957.

"History of 51st Engineer Combat Battalion (1944)." National Archives, n.d.

Hoge, General William M. *Engineer Memoirs.* Washington, DC: US Army Corps of Engineers Office of History, 1993.

Kays, Marvin D. *Weather Effects During The Battle of the Bulge and the Normandy Invasion.* White Sands Missile Range, NM: US Army Electronics Research and Development Command, Atmospheric Sciences Laboratory, 1982.

Kohli, Paul Eugene, "Interview With Paul Eugene Kohli (September 11)." By Jerri Donohue. Library of Congress Veterans History Project, 2008.

Kroen, Charles. Interview by John Racoosin. n.p. September 10, 2017.

Lengel, Edward G. *To Conquer Hell: The Meuse-Argonne, 1918, The Epic Battle That Ended the First World War.* New York: Henry Holt Publishing, 2008.

MacDonald, Charles B. *A Time For Trumpets: The Untold Story of the Battle of the Bulge.* United Kingdom: Endeavor Press, 2015.

Marshall, S. L. A. *The Battle of the Bulge: The First Eight Days.* Arden, UK: Coda Books, 2011.

Martin, Colonel Edward, and E. S. Wallace, eds. *The Twenty-Eighth Division: Pennsylvania's Guard in the World War.* Pittsburgh: 28th Division Publishing, 1924.

McKinsey, Captain William L., ed. *Battalion History: 291 Engineer C BN. Unit History*, Washington, DC: US Army Military History Institute, 1945.

Merriam, Robert E. *Dark December: The Full Account of the Battle of the Bulge.* Chicago: Ziff-Davis Publishing, 1947.

Metz, Leon C. *Desert Army: Fort Bliss on the Texas Border.* n.p: Mangan Books, 1988.

Parker, Danny S. *Battle of the Bulge: Hitler's Ardennes Offensive, 1944–45.* Cambridge, MA: Da Capo Press, 2004.

Parker, Danny S., ed. *Hitler's Ardennes Offensive: The German View of the Battle of the Bulge.* Mechanicsburg, PA: Stackpole Books, 1997.

Passion, Rex. *The Lost Sketchbooks: A Young Artist in the Great War.* Cambridge, Massachusetts: Komatik Press, 2014.

Pergrin, Colonel David E. *Engineering the Victory.* Atglen, PA: Schiffer Publishing, 1996.

———. *First Across The Rhine.* New York: Macmillan Publishing, 1989.

Pershing, John J. *My Experiences In The World War.* New York: Frederick A. Stokes, 1931.

Phillips, Henry J., ed. *202 Engineer Combat Battalion Unit History.* US Army Military History Institute, 1945.

Proctor, H. G. *The Iron Division, National Guard of Pennsylvania, in the World War.* Philadelphia: The John C. Winston Company, 1919.

Racoosin, Helen Anderson. "Memoirs." n.d.

Radford, Albert E. and Laurie S. Radford. *Unbroken Line: The 51st Engineer Combat Battalion From Normandy to Munich.* Woodside, CA: Cross Mountain Pulblishing, 2002.

Ramsey, Winston G., ed. *After The Battle Quarterly, Number 4: The Battle of the Bulge.* London: Plaistow Press, 1974.

Reynolds, Michael. *Men of Steel: I SS Panzer Corps, The Ardennes and Eastern Front 1944–45.* South Yorkshire: Pen & Sword Books, 2009.

The General Service School. "The German Offensive of July 15, 1918." Fort Leavenworth, KS: The General Service School Press, 1923.

Unit History: 1111th Engineer Combat Group (1945). US Army Military History Institute, n.d.

War Department. "FM 21-105 Basic Field Manual: Engineer Soldier's Handbook (1943)." Washington: Government Printing Office, n.d.

———. "FM 5-25 Engineer Field Manual: Explosives and Demolitions (1942)." Washington: Government Printing Office, n.d.

———. "TM 5-272 Steel-Treadway Bridge M2." Washington: Government Printing Office, 1944.

———. "TM 5-273 Technical Manual: 25 Ton Ponton Bridge Model 1940." Washington: Government Printing Office, 1942.

———. "TM 9-1901 Artillery Ammunition." Washington: Government Printing Office, 1944.

———. "TM 9-1904 Ammunition Inspection Guide Technical Manual," Washington: Government Printing Office, 1944.

Weiss, Wilhelm. *Battle of the Bulge '44: 1st SS Panzer Division Kampfgruppe Peiper.* Weitere Publikationen, 2012.

———. ed. *Battle of the Bulge: Standartenfuhrer Joachim Peiper (The Interview).* n.p. Kindle Edition, 2012.

INDEX

PEOPLE

A

Anderson, Harry Wallis
    birth and early life, 7-14
    college degrees, 13-14
    enlistment, National Guard of
    Pennsylvania, 14
    commissioning and early
    service, 15, 17
    promotions, 15 (through
    captain), 52 (major), 66
    (lieutenant colonel), 68
    (colonel)
    initial fulltime railroad
    employment, 16-17
    service along Mexican border,
    22-25
    marriage, to Elizabeth Cobb,
    25, 31; to Marietta Jones, 67
    mobilized with PNG, 31
    appointment as engineer
    officer, 32
    to France (World War I), 35,
    37-40, 42-43, 47-52
    renewed PRR service, 56-57,
    59-65, 67-68
    WWI service awards, 58-59
    death of wife, 61
    broken service, 62
    PRR career derailment, 64
    nationalized for WWII, 68
    assignment as commanding
    officer, 51st Engineer Combat
    Regiment, 76
    at Camp Bowie, 76-82
    at Plattsburgh, 83-96
    at West Virginia Maneuver
    Area, 96-97
    designated as commanding
    officer, 1111th ECG, 93
    deployed to Europe (WWII),
    98, 102
    pre-invasion, 103-105
    Highnam Court, 107, 110-112
    Normandy (Utah beach),
    116-118
    1111th ECG staff, 119
    operations in Normandy,
    120-125
    Operation Cobra and
    breakout, 126-129
    operations across France and
    Belgium, 131-134
    at Trois-Ponts, 142-147
    at Battle of the Bulge

(Ardennes), 4-6, 200-203, 206, 208-209, 215-216, 219, 221-224, 228-231, 233-242, 244, 246-259, 261-269, 273-277, 279-280, 282

into Germany, 283-290

at Remagen, 294-300, 302-306, 308-309

war's end, 310-315

post-war, 319-322

death, 7, 322

Anderson children

Bettie, 34, 67

Harry, jr (Bud), 57, 67

Helen, 60, 67, 100

Audrey, 61, 67, 100

Anderson, Ida Woodington, 7

Anderson, John Henry (J.H.), 7-11

Anderson, Marietta (née Jones), 67, 281, 306

Arnold, Clifford (and wife, Audrey), Medical Corps, 35, 61, 71

B

Bieker, Ralph, 252-253

Billington, R. C., 266

Bouck, Lyle, 213

Bradford, James, 33, 42, 53

Bradley, Omar, 110, 121, 129, 241, 293-294

Buchannan, Dallas, 253

C

Carter, William (First Army engineer), 111, 113, 126, 144, 202, 208, 238, 298

Carville, Richard, 119, 221-222

Chapin, Fred, 266, 268, 276, 281

Chinlund, Joe, 233-234, 247

Churchill, Winston, 108

Clausewitz, Carl von, 155

Cobb, Elizabeth Elsie ("Betsey"), 11

marriage to Anderson, 25, 31

death, 61

Collins, Lawton, 123

Conlin, John, 209

Connelly, Oliver jr, 291

Cooke, David (author of *Kampfgruppe Peiper at the Battle of the Bulge*), 230

D

Davis, Donald, 231

Dietrich, Josef "Sepp", 3, 157-158, 161, 168, 178, 180, 204

Duffy, Frank, 42, 81

E

Edelstein, Alvin, 262, 266-268, 301

Eisenhower, Dwight D., 114, 135-136, 144-145, 151, 174, 241, 243, 294

Engel, Gerhard, 207

F

Foch, Ferdinand, 43-44, 48
Fraser, Harvey, 202, 206, 222, 235-236, 274-275, 289, 292, 310-311
Frazier, Bruce, 252-253

G

Gamble, James H., 208, 213, 220-221, 223-224, 245-246, 301
Gavin, James, 244, 264, 266-267, 274
Gerow, Leonard T., 146
Giles, Henry, 300, 307, 317
Giles, Janice Holt (author of *The G.I. Journal of Sergeant* Giles and *The Damned Engineers*), 256, 279-280
Goebbels, Joseph, 152
Goldstein, Bernard, 232-233, 246
Green, Richard, 252-254

H

Hansen, Max, 162-164, 173. 220-221, 224, 260
Hechler, Ken (author of *Holding the Line* and *The Bridge at Remagen*), 242, 280, 295
Hensel, Charles, 231-234, 244, 246
Higgins, James, 253
Hill, E.D., 47
Himmler, Heinrich, 152, 168-169
Hinkel, Paul, 256
Hitler, Adolph, 129-130, 137, 149-155, 157, 160, 167, 169, 172, 174-175, 177, 204, 243, 251, 277, 306, 308
Hobbs, Leland, 261, 264, 270, 281
Hodges, Courtney, 129-130, 174-175, 228, 238, 264, 267
Hodges, Preston, 275, 282
Hoge, William, 295-296, 298
Hollenbeck, Donalde, 253

I

Irwin, Carlisle, 245
Ishmael, Lee, 275, 281-282

J

Jewett, Robert N., 119, 250, 252-254, 279

K

Kirkland, James
    assignment, appointment as
    executive officer, 51st Engineer
    Regiment (Combat), 86
    executive officer, 1111th
    Engineer Combat Group, 95,
    112, 119, 186
    temporary assignment as
    acting commanding officer,
    288
    at Remagen bridge, 302
Knittel, Gustave, 162-164, 173,
224, 260-261
Krämer, Fritz, 158-159, 166, 204
Krueger, Walter, 15

L

Lampp, Edward, 229, 231, 262, 265, 269

Lary, Virgil, 226

Liparulo, Lorenzo, 246

Ludendorff, Erich, 38, 41, 48

Lundberg, A. P., 259, 264, 267, 279

Lyons, F. H. "Rusty", 297, 302

M

Marshall, S.L.A., 294

Massoglia, Martin F., 75, 94

McCollum, Albert, 77, 86

McCollum, Lillard, 253

McKinley, William, 9

Middleton, Troy, 123

Milgram, Joseph, 236

Miller, Jean, 249, 260

Milliken, John, 289

Mohnke, Wilhelm, 161-162, 180, 204, 227

Montgomery, Bernard, Field Marshal, 136, 293-294

Moyer, Lawrence, 225, 229, 231, 242

Muir, Charles H., 37, 54

N

Nabors, Fred, 252, 256, 259

O

Oberdorf, Fred, 86

P

Parker, Danny, 158

Patton, George, 129-130, 289, 310

Peiper, Joachim (aka Jochen), 2-3, 162-166, 167-173, 176, 180, 203-205, 207, 210-213, 217-221, 224-227, 230, 232-235, 239-241, 244, 246-247, 251, 253-256, 258-262, 264-265, 267-271, 276, 279, 286

Pergrin, David E., 105-107, 120, 122, 126, 129, 143, 203-204, 206, 208-209, 222, 224-227, 229, 231, 238, 241, 262, 270-273, 290, 297-301, 303-305, 308-309

Perkins, John 242

Pershing, John J.
    career service, 20
    incursion into Mexico, 21
    command of American Expeditionary Force, 34-35, 41
    Meuse-Argonne Offensive, 44, 48
    reviewed the 28th Division, 51

Pigg, Edwin, 262, 265-266

Priess, Herman, 160

Q

Quesada, Elwood "Pete", 265

R

Radford, Albert E., 206, 311

Raper, Lee, 124

Reafsnyder, Victor, 94, 97, 109,

120, 123, 129, 143, 202, 206

Reynolds, Michael (author of *Men of Steel*), 173, 218, 221

Rhea, Frank, 220

Rombaugh, Warren, 231, 234-236, 242

Roosevelt, Franklin, 108

Roosevelt, Theodore, 9, 20

Roosevelt, Theodore, jr, 137

Rundstadt, Karl von, 177

S

Sandig, Rudolf, 162, 166, 173, 260

Sapp, Burt, 33, 40, 42, 47

Scheuber, Sam, 201, 236-237, 242, 248, 252, 257, 279-280, 287, 289

Sheetz, Lloyd, 234, 246

Simpson, William, 174

Skorzeny, Otto, 216, 240, 271-272

Smith, William, 220

Snow, James jr, 259, 267

Snyder, Frederic, 32, 37, 47, 54, 183

Solis, Paul, 245-248, 251, 279

Stalin, Joseph, 108, 114, 171, 180

Sternebeck, Werner, 226

Student, Kurt, 135

Sweitzer, Charles, 304-305

T

Taylor, Archibald, 245-246

Truman, Harry, 54

V

Villa, Francisco ("Pancho"), 20-21

W

Walters, Albert W. ("Bucky"), 209, 221, 249, 256-257, 259

Webb, Henderson O., 95, 103, 119, 124, 254-255, 259, 264, 267

Williams, Thomas J.C., 95, 119, 142, 216, 279, 311

Wilson, Cliff, 231, 234, 245-246

Wilson, Woodrow, 20-21, 27, 35

Wright, Floyd D., 310

Y

Yates, Robert ("Bull"), 86, 94, 124, 132-133, 143, 203, 263, 273-275, 280

PLACES

A

Amblève (town. aka Amel), 163, 208, 216, 220-221

Amblève River, 147, 166, 229-230, 232, 235, 237, 246-248, 251-255, 257-258, 260-265, 269-270, 278, 286, 294

Antwerp, Belgium, 135, 155, 158, 166, 230, 241, 248, 308

Ardennes 2-4, 145-147, 149, 151, 155-156, 160-161, 165, 222, 251, 272, 275-276, 283

Audouville-la-Hubert
(Ammunition dump fire), 124

B

Basse-Bodeux, Belgium, 143, 166,
201, 206, 255

Bastogne, Belgium, 134, 140, 155,
235, 264, 277, 289

Baugnez, Belgium (aka Five
Points), 225-227, 255

Bois de Rougis, France, 39-40

Born, Belgium, 208

Buchholz Station, 210, 217-218

Butgenbach, Belgium, 201, 220-
221, 223, 228, 239, 270

Büllingen, Belgium, 218-220, 224

C

Camp Bowie, Texas, 75-76

Camp Dix, New Jersey, 51, 97-98

Camp Hancock, Augusta,
Georgia, 31

Camp Stewart, El Paso, Texas, 23

Camp Swift, Texas, 105

Carentan, Normandy, 122-123;
bypass road, 125-126

Château-Thierry, 36-38

Cheneux, 258, 261-262, 265, 267

Columbus, New Mexico, 20

Cotentin peninsula, Normandy,
115, 118

E

Elsenborn, Belgium, 161, 221, 224,
228, 271

F

Fort A.P. Hill, Virginia, 68-69

Fort Bliss, El Paso, Texas, 23-25

Fort Ord (Monterey, California),
321

Francorchamps, Belgium, 251, 279

H

Habièmont (Neufmolin bridge),
Belgium, 166, 262, 264-269, 276-
277, 281, 301, 323

Haute-Bodeux, 206, 208, 215, 217,
221, 225, 231, 249, 255, 262, 266

Hébert, 118, 120, 123-124, 126

Highnam Court, Gloucester,
England, 107, 110

Honsfeld, Belgium, 218

Hotton, Belgium, 146, 235, 269,
275, 282

Hürtgen forest (Hürtgenwald),
145, 174

Huy, Belgium, 262, 266

I

Indiantown Gap, Pennsylvania,
NGP training center, 66

Ingolstadt, Germany, 311

L

La Gleize, Belgium, 208, 236, 255, 264-265, 286, 291

La Lienne creek, 2, 166, 262, 269, 276

Lanzerath, Belgium, 159, 166, 211-213, 217

Ligneuville, Belgium, 225-227

Losheim, 159, 166, 204, 208, 211, 217

Losheimergraben, Belgium, 159, 207, 211

M

Macomb Reservation, New York, 86, 90-92, 94-96, 100

Malmedy, Belgium, 143, 146, 201, 208-209, 220, 222-231, 234-235, 238-240, 242, 245, 248, 257, 261-262, 270-273

Marche-en-Famenne (Marche), Belgium, 143, 146, 201-203, 206, 235-236, 248

Marne River, 36

Meuse River, 2-3, 147, 155, 158-166, 205, 224, 244, 258, 261-262, 268-269

Modave, Belgium, 238, 254, 266, 269, 272, 283-284

Montfaucon, 44

Mount Gretna, Pennsylvania, 15, 23

N

Normandy (invasion beaches), 111-118, 125, 135, 158

O

Omaha beach, Normandy, 115-116, 118, 120-122

Ourthe River, 147, 235, 274-275, 284, 291-292

P

Plattsburgh Barracks, New York, 83-96

R

Reims, France, 38, 44

Remagen, Germany, 290, 293, 295-296, 298-300, 302-303, 308-309

Rhine River (Rhein), 288, 290, 294-295, 297, 300-301, 305-307, 309

Roer River, 144-145, 156, 174-175, 208, 288-289

Ruhr (German industrial area), 294, 310, 313

S

Saint-Lô, France, 126, 150

Saint-Marie-du-Mont, 120

Salm River, 147, 237-238, 248-249, 253, 256, 258-260, 263, 273-274, 280

Sourbrodt, Belguim, 144, 146, 160, 201, 242

Spa, Belgium, 144, 201-202, 228, 233-234, 238-239, 251, 259, 261, 264, 267, 279

St. Agnan, France, 39-40, 42, 55, 58, 81, 182, 189, 192, 317

St. Mihiel, France, 49

St. Vith, Belgium, 221, 226, 228, 241, 249, 273, 277

Stavelot, Belgium, 143, 146, 159, 166, 225, 227, 229-235, 237, 239-240, 244-247, 250-253, 255, 260-261, 264-265, 269-271, 278-279

Stoumont, Belgium, 254, 261, 268, 271, 286

T

Thirimont, 224-225

Trois-Ponts, Belgium, 142-147, 166, 208, 216-217, 221, 225, 228-230, 234-237, 239-240, 242, 245-251, 253-258, 260-264, 267, 269, 273-275, 277-280, 286-287, 294

U

Utah beach, Normandy, 115-116, 118, 120-122, 137

V

Vera Cruz, Mexico, 20

Vielsalm, Belgium, 237, 249, 260

W

Wanne, Belgium, 247-248, 256

Werbomont, Belgium, 143, 147, 166, 201, 223, 252, 259, 262, 264-266, 270

West Virginia Maneuver Area, 95-96

MILITARY UNITS

American

1st Infantry Division, 243, 295, 308

101st Airborne Division, 244, 277, 289

103rd Engineer Regiment (28th Division), 32-37, 41-43, 65, 68

105th Engineer Combat Battalion, 270

106th Infantry Division, 209, 218, 220, 241

109th Infantry Regiment (28th Division), 32, 38-41

1110th Engineer Combat Group, 123

1111th Engineer Combat Group (née 51st Engineer Regiment (Combat))

    formed as 51st Engineer Regiment, 70, 75, 77

    training, Camp Bowie 78-83

    training, Plattsburgh Barracks, 83-96

training at West Virginia Maneuver Area, 96

designation as 1111th ECG, 93

preparation for overseas deployment, 97-98

to England for pre-invasion training, 102-105

working with Royal Engineers, 103-104

at Highnam Court, UK, 107, 110-112

to Normandy, 116-119

staff, 119

operations in Normandy, 120-126

breakout, 127-128

operations after Mortain, 131-134

preparations in Belgium, winter, 140-142

Trois-Ponts, 142-147

Ardennes counteroffensive, 200-201, 206, 208-209, 215, 219, 221, 223, 228, 233-234, 238, 240-241, 249-250, 255, 266-270, 272, 274, 277

into Germany, 284-286, 288-290

Remagen, 295, 306-307, 309

end of the war, 310, 312-314

117th Infantry Regiment, 261, 270

119th Infantry Regiment, 261, 264

120th Infantry Regiment, 261

125th Engineer Squadron (PNG inactive reserve), 65

13th US Cavalry Regiment, 20

14th Cavalry Group, 159, 218, 220, 224

16th Infantry Regiment, US Army, 23

2nd Division (aka 2nd Infantry Division), 37, 219, 223, 243

202nd Engineer Combat Battalion, 201, 233-234, 239, 244-245, 251, 269, 276, 279

238th Engineer Combat Battalion (née 2nd Battalion, 51st Engineer Regiment (Combat)), 75, 93-95, 129, 286

254th Engineer Combat Battalion, 219, 240

28th Division

nationalized for World War I, 31

at Second Battle of the Marne ("The Iron Division"), 36-41

Meuse-Argonne Offensive, 43, 46-49

re-designated as 28th Infantry Division for WWII, 69

operations in Hürtgen forest, 145

Ardennes, 156

285th Field Artillery Observation Battalion, Company B (7th Armored Division), 226

291st Engineer Combat Battalion (née 2nd Battalion, 82nd Engineer Regiment (Combat)), 4, 105-107, 110, 117, 120, 127-128, 133, 141, 143, 145, 201, 203, 206, 208-209, 215, 220, 222-224, 230-231, 234-236, 239, 241, 245-246, 248-249, 255-256, 262, 265-266, 269-274, 284-285, 289-290, 297-298, 300, 307, 309, 312, 320

296th Engineer Combat Battalion, 105, 110, 120, 128, 131, 143-145, 201, 239, 269, 276

299th Engineer Combat Battalion, 290, 299, 305

3rd Armored Division, 126

3rd Division, 38-39, 53

30th Infantry Division, 126, 243, 261, 264, 270-271, 281

300th Engineer Combat Battalion, 284-285, 289

325th Tank Destroyer Battalion

35th Division, 46

365th Fighter Group, 265

394th Infantry Regiment, 159, 208, 211, 217

4th Infantry Division, 156

467th Engineer Maintenance Company, 289

49th Anti-Aircraft Artillery Brigade, 227

492nd Railroad Operating Battalion, 59

501st Engineer Light Ponton Company, 289

505th Light Ponton Company, 285

505th Parachute Infantry Regiment, 274

508th Light Ponton Company, 128

51st Engineer Combat Battalion (née 1st Battalion, 51st Engineer Regiment (Combat)), 4, 75, 86, 93-97, 105, 108-110, 117, 120, 127-129, 132-133, 141, 143, 145, 201-203, 222, 235-236, 239, 241-242, 248, 252, 256, 259, 263, 269, 274-275, 284-290, 299, 307, 309-311, 320

51st Engineer Regiment (Combat), see 1111th Engineer Combat Group

526th Armored Infantry Battalion, 245-246, 248-249, 252-254

629th Light Equipment Company, 128, 144-145, 201, 221, 289

7th Armored Division, 221, 226, 241, 249, 260-261, 277, 288

738th Tank Battalion (ME – mechanized engineer), 289

767th Dump Truck Company, 128, 145, 201, 270

77th Division, 46

78th Infantry Division, 295, 298

82nd Airborne Division, 244, 264, 266, 271, 274, 286

825th Tank Destroyer Battalion,

245-246, 278

86th Engineer Heavy Ponton Battalion, 110, 299

9th Air Force, 272

9th Armored Division, 156, 208, 295

9th Infantry Division, 295

962nd Engineer Maintenance Company, 128, 145, 201, 223

988th Engineer Treadway Bridge Company, 299, 307

99th Infantry Battalion (separate), 238

99th Infantry Division, 157, 159, 208, 211, 218-222, 241, 277

994th Engineer Treadway Bridge Company, 289

998th Engineer Treadway Bridge Company, 290, 299, 307

III US Corps, 288, 289-290, 292

  Capture of Remagen bridge, 295-298, 302, 309

  final stages of the war, 310

IX Tactical Air Command, 265

American Army policy concerning service by African Americans (1916), 23

American Expeditionary Force, 34

Army Corps of Engineers (combat)

  mission, 32-33

  modernization for WWII, 73-75

Normandy invasion, 114-116, 121

  bocage fighting, 125

  across France, 131

First US Army (aka American First Army, FUSA), 2, 4, 105, 111, 120-121, 123, 126, 129-131, 134-135, 144-145, 156, 174, 201, 203, 206, 208-209, 216, 219-220, 222-223, 228-230, 234-236, 238-239, 241, 243, 245, 250-251, 255, 259, 261, 264, 277, 279, 284, 292, 295, 297

National Guard of Pennsylvania (NGP) (aka Pennsylvania National Guard, PNG)

  Company K, 6th Infantry Regiment, 10, 14

  nationalized for Mexican border, 22

  nationalized for WWI (28th Division), 31

  created combat engineer component, 32

  postwar reorganization and modernization, 58

  nationalized for WWII (28th Infantry Division), 68

Ninth US Army, 145, 156

Pennsylvania National Guard, see National Guard of Pennsylvania

Third US Army, 129-131, 135, 145, 292, 310-311

Twelfth US Army Group (aka 12th Army Group), 129, 157, 241, 293

V Corps, 121, 146, 175, 201, 206, 209, 218, 221

VII Corps, 121, 123, 128, 156, 175, 201, 284-285, 321

VIII Corps, 123, 201, 218

XVIII Corps (Airborne), 243-244, 264, 284-285, 287-288

German

1st SS Panzer Division (née Regiment; Leibstandarte Adolph Hitler), 160-162, 168-173, 180, 204, 221, 223-224, 227, 261, 267-269, 284

116th Panzer Division, 275

12th SS Panzer Division (Hitlerjugend), 160-161, 166, 179, 204, 223-224, 228, 243, 270

12th Volksgrenadier Division, 159, 205, 207, 210-211, 213, 217

15.Armee, 156, 178

2nd SS Panzer Division (Das Reich), 160

272nd Volksgrenadier Division, 160

277th Volksgrenadier Division, 159

3rd *Fallshirmjäger* Division, 159, 179, 211

320th Infantry Division, 170

326th Volksgrenadier Division, 159

5.Panzerarmee, 156-157, 277, 283

501st SS *Schwere Panzer Abteilung* ("SS Heavy Panzer Battalion"), 165

6.Panzerarmee, 3, 156-158, 161-162, 166, 204, 217, 271, 277, 283

7.Armee, 156

9th *Fallshirmjäger* Regiment, 211-212, 217

9th SS Panzer Division (Hohenstaufen), 160, 269

Das Reich, see 2nd SS Panzer Division

Hitlerjugend, see 12th SS Panzer Division

Hohenstaufen, see 9th SS Panzer Division

I-SS Panzerkorps, 158, 160-161, 204

II-SS Panzerkorps, 160, 269

Kampfgruppe Hansen, 162-163, 220-221, 224, 260

Kampfgruppe Peiper, 2, 162, 164-166, 205, 211, 213, 217-219, 221, 224, 226-227, 232-233, 235, 239, 244, 246-247, 254-255, 259, 264-265, 267-270, 274, 286

Kampfgruppe Sandig, 162, 166, 260

Leibstandarte Adolph Hitler, see 1st SS Panzer Division

Schnellgruppe Knittel, 162-163, 224, 260

SS Panzer Brigade 150 (aka 150th Panzer Brigade), 216, 271

SS Panzer Lehr Division, 126

EVENTS

A

Air attacks against Peiper's column, 219-220, 265

Air attacks against Remagen bridge sites, 303-306

Ardennes counteroffensive (aka Battle of the Bulge; Eifel Offensive), 2-4, 6, 149-284

B

Battle of the Bulge, see Ardennes counteroffensive

C

Citadel, Operation (Kursk), 171

Cobra, Operation, 126-127

D

D-Day, see Overlord, Normandy

Herbstnebel, 160

L

Lumberjack, Operation, 295

Lüttich, Operation (Mortain), 130, 150, 152

M

Malmedy Massacre, 226, 241

Market-Garden, Operation, 135-137, 140, 153

Marneschutz ("Marne Defense"), 38

Meuse-Argonne Offensive, 43-45, 48-49, 59, 95, 133, 208

Mexican-American War, 19

N

Nivelle Offensive (April-May 1917), (Second Battle of the Aisne), 28, 30

O

Overlord (Allied invasion, Normandy), 114-116

S

San Juan Hill, battle of, 9, 20, 30

Second Battle of the Marne, 36

Spanish-American War, 10, 30

V

Villa raid, 20-21

W

Wacht Am Rhein, 155-156, 158, 178, 204, 277

THINGS

A

Amalgamation, 35

Andes, HMS, 109

B

B-24 heavy bomber, 273

B-26 medium bomber, 272-273

Battle of the Bulge (book), 158

Bailey bridge, 93, 100, 134, 286, 288-289

Bocage, 125

Bulldozer (Caterpillar, D-7), 124; tankdozer variant, 126, 138, 291

C

Campbell Soup Company, 62, 71

Central Manual Training School (CMTS), 12-13

D

DUKW amphibious vehicle, 288, 292

F

Fallshirmjäger, 159, 179, 218, 260

Flakpanzers, 165, 265

Floating treadway bridge, 134

G

Group Control Council (GCC), 312, 319

J

JagdPanzer IV tank destroyer, 163, 179, 278; JagdPanzer V, 179

L

Liberty ships

    Calvin Coolidge, HR 650, 108

    Richard Rush, HR 656, 108

    Charles M. Hall, 117-118

    Arthur Moore, 320

Ludendorff Bridge, 296-298, 302-303, 308-309

M

M2 Treadway bridge (US Army), 301, 307

M4 Sherman US medium tank, 272

M5 Stuart light tank, 278

M7 Priest Howitzer Motor Carriage (HMC), 278, 311

M8 Howitzer Motor Carriage (HMC), 274, 278

Main Supply Route (MSR) (Normandy), 121, 126

Metagama, CPSS, 34

Mongolia, SS, 51

N

National Defense Act of 1916, 30

O

Oberbefehlshaber West (OB West), 160, 177

Oberkommando der Wehrmacht (OKW—German High Command of the Armed Forces), 153

Officer Candidate School (OCS), 76

P

P-47 Thunderbolt American fighter-bomber ("Jabos" to the Germans), 219-220, 240, 265, 281

Panzergrenadiers, 162, 218, 247, 268

Panzerkampfwagen (*Pzkw*)
  Mark IV, 164, 179, 205, 217, 226, 247, 255-256, 259-260, 272
  Mark V (Panther), 128, 164, 179, 205, 211, 217, 227, 247, 251, 253, 265, 267, 272
  Tiger Ausf. B (*Königstiger*), 165, 205, 280

Pioneers (German combat engineers), 162, 247, 260

Ponton (pontoon) bridge (Army Model 1940 twenty-five ton), 89, 100

Pennsylvania, University of (Penn), 13
  Wharton School of Finance and Commerce, 14, 18
  Alumni dinner, El Paso, 24

Pennsylvania Military College (PMC), 9-10, 18

Pennsylvania railroad (PRR), 7, 13, 16-17

furloughed employees for military duty, 22

management rivalries, 63

Primacord, 266, 281

Q

Queen Mary, RMS, 98

R

Rollbahns, 159-164, 166, 204, 207, 211, 217, 220, 260

S

Santa Elena, SS, 107, 113

Society of American Military Engineers (SAME), 74, 98, 322

Sonderkraftfahrzeug 251 (Sd.Kfz 251, German halftrack armored vehicle, SPW), 163, 217, 226, 265, 268, 276

The 51st Again!, 82, 85

T

Triple Entente, 27

Tucker bridge, 122, 138

U

U-boats (German submarines), 34, 102, 150, 154

Ultra, 154

Unbroken Line, 82, 91

USS *Maine*, 10

V

V-1 rocket, 141, 144, 200, 206

V-2 rocket, 154, 308

Volksgrenadiers, 152, 177, 210

Waffen-SS, 2, 122, 157-158, 161,
167, 178, 204-205, 269

Wehrmacht, 131, 135, 149, 154,
158, 204, 210, 283-284, 291, 293

CPSIA information can be obtained
at www.ICGtesting.com
Printed in the USA
LVHW020057230321
682109LV00011B/343